SUPREME WHISPERS

ALSO BY ABHINAV CHANDRACHUD

Republic of Rhetoric: Free Speech and the Constitution of India

SUPREME WHISPERS

CONVERSATIONS WITH JUDGES OF THE
SUPREME COURT OF INDIA

1980–1989

ABHINAV CHANDRACHUD

PENGUIN
VIKING
An imprint of Penguin Random House

VIKING

USA | Canada | UK | Ireland | Australia
New Zealand | India | South Africa | China | Singapore

Viking is part of the Penguin Random House group of companies
whose addresses can be found at global.penguinrandomhouse.com

Published by Penguin Random House India Pvt. Ltd
4th Floor, Capital Tower 1, MG Road,
Gurugram 122 002, Haryana, India

Penguin
Random House
India

First published in Viking by Penguin Random House India 2018

ISBN 9780670090327

Typeset in Minion Pro by Manipal Digital Systems, Manipal
Printed at Replika Press Pvt. Ltd, India

www.penguin.co.in

MIX
Paper from
responsible sources
FSC® C016779

This is a legitimate digitally printed version of the book and therefore might not
have certain extra finishing on the cover.

To the memory of the great
Professor George H. Gadbois, Jr.,
scholar, mentor and friend

Contents

The Gadbois Interviews

In the cold Delhi winter of January 1980, a young American scholar met five judges of the Supreme Court of India. His name was George H. Gadbois, Jr. He had come to India with a reputation as a serious scholar who had written about the Indian judiciary in well-known journals like the *Law and Society Review* and *Economic and Political Weekly*. The judges he met gave him astonishing details: about what they actually thought of their colleagues, about the inner workings and politics of the court, their interactions with the government, and the judicial appointments process, among many other things. This was only the beginning. Over the course of that decade, Gadbois came to India on two more occasions and conducted over[1] 116 interviews with more than sixty-six judges of the Supreme Court of India (nineteen of whom held the post of chief justice), and others such as senior lawyers, politicians, relations of deceased judges, and court staff.[2] Each interview yielded a fascinating glimpse into the secluded world of the judges of the Supreme Court.

For instance, the wife of a Supreme Court judge, S.C. Roy, informed Gadbois that after her husband was appointed to the

Supreme Court, Prime Minister Indira Gandhi asked him to take care of some legal work concerning her family property in Allahabad. When that judge died in office shortly after being appointed, some people[3] rushed to his house and whisked away all the files so that nobody would know about this.[4] Chief Justice P.N. Bhagwati told Gadbois that a law minister, also a senior lawyer, with whom he had an uneasy equation[5] was not known to tell the truth;[6] he had once feigned heart trouble during an ongoing case at the Supreme Court in order to get that case adjourned, only to then rush to the Delhi High Court to participate in another case.[7] Perhaps most interestingly, one chief justice of the Supreme Court told Gadbois that he had vetoed the appointment of a judge serving at a high court in a northern state to the Supreme Court, despite the fact that the President of India had signed the warrant of appointment, because there was a credible allegation that the judge had committed sexual assault. Prime Minister Indira Gandhi was said to have been very upset with this story,[8] not in the least because that judge was related to a minister in her government.[9] These and scores of other stories, discussed in this book, would have been lost to history had it not been for Gadbois's interviews.

Gadbois prepared for each interview by reading everything that he could lay his hands on about the judge. As we shall soon see, this yielded rich dividends, because the judges were incredibly frank and forthright in the answers they gave him. For instance, Gadbois learnt that in the 1980s, though Chief Justice Y.V. Chandrachud wanted to appoint M.N. Chandurkar, chief justice of the Madras High Court, to the Supreme Court, Prime Minister Indira Gandhi decided to reject that appointment merely because Chandurkar had attended the funeral of (and eulogized) an RSS leader, M.S. Golwalkar, who had been a friend of Chandurkar's father.[10] His attendance at a funeral was enough for the government to brand him ideologically unsuitable for appointment to the Supreme Court. Similarly, Gadbois was told by Chief Justice R.S. Pathak that a sitting Supreme Court judge did not want Delhi High Court Chief Justice T.P.S. Chawla to be appointed to the Supreme Court because Chawla, who was that judge's neighbour, had threatened to shoot one of his dogs.[11]

Each interview lasted anywhere between forty-five minutes and several hours. Though they began in 1980, most interviews were conducted between April to July 1983 and March to December 1988. During each meeting, Gadbois diligently took down handwritten notes, which he later typed up on his typewriter. He recorded nearly every detail of what the judge had told him, sometimes to a fault. For instance, Gadbois wrote that Justice S. Natarajan, a 'hospitable fellow', had served him a 'pureed watermelon drink'.[12] He wrote that the reclusive Chief Justice A.N. Ray (who had become very unpopular for superseding three judges who had voted against the government in the *Basic Structure* case[13]), seemed 'very nervous' throughout the interview, and that Gadbois had 'serious doubts' about whether he had told Gadbois the truth during the interview.[14] He even recorded that a retired Supreme Court judge from Bombay had been drinking alcohol before Gadbois arrived to meet him, that he 'drank heavily' during the interview and became 'loud and rather obnoxious'.[15] He wrote, perhaps with some amusement, how Justice R.S. Sarkaria pronounced the word 'lawyer' as 'liar'.[16] He noted that he saw photographs of two famous American Supreme Court judges, Benjamin Cardozo and Oliver Wendell Holmes, in the office of Justice

M.N.R. Venkatachaliah, and that Venkatachaliah 'virtually [worshipped]' these judges.[17]

These typewritten interview notes now survive Gadbois who passed away of a terminal disease at the age of eighty in February 2017. They provide an invaluable insight into a decade of politics, decision-making and legal culture in the Supreme Court of India. Gadbois sent me his notes shortly before he passed away, without imposing any condition on how I could use them.[18] He was a mentor and guide to me in my own research, and had informally supervised two books on India's judiciary which I wrote in 2014 and 2015 respectively.[19]

Some of the contents of the interviews were off the record and most have never been written about, not even in the monumental book[20] Gadbois published a few years ago about the judges of the Supreme Court. This was understandable, because Gadbois did not want to upset the judges with whom he had spoken—many of them were sitting judges, and they were, after all, speaking about their own colleagues, contemporaries and times, about ongoing situations in court which were still unfolding as the interviews were being conducted. Revealing these stories in the 1980s would have been like lighting a spark in a powder keg.[21] Today, however, the keg no longer holds any powder. Nearly thirty years have gone by since the last interview took place. Most of the judges who were interviewed have passed away. The stories contained in the interviews, though incredibly fascinating and still highly relevant today, are now decades old. As such, the notes of the interviews now belong to history and it is only fair to finally make their contents publicly known.[22]

* * *

After graduating from high school, Gadbois served as a sergeant in the US army for three years, between 1953 and 1956.[23] He went on to get his undergraduate degree in political science and history from Marietta College in Ohio in 1959, and an MA and PhD from Duke University in 1962 and 1965. It was at Duke that Gadbois first developed an academic interest in India. His MA thesis, written entirely in the US,[24] explored the fundamental rights under the Indian Constitution.[25] As a PhD student, he made his first trip to India in 1962, taking advantage of a fellowship offered by the American Institute of Indian Studies at New Delhi. His doctoral dissertation explored the early years of the Supreme Court, including the establishment and working of its precursor, the Federal Court of India. Two[26] of the chapters of his dissertation were published in the journal of the Indian Law Institute, which was then a prestigious and well-read law review.[27] After going back to the US, he got a teaching job in the department of political science at the University of Kentucky, which he held for the rest of his career.

Gadbois made his second trip to India between 1969 and 1970, once again on a fellowship from the American Institute. It was in these two years that Gadbois first took a serious interest in the judges of the Supreme Court. Though he did not substantially[28] conduct any interviews with judges at that time, he wrote two papers which perhaps became the defining works of his career, until his book was published decades later. In the first of these, an article published in the *Law and Society Review* in the late 1960s,[29] Gadbois prepared a 'portrait' of the thirty-six judges who had served in the Supreme Court between 1950 and 1967, examining their educational backgrounds, career patterns prior to getting on the bench, seniority, age, religion, caste and other details. In the second,

an article published in the *Economic and Political Weekly* in
1970,[30] Gadbois carefully studied 3272 reported judgments
delivered by the Supreme Court between 1950 and 1967, and
tried to work out the voting pattern of the judges, classifying
them as 'Modern Liberals', 'Modern Conservatives', 'Classical
Liberals' or 'Classical Conservatives'. In this paper, Gadbois
also studied the dissenting patterns of Supreme Court judges.
He discovered a pattern which many subsequently found very
interesting: As a puisne judge of the Supreme Court (a puisne
judge is any judge apart from the chief justice), Justice K. Subba
Rao had dissented forty-eight times during his nine-year term
in the court, making him 'the greatest dissenter in the history
of the Supreme Court' until then, but as the chief justice of
India, Subba Rao had not dissented even once. This suggested
that the chief justice of India had a critical role in determining
the outcome of cases decided by the court, by selecting the
judges who would sit with him on the bench.

Both these articles were read by several judges of the
Supreme Court.[31] When Gadbois later met Justice Bhagwati
for the first time in January 1980, the very first thing Bhagwati
said to him was that he had wrongly identified Bhagwati as a
Brahmin in his *Law and Society Review* portrait of Indian judges.
When he met Justice G.K. Mitter, the judge complimented
him on his articles.[32] In their classic autobiographies, Justice
P.B. Gajendragadkar[33] and M. Hidayatullah,[34] early and iconic
judges of the Supreme Court, referred to Gadbois's work,
particularly the dissenting patterns of judges. Another Supreme
Court judge, R.M. Sahai, referred to an exchange he had
with Gadbois in his autobiography.[35] Gadbois's trip between
December 1979 and February 1980 was his third to India. This
time, he was here on an exchange programme between US and
Indian scientists.[36] Both his trips to India thereafter, in 1983 and

1988, were funded by the American Institute.[37] The interviews were conducted in interesting political times. The Emergency had come to an end. The Janata government had been voted in and out of power. Indira Gandhi was back in the government and the independence of the judiciary was under attack, which continued under her son, Rajiv.

Many judges thought very highly of Gadbois, which is why they agreed to meet him in the first place. Justice A.P. Sen informed Gadbois that during the hearings of the *Waman Rao* case[38] (decided in November 1980) at the Supreme Court, both Chief Justice Chandrachud and Justice Bhagwati kept referring to Gadbois and wondered if he was around in India. Chandrachud, in particular, had enormous respect for his work, and considered him comparable to another American scholar of Indian constitutional history, Granville Austin.[39] Justice K.S. Hegde sent Gadbois an invitation to his daughter's wedding in June 1971. Even today, Gadbois's scholarship remains relevant and well regarded. Gadbois's work was recently cited by the majority judgment written by Justice J.S. Khehar (as he then was) in the fourth *Judges* case,[40] where the court struck down the 99th amendment to the Constitution[41] which sought to introduce a 'National Judicial Appointments Commission' for appointing judges.

It was on account of his academic credentials and good reputation with the Supreme Court's judges that Gadbois succeeded in interviewing nearly every judge of the court. An interesting story illustrates this. Justice V.D. Tulzapurkar, in a short meeting with Gadbois in his chamber, refused to be interviewed by him and told him to go away. At the time, Tulzapurkar was very weary of scholars, because he had been heavily criticized by Upendra Baxi, doyen of Indian legal academia, for some of the speeches he had made about the court.

Baxi had called Tulzapurkar the 'chief public flagellator of the Supreme Court', and said that he was 'knowingly hastening [the court's] disintegration'.[42] After the incident in Tulzapurkar's chamber, Gadbois wrote a letter to the judge in April 1983 to try to get an audience with him. Gadbois wrote that Tulzapurkar might have been reluctant to meet him because of the 'grossly unfair way some Indian scholars and journalists have treated [him]',[43] but assured him that he (Gadbois) was not party to these criticisms. Tulzapurkar sent Gadbois a short reply,[44] saying that he was sorry for hurting Gadbois. But Tulzapurkar still did not agree to give Gadbois an interview. But then, Justices P.K. Goswami and E.S. Venkataramiah spoke to Tulzapurkar on Gadbois's behalf, and Tulzapurkar eventually agreed to meet Gadbois in July 1983, for a very frank and 'excellent' interview, which lasted two hours.[45]

Indeed, many of the interviewed judges were very aware of the writings of two prominent legal scholars at that time, H.M. Seervai (former advocate general of Maharashtra, and author of the magnum opus, *Constitutional Law of India*), and Upendra Baxi. Judges like Justice A.N. Grover, Krishna Iyer, P.S. Kailasam, Tulzapurkar, and A.P. Sen urged Gadbois to read what Seervai had written about them, their own decisions, or others' decisions. Similarly, when Gadbois mentioned to Justice D.P. Madon that Baxi had criticized him in a journal called *Mainstream*, Madon promptly told Gadbois that the title of the article was 'The Horse and the Rider', indicating that he was familiar with it.[46] Justice D.A. Desai told Gadbois that Baxi had written an article about one of his decisions, *D.S. Nakara v. Union of India*,[47] in which the court had struck down a pension scheme introduced by the central government for its employees on the grounds that it was discriminatory.[48] Baxi wrote a paper praising the decision, called 'Socialism for the

Superannuated'.[49] Justice Krishna Iyer said that he had been criticized either by Baxi or by another scholar, Rajeev Dhavan, for writing concurring judgments which were veiled dissents.[50] Some judges were sceptical of Baxi's writings. Apart from Tulzapurkar, Justice Grover told Gadbois not to trust what Baxi wrote, that he had 'axes to grind'.[51] Interestingly, therefore, the judges were not completely aloof from the world of academic writing.

At the same time, many agreed to meet with Gadbois because they also thought of him as a useful contact to have in the US. At a time, without the Internet, when it was not possible to get an esoteric judgment of a foreign court at the click of a button, some asked Gadbois for his help to obtain foreign reading material. For example, Justice Baharul Islam asked Gadbois for a copy of William M. Thayer's biography of American president, James A. Garfield, titled *From Log-Cabin to the White House*. Gadbois told him that he would try to get it for him from the American Center, or else he would send him a photocopy from Kentucky once he got back.[52] Gadbois made a note that he must try and send Fali S. Nariman, who he met in July 1983, a copy of a Canadian judgment on taxing judicial salaries if he could find it.[53] Many judges had children who had moved to and settled in the US,[54] and they thought that Gadbois might be a useful person to know. They perhaps thought that Gadbois's University of Kentucky might invite them for a lecture, giving them an opportunity to visit their children.[55] Some wanted Gadbois's help to get their children to the US. Justice M.M. Dutt asked Gadbois how his son, who was studying law in Calcutta, could go to the US for an LLM.[56] Some interviewees probably thought that Gadbois would get them a professorship or lectureship in the US. In December 1988, for example, Law Minister Asoke Sen told Gadbois that he wanted to get a teaching job in the US, no doubt, thought Gadbois, because he expected to lose the next election. Justice Hidayatullah (who was known by his nickname 'Haddi') also spoke to Gadbois about the possibility of his teaching at an American university for two years, after retiring as vice president of India.[57] Likewise, prior to travelling to the US in 1990, Justice Madon wrote to Gadbois and asked him whether he would be interested in Madon 'giving some lectures in your University on the Indian judiciary as also the Indian Constitution'. If so, asked Madon, '[h]ow long would each lecture be?', and '[h]ow much would your University pay?'[58] Some, like Justice Vivian Bose, were interested in Gadbois's research. 'As you are compiling a list of Judges,' Bose wrote to Gadbois in 1983, 'I wonder whether you could have 50 copies made out for me. I will of course pay for them on hearing from you.'[59] Justice R.B. Misra kept telling Gadbois during the interview that Gadbois knew more about Supreme Court judges than even he did.[60] Others, like Chief Justice A.N. Ray, probably met Gadbois in order to improve their image. Ray had been an unpopular chief justice, and he probably wanted some control over the version of history that Gadbois was going to write.

* * *

In Chapter 1, we will see that some judges of the Supreme Court have had intense professional, ideological and personal rivalries with one another, often over the question of succession to the post of chief justice of India. In fact, whether it was Chief Justice B.P. Sinha and Justice S.J. Imam, Chief Justice Gajendragadkar and Justice A.K. Sarkar, or, perhaps most famously, Chief

Justice Chandrachud and Justice Bhagwati, the number one and number two judges of the Supreme Court, the chief justice and most senior judge have often been unable to get along. This chapter is faintly reminiscent of the tussles that continue to be seen in the court today.

However, in Chapter 2, we will see that despite these rivalries, there is a puzzling lack of dissent in the day-to-day decision-making of the court. The near-absence of dissenting judgments makes the Supreme Court straddle the divide between the civil law tradition (where courts in continental European countries like France typically write unanimous and anonymous judgments) and the common law tradition (where the court of the King's Bench delivered judgments seriatim, with each judge delivering a separate judgment published according to seniority).

Chapter 3 suggests that a part of the reason why dissenting judgments are not written today is because the judges are overworked. Over 40 per cent of the court's productive time is spent on hearing admissions of 'special leave petitions'. Most judges in the 1980s found that hearing these petitions, or 'SLPs' as they are called, was the most taxing and unpleasant part of the job. In the colonial period, litigants who lost their cases at the Indian high courts could file petitions seeking 'special leave' from the Privy Council in London to file an appeal there. However, going to London was expensive, and the Privy Council exercised this jurisdiction sparingly. By contrast, filing SLPs in Delhi is relatively inexpensive, and the Supreme Court is far more liberal in admitting them. Worse, judges who attempted to reform the system were prohibited from doing so by the powerful Supreme Court Bar, which has vested interests in ensuring that the system remains as it is.

Chapter 4 studies the 'decliners'—those who declined offers of elevation to the Supreme Court. We will see that over the years, the status and prestige of the high courts of India have been diluted, while there has been a corresponding increase in the stature and prominence of the Supreme Court. This is exactly what the Law Commission, in its famous 14th report,[61] had feared. In the colonial period, lawyers who were offered judgeships of high courts did not turn them down, especially because the salaries paid to judges were quite handsome during that time. The chief justice of the Calcutta High Court in the colonial period earned more than puisne judges in England, while the Bombay High Court chief justice drew a higher salary than the chief justice of the US Supreme Court.[62] This led to a tradition that a lawyer would not refuse an offer to become a high court judge. On the other hand, chief justices of prominent high courts like those at Bombay, Calcutta, Madras and Allahabad, would refuse offers to be elevated as puisne judges of the Supreme Court, because their own posts had more status than a junior Supreme Court judgeship. Over the years, however, this situation reversed itself. Judges' salaries were actually reduced under the Constitution of independent India, and they were not thereafter increased for a long time. This led to the strange situation that a chief justice of the Supreme Court who retired in 1985 earned less than what the chief justice of the Calcutta High Court earned in 1893, nearly 100 years before. Consequently, we will see that top-ranking lawyers often declined offers to become high court judges. On the other hand, as the years rolled on, very few high court chief justices turned down offers to be elevated to the Supreme Court, which started being seen as a promotion. Since a person can no longer become the chief justice of his parent high court (i.e. the high court where he was first appointed a puisne judge) and since high court chief justices can be transferred from one state to another (i.e. since there is no guarantee that a person will serve as chief justice in any particular high court), virtually no high court chief justice today will turn down an offer to move to the Supreme Court.

In Chapter 5, we will see that there was executive interference in judicial appointments even between 1950 and 1971, contrary to popular belief. During those years, the executive at times had its way over the judiciary when it came to appointing judges. For instance, Home Minister Sardar Vallabhbhai Patel convinced Chief Justice Harilal J. Kania to appoint Justice Basheer Ahmed Sayeed to the Madras High Court against Kania's wishes. During those years, even when the chief justice disagreed with a judicial appointment, he nominally signed off on it, thus preserving the theoretical fiction that all judicial appointments were made with the concurrence of the chief justice of India. We will see that after 1971 the method of appointing judges changed in three ways. Firstly, where political appointments in earlier years had been made only on the basis of political patronage or what the Law Commission called 'extraneous' considerations (like region or religion), after 1971, the government started openly looking at the ideology of judicial nominees and seeking out 'committed' judges. Secondly, the extent of executive interference in judicial appointments was also much greater in the post-1971 period than it had been before. Thirdly, the government used tactics to intimidate judges after 1971, using weapons like supersessions, transfers and non-confirmation of additional and acting judges, to undermine the independence of the judiciary, which had not been done before.

We will also see in this chapter that the collegium system of judicial appointments which is presently in place made three important breaks from the past. Firstly, it gave the senior colleagues of the chief justice of India an institutionalized role in making appointments, which existed only informally, if at all, before. Secondly, it made the recommendations of the chief justice of India and his colleagues binding on the executive government. Thirdly, it took away the government's power to intimidate judges through transfers, etc. However, the collegium does not control how the government allocates post-retirement jobs to judges, and the independence of the judiciary is therefore still at risk today.

Chapter 6 examines the criteria which were employed for selecting and appointing judges. We will see that, over the years, these have not changed much. Judges are still appointed to the Supreme Court on the basis of region, religion, caste and gender, as they were in the 1980s and before. In other words, an attempt is made to preserve a rough regional balance in the court, and to ensure that some judges belonging to religious minorities and backward castes, and women, are appointed. A host of other factors were taken into account to determine whether or not to select a person as a judge, many of which are still relevant and in play today—merit, integrity and family background, among others. Interestingly, we will see that the personal life of a judicial candidate was also investigated by government intelligence-gathering agencies, in order to determine whether the candidate was, say, having an extra-marital affair, or prone to drinking excessively. One wonders whether this does not amount to an intrusion of privacy, now a fundamental right, and whether such factors should at all be taken into account if they do not otherwise have an impact on the professional performance of the candidate. Interestingly, we will see that in the early years, a person's familiarity with English and American cases was counted in his favour while determining whether or not he should be appointed to the Supreme Court.

In the 1970s and 1980s, the political ideological leanings of a judge were explicitly taken into account in determining whether he was fit for elevation to the Supreme Court. It was for this reason that Chandurkar was rejected; his mere attendance at an RSS leader's funeral got him associated with an opposition party, and the government did not want someone who would not be helpful to it. Today, with the advent of the collegium, the ideology of a judge seldom makes its way into the judicial appointments process. However, in 2017, Justice Jayant Patel, a judge of the Gujarat High Court who was serving at the Karnataka High Court, resigned when the collegium sought to transfer him to the Allahabad High Court, about ten months prior to his retirement.[63] As a Gujarat High Court judge, Patel had ordered a CBI probe of the politically loaded Ishrat Jahan 'fake' encounter case, in which it was alleged that the police had carried out extrajudicial killings of suspected terrorists in fake encounters. This made some wonder whether the collegium was bending to the wishes of the executive government in matters of judicial appointments. Even in the 1980s, it was not merely the government which selected judges based on their views (Chief Justice Bhagwati, for example, looked at the social and economic philosophies of judges while appointing them, and sought out activist judges in his own image). However, factors like the age and seniority of judicial candidates, though not entirely irrelevant in the 1980s, have now become far more prevalent in the judicial appointments process at the Supreme Court.

Though this book is based on interviews which were conducted in the 1980s, much of it still rings true today and the book continues to be a commentary on the modern-day Supreme Court of India. Many things remain the same. The highly public tussle between Chief Justice Dipak Misra and the four other members of the collegium, led by Justice Jasti Chelameswar, over the assignment of cases at the Supreme Court, is perhaps one of the most public judicial disagreements in recent memory. Dissent is still infrequent, though not absent, at the court. The SLP is still overworking and overburdening the typical Supreme Court judge. Prominent lawyers still decline offers to become high court judges (though there are, of course, eminent exceptions), while high court chief justices still don't refuse elevation to the Supreme Court. The criteria for appointing judges have mostly remained the same, despite the collegium system.

I must conclude this introductory chapter, however, on a note of caution. Anyone who reads this book must understand the inherent limitations of its source material. This book is primarily based on conversations that took place between Gadbois and the judges of the Supreme Court in the 1980s. However, this has a few shortcomings which the reader must bear in mind. Firstly, in answering the questions that Gadbois posed them, judges may not have necessarily been telling the whole truth. Perhaps unwittingly, or otherwise, they may have portrayed facts that best suited their side of the story. Therefore, while reading the episode, say, about the rivalry between Chief Justice Sinha and Justice Imam, readers ought to note that the story is based entirely on the version narrated by Chief Justice Sinha, as Justice Imam had passed away in 1964. Of course, Gadbois himself indicated in his interview notes whenever he thought that a judge was not telling him the truth (as was the case, for example, with Chief Justice A.N. Ray, or Law Minister Asoke Sen). Such instances have been highlighted in this book.[64] Secondly, this book assumes that the judges' memories were fine when they were being interviewed by Gadbois. This is a fair assumption because when Gadbois thought that the judges were unable to recount facts correctly (which is what happened, for example, with Chief Justice J.C. Shah), he wrote this down in his notes. For instance, the oldest judge Gadbois met, Vivian Bose, was ninety-two years old. Bose had retired from the Supreme Court in the 1950s, and the interview was conducted in 1983. Though his 'speech [was] affected by strokes,' wrote Gadbois in his notes, his 'mind [was] fine'.[65] Every attempt has been made in this book to cross-reference what one judge told Gadbois against what others told him and against publicly available information. However, readers ought to bear in mind that the stories narrated in this book mostly come from first-hand oral accounts and not from primary historical documentary sources like letters and memoranda in government files. At the same time, apart from the Gadbois interviews, this book relies on published sources (like the private papers of Rajendra Prasad and Sardar Vallabhbhai Patel and autobiographies written by judges over the years), and unpublished publicly available sources (like the papers of Chief Justice P.B. Gajendragadkar at the Nehru Memorial Museum and Library, the papers of President Rajendra Prasad at the National Archives of India, and the Granville Austin papers at the University of Princeton). Thirdly, I have assumed that Gadbois recorded the contents of each interview faithfully and correctly. I have no hesitation that this assumption is fair.

Gadbois was a reputable, serious and established scholar with an unblemished record for outstanding and meticulous social science research.[66] However, since the interviews were not voice-recorded, Gadbois may have paraphrased much of what the judges told him.

1

Judicial Rivalries

Over the years, there have been several personal (sometimes petty) rivalries, jealousies and tensions between judges of the Supreme Court of India, apart from intellectual disagreements over ideology and substance. Disagreements have often occurred between the chief justice of India and the most senior judge of the court who, historically, have been unable to get along. These disputes usually involved matters relating to succession to the post of chief justice of India or post-retirement positions. There have been disputes about the proper role and function of a judge in India: whether a judge should be a mere arbiter of disputes or an activist who sets up a parallel government. At a broader level, stories of these rivalries and disagreements are immensely valuable, not merely because they are anecdotally interesting, but also because they stand in stark contrast to the general lack of dissent in the Supreme Court's decision-making, which we will see in the next chapter. The episodes narrated in this chapter still ring true. In January 2018, the four most senior judges of the Supreme Court of India[1] held an unprecedented press conference in which they complained that the chief justice of India, Dipak Misra, was not assigning cases to benches in a transparent manner. The incidents set out in this chapter reveal that such tussles have historically not been uncommon in the Supreme Court.

Sinha–Imam

The first known, significant rivalry at the Supreme Court was between B.P. Sinha (1899–1986) and S.J. Imam (1900–1965), who served in the court in the 1950s and 1960s. Sinha and Imam began their careers as lawyers at the Patna High Court, and they were appointed judges there in January 1943 and October 1943 respectively. They came to the Supreme Court in quick succession, in December 1954 and January 1955 respectively. Sinha probably disliked Imam because he went ahead of Sinha at the Patna Bar and became the advocate general of the state while Sinha was only an assistant government advocate.[2] Imam clearly had the more distinguished academic background of the two—he had studied at Cambridge and was called to the bar in London.

Imam could actually have come to the Supreme Court before Sinha. Ghulam Hasan, a Muslim Supreme Court judge, died in November 1954. Thereafter, Prime Minister Jawaharlal Nehru was keen on a Muslim judge replacing Hasan, and Imam was the most senior Muslim judge in the country at that time. However, Chief Justice M.C. Mahajan, after consulting his colleagues, recommended the appointment of Sinha for the vacancy created by Hasan's death, and the government accepted the nomination. Sinha believed that Mahajan appointed him over Imam because he wanted him (i.e. Sinha) to become the chief justice of India when S.R. Das retired in October 1959.[3]

Interestingly, Chief Justice S.R. Das hilariously lampooned his colleagues in the speech he gave at his farewell function in September 1959. He referred to his colleague, Justice J.L. Kapur, and said, 'When an argument is in full swing, he distinctly remembers that there is a decision, either of the House of Lords or of the Privy Council, which is pat on the point under discussion, but unfortunately that decision he cannot, for the moment, lay his hands on and all the members of the Bar appearing in the case cannot find it till the case is over.' He referred to Justice P.B. Gajendragadkar, the pro-labour judge, and said, 'His heart is literally bleeding for the under-dogs, and unless the bleeding can be stopped the under-dogs will very soon become top dogs.' He referred to Justice A.K. Sarkar, a bachelor, and said, 'My brother Sarkar has been an onlooker on the highway of life. He attends dinners but does not eat; he sees other people eat. He has joined many bridal processions but has not married. But I do not know whether he will change his mind.' He referred to Justice K. Subba Rao who, as chief justice of India many years later, would pen the majority judgment in the controversial *Golak Nath* case. Das said that Subba Rao 'is extremely unhappy because all our fundamental rights are going to the dogs on account of some ill-conceived judgments of his colleagues which require reconsideration'. He also referred to the Cambridge-educated Justice M. Hidayatullah and said that he 'has given us three Gospels. Stroud's Judicial Dictionary, Wilson's Glossary and Words and Phrases by some author whose name I forget. I do not know when he will produce the fourth Gospel.'[4]

When the time came for B.P. Sinha to be appointed chief justice according to the seniority convention, Sinha believed that a member of Imam's family started spreading false rumours that Sinha was three years older than the records showed.[5] The accusation gained some currency. Alarmed by this, Sinha went to

President Rajendra Prasad, himself a lawyer from Bihar, and told him to conduct an inquiry about Sinha's age. After an informal inquiry, Prasad announced that Sinha would become the next chief justice, about a month prior to Chief Justice Das's retirement.[6]

Justice Rajagopala Ayyangar, who was appointed to the Supreme Court in 1960, said that most judges got along well in his day, except Sinha and Imam.[7]

Later, in January 1964, B.P. Sinha was due to retire as the sixth chief justice of India. Imam was the most senior judge on the court at the time. However, Imam was superseded and his junior colleague, Justice P.B. Gajendragadkar, was appointed to the post of chief justice when Sinha retired. The following story, of Imam's supersession was narrated by Sinha to George H. Gadbois, Jr. during an interview in July 1983. Some of it must perhaps be taken with a pinch of salt because, as we have seen, Sinha and Imam themselves were rivals, having had some bad blood between them.

Imam had been very sick for three years, having had heart problems and strokes. Chief Justice Sinha was very kind to him during that time, giving him little work and stretching the rules about paid leave. But Imam's poor mental health was an open secret among the judges and the bar.[8] Justice Subba Rao, who sat with Imam on the bench, complained that Imam was not able to concentrate. He was not able to follow arguments, asked unintelligible questions to lawyers, and even fell asleep in court.[9] Imam's mind, by that time, was weak. If he wanted to say that something cost Rs 300, he would say that it cost Rs 30,000.[10] He was very ill, and couldn't function as any kind of judge, much less as the chief justice.[11]

Actually, there had been some concern among the judges for several months about Imam's health, because everyone knew that Imam was staying on and not resigning despite his mental incapacity, in order to get promoted to the position of chief justice. Sinha believed that he and Imam were good friends, that the problem was not Imam, who was a 'nice man', but his wife,[12] who wanted him to become the chief justice. Each day, his wife and nurse had to accompany him to the court. When the government came to know about Imam's health, Nehru was worried about what Pakistan would say if a Muslim were bypassed for the position of chief justice. Nehru had a soft corner for minorities. Imam's family had been very close to the Nehru family, and had played a prominent part in Congress politics.[13]

A few weeks before his retirement, Sinha went to Nehru and suggested to Nehru that he invite Imam over for a cup of tea without his wife. Sinha told Nehru to ask Imam to pronounce the words 'Supreme Court' during the tea. If Imam succeeded, Sinha said, Nehru should appoint him as the chief justice. Sinha also suggested to Nehru that a medical examination be conducted for Imam. Sinha and Gajendragadkar also convinced Attorney General C.K. Daphtary and former Attorney General Motilal C. Setalvad to see Nehru about this, in order to convince him to supersede Imam.[14] Nehru informed them that the doctor (a medical examination was conducted by a doctor at the All India Medical Institute[15]) said that Imam did not have, in Sinha's words, as noted down by Gadbois, 'the intelligence of a high school boy'. They gave him three simple math equations to do, which he was not able to handle.[16] Upon receiving the medical report, Nehru agreed that Imam could not be the next chief justice, and Gajendragadkar was appointed instead.

Sinha–Gajendragadkar

P.B. Gajendragadkar (1901–1981) began his career as an advocate at the Bombay High Court. He served as a judge in that court and was thereafter a Supreme Court judge in the 1950s and 1960s. He was reputed to be a pro-labour judge, and served as the chief justice of India after Sinha. Some years after his retirement from the court, he was appointed the chairman of the Law Commission.

As chief justice of India, B.P. Sinha wanted to set up a separate high court for Delhi. Back then, there was a circuit bench of the Punjab High Court in Delhi. However, Sinha's successor in office, Gajendragadkar, 'was of the opinion that a High Court [in Delhi] was neither constitutionally feasible nor expedient'.[17] After Sinha retired, when Gajendragadkar took over the reins of the chief justiceship of the Supreme Court, he wrote to Home Minister Gulzari Lal Nanda and requested him 'not to take any further steps' in setting up a high court at Delhi, adding that all the judges of the Supreme Court, at a 'Chamber Meeting', were 'unanimously inclined to take the view that all things considered, a separate High Court for Delhi would be inexpedient and undesirable'.[18] The Delhi High Court was eventually set up in October 1966,[19] under Chief Justice Subba Rao.

One of the first things that Gajendragadkar did after assuming the office of chief justice of India was to revoke the approval which had been given by Sinha for transferring four judges: Harbans Singh of Punjab and S. Murtaza Fazal Ali of Kashmir, both to Allahabad; and M. Hameedullah Beg and G.C. Mathur, both of Allahabad, to Kashmir and Punjab respectively.[20] Gajendragadkar believed that such transfers would be 'ethically improper' and would 'materially affect the independence of the Judiciary'.[21]

After retiring from office, Sinha wanted to be a part of the Indian Law Institute (ILI), and became its executive chairman.[22] However, Gajendragadkar and he differed on what ILI ought to be doing. Sinha wanted ILI to be an independent body, not under the control of the chief justice, and wanted it to focus on constitutional law research. Gajendragadkar disagreed with this approach, and Sinha eventually left ILI.[23] Without mentioning any names in his autobiography, Sinha wrote that 'petty jealousies and big egotistic personalities combined to put me out of the picture'.[24]

Sinha was of the view that there had to be a code of conduct for judges, but Gajendragadkar, said Sinha, 'summarily rejected the idea of such a code observing that every Judge was expected to know the proper standards and that such a code was redundant'.[25] Influenced in part by his opinion of Gajendragadkar, Sinha believed that all Maharashtrians thought that all non-Maharashtrians were no good. Gajendragadkar was known to be a pro-labour judge (i.e. a judge who decided workmen's cases against the management),[26] so Sinha put Justice K.N. Wanchoo (who was known not to be a pro-labour judge) with him on the bench (though Gajendragadkar claimed that he asked Sinha to put Wanchoo and K.C. Das Gupta with him on the labour bench).[27] However, Sinha said that there was no rift between himself and Gajendragadkar.[28]

Gajendragadkar–Sarkar

Justice P.B. Gajendragadkar did not get along with his number two, Justice A.K. Sarkar (1901–1993). Sarkar, a judge who came to the Supreme Court from Calcutta,[29] served in the court in the 1950s and 1960s. The following is an account narrated by Sarkar to Gadbois. Sarkar believed that Gajendragadkar did not want him to become the chief justice of India once he (i.e. Gajendragadkar) retired. Apparently, Gajendragadkar wanted Sarkar to be superseded, since Sarkar would only get a little over three months as chief justice of India. However, the government was not interested in Gajendragadkar's position, as it was not worried about chief justices having short tenures. Gajendragadkar tried to get other sitting Supreme Court judges to agree that Sarkar should be superseded, but nobody agreed. Eventually, Sarkar learnt that he would become the chief justice a few weeks before Gajendragadkar retired. Sarkar didn't have a very high opinion of Gajendragadkar. In fact, according to Gadbois's notes, Sarkar believed that with the exception of Gajendragadkar, no judge in his generation was interested in publicity-mongering. He said that Gajendragadkar, who is perhaps best known for his judgments in the field of labour law, was able to influence judges like Justices Wanchoo and Das Gupta on the labour bench into deciding cases the way he desired them to be decided. Sarkar dissented from judgments written by Gajendragadkar a lot. While there were never any bad words exchanged between the two, one cannot say that Sarkar was fond of Gajendragadkar.[30]

Appointed to the Supreme Court in the mid-1960s, Justices R.S. Bachawat and V. Ramaswami agreed that Justices Gajendragadkar and Sarkar did not get along, but then again, Bachawat also said that the chief justice and his number two often do not get along.[31]

Gajendragadkar's version of events, however, was different. According to him, Prime Minister Lal Bahadur Shastri wanted to supersede Sarkar because he was likely to have a very short tenure as chief justice of India.[32] However, Gajendragadkar told Shastri not to do so, and said that 'the selection of the Chief Justice must necessarily and always be governed by the rule of seniority'.[33] Before retiring as the chief justice of India, Gajendragadkar recommended to both Prime Minister Indira Gandhi and Home Minister Gulzari Lal Nanda that Sarkar should be appointed to replace him, and that the 'convention which has been invariably followed . . . to select for appointment as Chief Justice of India the Judge of the Supreme Court who happens to [be] the seniormost Judge at the time when the vacancy occurs' must not be departed from, even though Sarkar would 'have a very short tenure as Chief Justice of India'.[34] Later still, Gajendragadkar unsuccessfully tried to persuade Prime Minister Indira Gandhi not to supersede four judges, J.M. Shelat, K.S. Hegde, A.N. Grover and H.R. Khanna.[35]

Hidayatullah–Shah

M. Hidayatullah (1905–1992) and J.C. Shah (1906–1991) were judges of the Supreme Court between the late 1950s and early 1970s. In his well-known autobiography, *My Own Boswell*,[36] Justice Hidayatullah wrote that one of his colleagues was jealous of him. In his own words: 'One colleague wrote a separate opinion every time I wrote what others considered a well-written Judgment. I attributed this to jealousy.' Though he did not name the judge in his autobiography, he was referring to Justice J.C. Shah.[37] For instance, in *Maganbhai Ishwarbhai v. Union of India*,[38] Chief Justice Hidayatullah wrote the majority judgment for himself and three other judges. In that case, the Supreme Court was considering whether the Government of India could give up territory in the Rann of Kutch to Pakistan, after the 1965 war, without the approval of India's Parliament. Shah wrote a separate concurring judgment. Hidayatullah said that Shah also disagreed[39] with his famous judgment in the *Lady Chatterley's Lover* case,[40] though no dissent was formally recorded. In that case, the Supreme Court upheld the conviction of a bookseller in Bombay for selling D.H. Lawrence's novel *Lady Chatterley's Lover*, on the grounds that it was obscene.

However, Hidayatullah was proud of the fact that he 'saved' Shah from being superseded.[41] Hidayatullah was due to retire as chief justice of India in December 1970. Shah was the next most senior judge at the time, and was supposed to replace Hidayatullah as chief justice. However, the government was contemplating superseding Shah for having written the majority judgment against the government in the *Bank Nationalization* case,[42] and replacing him with the cabinet minister of steel and mines, S. Mohan Kumaramangalam,[43] or possibly with Calcutta lawyer S.C. Roy, who later became a Supreme Court judge.[44] However, the government never formally acknowledged whether this rumour was true. Hidayatullah went to Prime Minister Indira Gandhi and told her that there was going to be an international convention of lawyers from around the world in Delhi within a few days, that if Shah were superseded, all the judges of the court (but one) would resign,[45] and the world would know what had happened. The one judge who was not willing to resign was Justice A.N. Ray, who told Justice Hidayatullah that he could not afford to resign. However, there had never really been any formal vote among the judges on whether they were willing to resign. There had only been informal talks about resignation.[46] At the time, another judge who was serving in the Supreme Court, Justice Grover, went and met Nagendra Singh, who was the secretary to the President of India, to try and convince him not to go ahead with the supersession. Grover had good relations with Singh. Singh himself wanted to be a judge of the Supreme Court, and hoped that Grover would appoint him to the court when he became the chief justice.[47]

A motion had also been introduced by S.M. Joshi in Parliament to impeach Justice J.C. Shah. The move arose not merely on account of his decision in the *Bank Nationalization* case, but also because of some critical remarks Shah made about a litigant in a case.[48] That litigant happened to have some very powerful political friends, and the impeachment motion was brought about as a consequence. Hidayatullah believed that Joshi was a disreputable character, that many of the 199 MPs who had signed the motion of impeachment had done so under a misapprehension, and that they had later withdrawn their names. Speaker of the Lok Sabha, G.S. Dhillon, disallowed the motion of impeachment, and the statement made by Dhillon on the occasion was drafted by Hidayatullah himself.[49] Prime Minister Indira Gandhi claimed to have had nothing to do with the motion.[50] Contempt proceedings were initiated against the litigant, who went underground and was later sentenced to imprisonment.[51]

Thus, though relations may not have been good between judges in the 1960s and early 1970s, they were kept under wraps behind closed doors, and not displayed in the open.

Beg–Goswami

In the March 1977 Lok Sabha elections following the Emergency, the Janata Party routed the Congress. Thereafter, on 18 April 1977, the Union home minister, Charan Singh, wrote a letter to nine Congress-ruled states directing them to ask their governors to dissolve their assemblies and call fresh elections. Six[52] of those states filed suits in the Supreme Court of India, seeking a declaration that the directions contained in the minister's letter were illegal. On 29 April 1977, a bench of seven judges of the Supreme Court dismissed the suits, without giving reasons, and said that reasons would be given in separate judgments delivered later on. On 6 May 1977, the court delivered its judgments in the case, *State of Rajasthan v. Union of India.*[53] However, one of the judges, Justice P.K. Goswami (1913–1992), concluded his judgment with what he called 'a cold shudder'.[54] He wrote that Chief Justice Beg (1913–1988) had informed him and the others that the acting President of India, B.D. Jatti, had seen him after the 29 April order, and that 'there was mention of this pending matter during the conversation'. Goswami wrote that he had given this matter 'the most anxious thought' and that he hoped 'the majesty of the High Office of the President, who should be beyond the high watermark of any controversy, suffers not in future'.

When Chief Justice M. Hameedullah Beg read Goswami's judgment, he immediately issued a press statement on 6 May itself, and said that Goswami's observations seemed 'to be based on quite a wrong impression'. Jatti had visited Beg to invite him for his son's marriage reception and had not uttered 'a single word about the constitutional case'. The reception was scheduled to be held on 7 May. If Beg attended the reception, he was likely to meet Jatti and other ministers of the Union government. Jatti therefore wanted the judgment of the court to be delivered before his son's reception, in order to avoid awkwardness at the reception. He did not, clarified Beg, want to see the judgment itself. Beg said it was 'very regrettable' that Goswami 'should have misunderstood the Chief Justice', who was only 'anxious that the reasons should be delivered before the Court closes so that the Judges are not placed in any embarrassing situation during the vacation', i.e. while attending the reception.

During his interview with Gadbois, Beg was very critical of Goswami for his concluding paragraph in that case. He believed that Goswami had some political motivations for writing it. Jatti had been appointed under the Congress regime, and the case concerned the Janata government. However, the press release issued by Beg was not entirely accurate. Jatti had said more to Beg about the case than what was revealed in the press release. Jatti had telephoned Beg to ask him what would happen if he refused to sign the dissolution warrant. He believed that signing the warrant would be morally wrong. Beg said that he could deal with questions of law, not morality, that this was a legal question which would have to come to the Supreme Court, perhaps as a reference made by the President under Article 143[55] of the Constitution. It was Beg himself who revealed the meeting between him and Jatti at the judges' daily meeting in the chief justice's chamber one morning. That is where Goswami heard about it.[56] Beg contemplated initiating contempt proceedings against Goswami over this issue.[57]

Goswami, on the other hand, said that his colleagues on the bench agreed with his criticism of Beg about the Jatti meeting. Justice K.K. Mathew, in particular, said Goswami, supported him.[58]

The Beleaguered Justice Ray[59]

Chief Justice A.N. Ray (1912–2010) was appointed to the Supreme Court of India in August 1969. In the ordinary scheme of things, he was not in line to become the chief justice of India. According to the seniority convention,[60] after Chief Justice S.M. Sikri retired from the court in April 1973, the post of chief justice would go to Justice Shelat, who would retire in July 1973, after which Justice Hegde would hold the post until his retirement in June 1974. Hegde would then be followed by Justice Grover, who would retire in February 1977, one month after the scheduled retirement of Justice Ray in January 1977. In other words, Justice Ray was slated to retire as a puisne judge during the chief justiceship of Justice Grover. Destiny had other things in store for Ray. When Sikri retired in April 1973, the Indira Gandhi government decided to supersede Shelat, Hegde and Grover, and appoint Ray to the post of chief justice instead. The superseded judges had decided many cases against the government, including the most recent case of *Kesavananda Bharati v. State of Kerala*,[61] in which the Supreme Court decided, by a majority (which included the three superseded judges) of seven to six judges, that Parliament did not have the power to amend certain basic features of the Constitution. Ray became an unpopular figure at the court after he assumed the office of chief justice of India, because he was seen as someone who had betrayed his colleagues.

Gadbois met Ray in June 1983 in Calcutta. By then, it had been six years since Ray had retired from the Supreme Court. The interview lasted three hours, but could have gone on for longer. Ray's wife sat with him for two out of the three hours. Ray was 'very nervous, but tried to appear in control'. He answered every question which Gadbois asked, but only answered precisely what was asked. If Gadbois did not follow up on an answer, he got nothing more out of Ray. He seemed especially nervous when Gadbois discussed each of the judges who had been appointed to the Supreme Court during Ray's tenure as chief justice of India. Gadbois considered this to have been one of the most interesting interviews of all. 'Even after thinking about it for a few days,' wrote Gadbois in his private notes later on, 'I still don't know whether I was given a massive snow job or not.' A 'snow job' is 'an attempt . . . to persuade someone that something is good or true, when it is not'.[62] The first thing Ray asked Gadbois when he met him was his age, and he then said that Gadbois looked like Ernest Hemingway. Ray offered Gadbois mango and sweets during the interview.

Ray pointed out to Gadbois that though the supersession of Shelat, Hegde and Grover was announced on 25 April 1973,[63] the three judges did not resign from the court immediately.

He tersely said that Shelat and Hegde went on leave until 30 April, while Grover went on leave until 31 May.[64] He implied that this had something to do with their pensions; that the three judges did not resign immediately in order to ensure that they would have sufficient years in service so as to receive an enhanced pension upon retirement. Ray said that since the three judges were still members of the Supreme Court when he was appointed the chief justice, they should have accepted him in his new post, and treated him accordingly. He suggested that the three judges who had been superseded behaved selfishly regarding their pensions, and were immoral in their criticism of the supersession. In saying all of this, Gadbois thought that Ray came across as 'bitter and sarcastic and self-righteous'.

In fact, there does not appear to be much truth to the allegation that Shelat, Hegde and Grover hung on at the Supreme Court in order to become eligible to receive enhanced pensions. Under the prevalent rules at the time, judges had to have seven years in office in order to get higher pensions.[65] Shelat had the seven years in office, so holding on at the Supreme Court would not have helped him. Hegde and Grover did not have the seven years in office, but continuing at the court until 31 May did not give them seven years in office either. At the most, perhaps they went on leave, instead of resigning immediately, in order to make use of unutilized leave entitlement.

Ray said that many of those who had criticized the supersession 'didn't have the standing of a school leaving certificate'. He was very sarcastic and sharp-tongued, thought Gadbois. Ray even told Gadbois that he thought that the story about the contemplated supersession of Justice Patanjali Sastri in 1951, which we will see in a subsequent chapter, was made up by M.C. Chagla (chief justice of the Bombay High Court) and Motilal C. Setalvad (attorney general of India) in order to make themselves look good.

Ray informed Gadbois that if he had not accepted the chief justiceship upon the supersession of the three judges, he too would have been superseded. He said that while nobody had said this to him in so many words, he had understood that this was the situation. 'If I didn't accept [the Chief Justiceship],' he said, 'someone else would have been offered it. I did not hanker for it.' Ray said that he was asked on 24 April if he would take the job and was given two hours to decide. However, Justices Hegde and P. Jaganmohan Reddy[66] did not believe this to be true. They thought that Ray knew long before, well in advance of the pronouncement of the *Kesavananda Bharati* judgment, that he would be appointed chief justice after Sikri.[67] In fact, at a dinner held for the Russian ambassador a week before the supersession, P. Jaganmohan Reddy and his wife had heard cabinet minister of steel and mines, Kumaramangalam congratulate Ray on his impending appointment as chief justice of India.[68] Before Ray, Justice Mathew had been asked by someone junior in the Union law ministry whether he would be interested in accepting the chief justiceship of the Supreme Court after the supersession, but Mathew had declined because he thought that it would be wrong to supersede senior judges.[69] By failing to do what Mathew had done, Ray became unpopular among his colleagues.

Ray and Shelat used to carpool to the court together.[70] Before the supersession was announced, on 25 April, Ray asked Shelat whose car would be used the following day. Hegde thought that this was very crude of Ray.[71]

In his interview with Gadbois, Ray lost no time in defending his controversial decisions in the Supreme Court. He commented on his judgment in the infamous *Habeas Corpus* case,[72] in which the Supreme Court had essentially held that the government had the power to arbitrarily arrest any person during an emergency, that the right to life and to the writ of habeas corpus stood suspended during an emergency. While commenting on this judgment, he said that it was obvious to anyone with any sense that one cannot have the writ of habeas corpus during an emergency.

In November 1975, Ray had convened a controversial bench to reconsider the decision of the Supreme Court in *Kesavananda Bharati*. After a few days' arguments, the bench was mysteriously dissolved. When Gadbois asked him about this, Ray treated it as a matter of little consequence. He said that he dissolved the bench on the third morning of the case because his colleagues said to him that there were no live issues to consider,[73] and that the hearing of the case would take six months, which was a waste of time.

In fact, getting *Kesavananda Bharati* reversed seemed to be a priority for Chief Justice Ray. In October 1975,[74] Ray called on Justice R.S. Pathak who was, at that time, the chief justice of the high court of Himachal Pradesh. When Ray was appointed the chief justice of India in 1973, Pathak was one of the few (if only) high court chief justices who did not write Ray a congratulatory letter.[75] Ray quizzed Pathak about his views on the *Kesavananda Bharati* judgment to determine whether Pathak would be inclined to overrule it. When Pathak refused to answer, Ray decided not to appoint him to the Supreme Court, and instead he appointed Justice P.N. Shinghal in November 1975.[76]

He had very unflattering things to say about other members of his court. When asked about Justice Krishna Iyer, who was known for writing judgments in particularly dense jargon, Ray remarked, 'I am not responsible for his judgements.'[77] He criticized Justices P.N. Bhagwati and Krishna Iyer for releasing their concurring judgment in the 'presidential power case' (i.e. *Samsher Singh v. State of Punjab*[78]) to the press before Ray's judgment for the court was announced or publicized. In that case, the governor of Punjab had terminated the services of two subordinate judges, Samsher Singh and Ishwar Chand Agarwal. The question was whether the governor had the power to do so on his own personal authority, i.e., without consulting the council of ministers of the state government. Speaking for the majority of the court, Ray held that the governor must act on the aid and advice of the council of ministers while exercising functions like dismissing judges in the subordinate judiciary. Justices Krishna Iyer and Bhagwati agreed with Ray. Ray was particularly miffed with these two judges for 'hawking' their judgment to the press. Ray was critical of the generation of judges serving at the court in the 1980s, and said that they were trying to be popular. Gadbois got the impression that Ray was quite isolated and aloof from his colleagues.

Ray said that he was unhappy with Bhagwati because Bhagwati had never paid him a visit at his home in Calcutta after he had retired, that Bhagwati had not even spoken to him after his retirement. He said that this reflected a lack of courtesy on Bhagwati's part. He pointed out that both Y.V. Chandrachud and Krishna Iyer had visited him.

'I don't know what to think,' wrote Gadbois in his typewritten notes after the interview. 'He seemed at peace with himself, but then he seemed very nervous.' 'Was he telling me the truth?' he asked himself, 'I really have serious doubts . . .'

Some members of the legal profession did not have a very high opinion of Chief Justice Ray. L.M. Singhvi[79] informed Gadbois that he thought Ray was completely a 'Government man', that the judges who were appointed to the Supreme Court during Ray's tenure as chief justice were forced upon him by the government. Singhvi thought that the entire bar considered Ray to be a disaster, that few people had any respect for him, including his own colleagues.

Ray, a puisne judge of the Calcutta High Court, was appointed to the Supreme Court on virtually the same day that his patron, Justice Bachawat, retired from the court, in August 1969. Ray's appointment to the Supreme Court itself had come as a surprise to some at the Calcutta High Court.[80]

Bachawat had originally recommended Ray's name to Chief Justice Hidayatullah for appointment to the Supreme Court.[81] Hegde, who strongly disliked Ray, said that Ray used to praise Hidayatullah and 'Muslim nawabs like [him]' prior to 1969, and it was for this reason that Ray was appointed and sworn in as a Supreme Court judge before P. Jaganmohan Reddy and I.D. Dua, even though Reddy was senior to Ray, and both were older than Ray.[82] Years later, Jaganmohan Reddy and his wife were still very upset that Ray was sworn in ahead of Reddy. In this case, seniority was a matter of status, though nothing turned on it as neither was in line to be appointed the chief justice of India in the ordinary scheme of things.[83]

Bachawat settled in Delhi after he retired from the court, and Ray used to visit him. However, once Ray became the chief justice of India in April 1973, he never spoke to Bachawat again, who felt quite sore and hurt about this and held Ray in low esteem thereafter. He thought that the chief justiceship went to Ray's head. He even doubted whether Ray told Gadbois the truth during the interview.[84]

While Ray himself told Gadbois that he was instrumental in making judicial appointments during his term as chief justice, others like Hegde said that he was a weak chief justice who accepted whatever appointment the government pushed on

him.[85] Hegde was miffed with Ray for raising judges' pensions
from 1974;[86] having resigned from office in 1973, Hegde did
not get the benefit of an increased pension.[87] Both Hegde and
Grover felt that Ray's judgments after he was appointed to the
Supreme Court in 1969 were steadily pro-government, and that
he was angling himself or working towards the chief justiceship.[88]
Grover considered Ray to be the weakest chief justice of all
time.[89] Jaganmohan Reddy believed that Ray expected to be
rewarded with the post of President of India some day, and he
was bitter about not having been made the President. He also
believed that Prime Minister Indira Gandhi asked Ray's opinion
on the supersession of Justice Khanna, and that he urged her
to go ahead with it.[90] Chief Justice Chandrachud remembered
Ray to be a very elegant man who wore expensive suits and had
fourteen pairs of expensive shoes, and found it odd that, even so,
the government believed that he was a socialist.[91]

Of course, not everyone thought poorly of Ray. Justice
Ranga Nath Misra, for instance, said that Ray was a good man,
that he was very religious, that he had been unfairly criticized
by scholars and deserved to be vindicated.[92] Justice Bhagwati
thought that Ray was an enigma and an honest man who
genuinely believed that Prime Minister Gandhi was the nation's
saviour.[93]

Chandrachud–Bhagwati

Of all the rivalries among judges in the Supreme Court of India,
the one between Justices Y.V. Chandrachud (1920–2008) and
P.N. Bhagwati (1921–2017) perhaps stands out the most. Both
were Bombay lawyers who eventually served in the Supreme
Court in the 1970s and 1980s. Theirs was easily one of the most
public rivalries in the history of the Supreme Court of India.

The antagonism between Chandrachud and Bhagwati probably dated back to their days at the Bombay Bar. Chandrachud was older than Bhagwati and, having enrolled as a lawyer earlier, was senior to him. However, Bhagwati's father, N.H. Bhagwati, was a judge of the Bombay High Court, who would eventually go on to become a Supreme Court judge. Rumour had it that senior Bhagwati was not very nice to the advocates who were considered junior Bhagwati's competitors. Senior Bhagwati was transferred from the prestigious Original Side[94] of the High Court to the Appellate Side, because Advocate General H.M. Seervai complained about him to Chief Justice Chagla. N.H. Bhagwati did not like Chandrachud at all.[95]

Bhagwati was appointed a judge of the newly established Gujarat High Court in July 1960 by S.T. Desai, the first chief justice of the Gujarat High Court,[96] who was very close to Bhagwati's father. Desai had sent up Bhagwati's name in May 1960, when the Supreme Court was closed for the summer vacation, at a point in time when Justice Gajendragadkar, who might have blocked the appointment, had come back home to Bombay for the summer.[97] Initially, Bhagwati didn't want to go to Ahmedabad, even though he had been born there, because Bombay was home for him, but he reluctantly accepted when Desai spoke to his father to persuade him to accept.[98]

On the other hand, Chandrachud was appointed a judge at the Bombay High Court in March 1961. Bhagwati was thirty-eight years old when he was appointed a High Court judge, while Chandrachud was forty. Chandrachud's appointment to the Bombay High Court was stalled on account of a speech made by Chief Justice B.P. Sinha at that court. While visiting Bombay, Sinha had expressed the view that no advocate from the bar ought to be appointed to the bench unless he was between the ages of forty-five and fifty-five. Chief Justice H.K.

Chainani of the Bombay High Court took this as a formal rule, and refused to recommend Chandrachud's name for a high court judgeship. This was despite the fact that Sinha had not objected to Bhagwati's appointment as a high court judge below the age of forty. Gajendragadkar, a sitting Supreme Court judge at that time, learnt of this, and informed Sinha that his Bombay speech was being taken literally by the chief justice there. Sinha then told Gajendragadkar to tell Chainani to recommend Chandrachud's name without delay. Gajendragadkar conveyed the message to Chainani, and it was under these circumstances that Chandrachud became a high court judge, when he was forty years old.[99] Chandrachud's appointment to the Bombay High Court was also delayed by the fact that he was involved, as the government pleader, in arguing the famous *Nanavati* case at the high court.[100]

Many Supreme Court judges at the time believed that Bhagwati and Chandrachud would eventually be appointed to the Supreme Court.[101] They were identified as being among the three most brilliant judges in the country—the third one was Justice R.S. Pathak.[102] By September 1967, Bhagwati had also become the chief justice of the Gujarat High Court, while Chandrachud was still a puisne judge in Bombay. Though Bhagwati was younger than Chandrachud and had been junior to him at the Bombay Bar, there is no doubt that Bhagwati was senior to Chandrachud in the judiciary.

Chief Justice J.C. Shah, who served as the chief justice of India between December and January 1971, recommended Bhagwati's name for elevation to the Supreme Court. Both were Gujaratis. However, Justice J.M. Shelat, who was in the Supreme Court at the time, and who had served as chief justice of the Gujarat High Court, torpedoed Bhagwati's nomination. Shelat gave Chief Justice Sikri the impression that Bhagwati was interested in 'pleasing the Government'. Shelat had apparently heard that in 1970 or 1971, Bhagwati had made a speech at a public function in Ahmedabad, in the presence of Union Law Minister H.R. Gokhale, that all judges should be committed to the Congress. This embarrassed even Gokhale, who had stood up and said that this was not what the government wanted.[103] Sikri had known Bhagwati because Bhagwati would call upon him when he visited Delhi from Gujarat (though Sikri did not tell Gadbois that Bhagwati was canvassing for an appointment to the Supreme Court).[104] Sikri did not concur with Shah's recommendation.[105] When Shah realized that Shelat's opposition would prevent Bhagwati's appointment from going through, he withdrew his recommendation, as he didn't want to hurt Bhagwati's record (otherwise, Bhagwati's file would have had an entry showing that his appointment had been rejected).[106] Shah said that he had indeed 'sent Bhagwati's name over' for appointment, but that 'ultimately, the Government has the appointing power'.[107]

Years later, Bhagwati thought that Shelat had blackballed his elevation to the Supreme Court on account of a personal grudge. Justice Shelat's daughter had once wanted to marry one of Bhagwati's brothers, but his brother had declined. Bhagwati wondered whether this had something to do with Shelat's recommendation against him.[108] Bhagwati told Gadbois that Shelat didn't like him, which is why he halted his appointment.[109] If Bhagwati had been appointed to the Supreme Court on Chief Justice J.C. Shah's recommendation, he would have served in the office of chief justice of India between January 1977 (upon the retirement of Chief Justice A.N. Ray) and December 1986 (when he reached the retirement age of sixty-five), by far the longest term served by any chief justice of India.

Eventually, Chandrachud was elevated to the Supreme Court before Bhagwati, on account of the efforts of Law

Minister H.R. Gokhale.[110] Though Chandrachud thought of Gajendragadkar as his godfather, he may not have had a hand in Chandrachud's appointment to the Supreme Court.[111] Gajendragadkar had been very close to Chandrachud's uncle and father-in-law. In earlier days, the latter would send work from Pune to Bombay for Gajendragadkar when he was still a lawyer.[112] Yet, Chandrachud, said Chief Justice Sikri, was 'completely my choice'.[113] Chief Justice Sikri said that their relative ages were taken into account while deciding whom to appoint to the Supreme Court first, Chandrachud or Bhagwati. The fact that Chandrachud was older than Bhagwati held some weight. The fact that Shelat did not like Bhagwati also weighed against Bhagwati. Whenever Chandrachud's name was discussed for appointment to the Supreme Court, Bhagwati's name was also discussed. In fact, everyone was aware of the implications of appointing either Chandrachud or Bhagwati first; the fact that one or the other would have an enormous term as the chief justice of India.[114] In his autobiography, P. Jaganmohan Reddy wrote that after Chandrachud was elevated to the Supreme Court, '[t]here was . . . a grouse entertained by a Chief Justice of a High Court who, though junior, thought he should have been considered by reason of the office held by him. His attempts did not succeed.'[115] He was, in all probability, referring to Bhagwati.

Justice Hegde, on the other hand, wanted Bhagwati to be appointed to the Supreme Court before Chandrachud. He tried his best to convince Chief Justice Sikri to do so, and when his efforts failed, he let Bhagwati know that he would be appointed to the Supreme Court next.[116] He thought that Bhagwati was more competent than Chandrachud.[117] Hegde[118] and some others,[119] including Bhagwati[120] himself, thought that Gajendragadkar might have had a hand in Chandrachud's appointment to the Supreme Court as well. Never a fan of Chandrachud, Hegde regretted the fact that he did not oppose Chandrachud's appointment to the Supreme Court.

Hegde would go on to regret the enthusiasm he had shown for appointing Justice Bhagwati to the Supreme Court as well, put off by how ambitious Bhagwati would soon show himself to be.[121] When Indira Gandhi came back to power after the Janata government, Bhagwati wrote her a letter in which he said, 'Today the reddish glow of the rising sun is holding out the promise of a bright sunshine.' The letter was leaked to the press, and Bhagwati was criticized for writing the letter, among others, by Seervai, who pointed out that in a case decided a few years earlier,[122] Bhagwati had described the Indira Gandhi government's electoral defeat at the hands of the Janata Party in the harshest of terms, calling it a 'crushing defeat' and 'symptomatic of complete alienation between the Government and the people'. Gadbois thought that Bhagwati's letter was 'the most scandalous incident involving a [Supreme Court] judge'.[123]

When Chief Justice Beg was due to retire from the Supreme Court in February 1978, the Janata Party government contemplated superseding Chandrachud to punish him for his decision in the *Habeas Corpus* case.[124] Law Minister Shanti Bhushan wrote letters to all of Chandrachud's colleagues at the Supreme Court, as well as to all high court chief justices, asking their opinion on whether Chandrachud ought to be superseded.[125] Justice P.S. Kailasam, who was in the Supreme Court at the time, believed that Bhagwati (and Krishna Iyer) voted in favour of superseding Chandrachud.[126] However, Shanti Bhushan said that Bhagwati was the only judge who 'did not express any opinion on the point', whereas another Supreme Court judge (whom he did not name) and one high court chief justice said that seniority need not be adhered to.[127]

Rumour had it that the noted lawyer Nani A. Palkhivala was offered the chief justiceship of the Supreme Court at this time, but that he declined.[128]

Eventually, Chandrachud was appointed the chief justice of India in February 1978 (upon the retirement of Chief Justice M. Hameedullah Beg), and has served the longest term in office as such, up to July 1985, over seven years. By contrast, Bhagwati served as chief justice of India for only a little over a year.

Bhagwati made Chandrachud's tenure as chief justice somewhat difficult. He torpedoed two of Chandrachud's nominations for appointment to the Supreme Court: Justice V.S. Deshpande and M.N. Chandurkar.[129] Bhagwati had informed Chandrachud that he would support the Chandurkar nomination, but then he went to the prime minister and said things against Chandurkar.[130] Bhagwati went to President Sanjiva Reddy to blackball the Deshpande nomination.[131]

Chandrachud and Bhagwati tried to convey the impression that they got along fine.[132] In his judgment in the *First Judges* case,[133] for example, Bhagwati had cited an article written by Chandrachud's son, then a law student,[134] on evolving trends in the doctrine of locus standi. In an interview with *India Today* magazine, published after he retired from office, Chandrachud said that there had been 'no notable differences' between him and Bhagwati, that there was not a single incident between the two which reflected any 'personal animosity'. Chandrachud even referred to the 'word of praise' which Bhagwati lavished on his son's article in the *First Judges* case, saying that this was 'generous on [Bhagwati's] part'. 'The general impression,' said Chandrachud, 'that all is not well between us arose because of observations made by him in two of his judgments which, with respect, were somewhat harsh.' Chandrachud was probably referring to the *First Judges* case and the case of *Minerva Mills*, which we will see below. But Chandrachud said that he did not allow those observations to mar their relationship.[135]

However, most observers considered there to be real animosity between the two.[136] In the *First Judges* case itself, Chandrachud had been made to file an affidavit by Bhagwati,[137] which some considered unacceptable.[138] The affidavit justified the transfer of Chief Justice K.B.N. Singh of the Patna High Court to the Madras High Court.[139] Bhagwati then described the affidavit as 'delightfully vague'.[140] Justice D.G. Palekar, who had ceased to be at the court by that time, said that Bhagwati never got over the fact that Chandrachud was appointed to the Supreme Court before him.[141] Eventually, by a narrow majority of 4–3,[142] the Supreme Court held that the transfer of Chief Justice K.B.N. Singh was valid, thereby accepting what Chief Justice Chandrachud had said in his affidavit.[143]

Bhagwati himself considered Chandrachud to be a good judge but a weak leader.[144] He did not support the seniority convention, and believed that only a strong leader should have been appointed the chief justice.[145]

Bhagwati also criticized Chandrachud for not giving members of the bench in a case, *Minerva Mills v. Union of India*,[146] an adequate opportunity to consult with each other prior to delivering judgment. This case dealt with the important question of the validity of the 42nd amendment to the Constitution, enacted by the Indira Gandhi government in 1976 during the Emergency. One of the members of the bench, Justice A.C. Gupta, said that there had, in fact, been consultations between members of the bench in the *Minerva Mills* case.[147] He said that Bhagwati made those comments because he disliked Chandrachud and wanted him to resign so that he would become the chief justice of India.[148] In fact, after Bhagwati's comments, two of Chandrachud's colleagues

(N.L. Untwalia and Kailasam[149]) wrote letters to Chandrachud, saying that there had been a full discussion among the judges in the case, but Chandrachud decided not to take any action against Bhagwati, in an 'endeavour . . . to hold the court together, even at the cost of personal embarrassment'.[150] In fact, ironically, the judges who heard the *First Judges* case,[151] which was presided over by Bhagwati, were not given an opportunity by Bhagwati to circulate draft judgments among themselves.[152]

Though there had been personal rivalries among judges in the Supreme Court in the past, the Chandrachud–Bhagwati disagreement was unique for how incredibly public it was. It was as though the judiciary was washing its dirty linen in public. Several judges were highly critical of how publicly the court had polarized, and how it had developed two factions—a Chandrachud faction and a Bhagwati faction.[153]

In hindsight, perhaps there is some truth in saying that the friction between Chandrachud and Bhagwati was a little exaggerated or overstated. Relations between the two, especially after retirement, were very cordial. It is also hard to deny that the late Justice Bhagwati was one of the greatest judges the Supreme Court has ever seen. He remains, to this day, an inspiration to young lawyers and judges in India and overseas.

Activists and Conservatives

Apart from personal animosities and rivalries, the Supreme Court of the 1970s and 1980s had interesting ideological divisions. Ideological rivalries, however, became very personal at times. Substantively (and not personally) speaking, the court was divided among judges who identified themselves as activists, and those who did not. In 1983, Justice Pathak said that there were three distinct groups in the court at that time: firstly, there were the British-style legalists who looked only at the law, not social and economic conditions. These judges were essentially conservatives. Secondly, there was a centrist group, which was sensitive to changing circumstances and the need for change, but which wished to remain within the confines of the law and Constitution. These judges were unwilling to become judicial legislators, and were conscious of the limitations of judicial power. Thirdly, there were judges who considered themselves to be lawmakers, those who wished to initiate change, to make law, correct social problems and go beyond what the legislature had envisioned.[154]

There were, broadly speaking, two defining features of an activist judge: firstly, an activist judge interpreted the Constitution in a manner that stretched it beyond what the framers of the Constitution had intended. These activist judges were opposed to those who we refer to, in today's parlance, as 'strict constructionists'. They believed, in essence, in the idea of a living Constitution; that the words of the Constitution had to be given meaning according to the social realities of the times in which the court was sitting. Secondly, activists adopted procedural innovations: they converted letters and postcards into writ petitions, and relaxed rules of standing to enable petitions to be filed on behalf of those who could not come to the court. Both these limbs of judicial activism—expansionist interpretation and procedural innovation—were aimed at benefiting the poor. This emphasis on protecting the downtrodden and helpless is perhaps missing in modern-day activist judgments.[155] The most diehard activists of the 1980s particularly identified themselves as being pro-employee in labour disputes between labour and management, and as being pro-tenant in tenancy cases between landlord and tenant.

Judicial activism in India in the 1980s arose out of the famous dissent of Justice H.R. Khanna in the *Habeas Corpus* case.[156] The framers of the Constitution had specifically intended that the right to life and personal liberty, including the right to seek remedies against arbitrary arrest and detention (i.e. through the writ of 'habeas corpus'), could be suspended during an emergency. The idea was that if the existence of the State itself was at risk, then individuals could not claim to have rights until the State first secured itself. Consequently, when Indira Gandhi imposed the Emergency in the 1970s, a bench of five judges of the Supreme Court, by a majority of 4–1 in the *Habeas Corpus* case, held that the right to seek the writ of habeas corpus could be suspended during the Emergency. This was a conservative interpretation, one which accorded with the intent of the framers of the Constitution. Only one judge dissented in that case, Justice H.R. Khanna, whose judgment was essentially activist in nature. He invoked the idea that the right to life existed even before the Constitution, and therefore the suspension of Article 21 (the right to life and personal liberty) did not mean that the pre-Constitution right to life could be taken away by the government.[157] This was clearly an interpretation which went beyond the circumscribed limits of the Constitution, though commendably and courageously. After the decision was handed down, it was widely perceived that the majority of the judges in the *Habeas Corpus* case had failed in their duty to uphold the Constitution, and that Khanna's activist judgment was a legitimate one. It was this phenomenon—the legitimacy of judicial activism during the Emergency—which created the space for the activist judges of the 1980s.[158]

Four judges very openly identified themselves as activist judges: Justices P.N. Bhagwati, Krishna Iyer, D.A. Desai and M.P. Thakkar.

Bhagwati told Gadbois that he was consciously trying to create more rights than were available under the Constitution. He felt that the right to life under Article 21 of the Constitution ought to contain more freedoms than had been conventionally believed. For instance, he felt that Article 21 must give indigent accused persons the right to receive legal aid.[159] This was part of the doctrine of 'substantive due process', introduced in Indian constitutional law at this time.[160] In his discussions with Gadbois, Bhagwati was quite open about the fact that he had introduced the constitutional law doctrine of 'procedural due process' to Indian constitutional law (he was obviously referring to his famous judgment in *Maneka Gandhi v. Union of India,*[161] where the Supreme Court rejected the intent of the framers of India's Constitution to delete the American 'due process clause' from the Constitution[162]). Procedural due process, said Bhagwati, meant that procedures set up by the government for depriving rights must be fair, reasonable and acceptable to the Supreme Court.[163] Bhagwati believed that his brand of judicial activism differed from that of Krishna Iyer because Bhagwati stayed within the confines of the Constitution and law, while Krishna Iyer sometimes went beyond them.[164] However, by introducing the doctrines of substantive and procedural due process into Indian constitutional law, contrary to the intent of the framers of the Constitution, Bhagwati also went much past the limits of the Constitution.

Justice Krishna Iyer too described himself as a 'judicial activist'. Judicial activism, said Iyer, meant the 'furtherance of . . . social causes', 'advancing the cause of the backward classes, and not just those identified as such by the government'. Krishna Iyer said that he favoured the approach of 'benign discrimination', i.e. virtually twisting the law and Constitution in order to support and help the downtrodden.

However, Krishna Iyer too thought that he was being faithful to the Constitution. He said that the Constitution contained an approved social and economic philosophy, but most judges, because of their class backgrounds, were not able to apply the philosophy faithfully.[165] He said that the elite class backgrounds of many judges helped explain why so many of them decided cases in favour of landlords over tenants.[166]

D.A. Desai, another activist, was particularly proud of his judgment in *D.S. Nakara v. Union of India*.[167] The Government of India had introduced higher pensions for some retired government employees—only those who retired after March 1979. Anyone who retired before that date got the older, lower pension. Invoking socialism, Justice Desai struck down the government's policy of a different pension based on a different retirement date, and said that the new pensions would be payable to all the retired employees,[168] regardless of their date of retirement. Desai told Gadbois that he thought that his conservative colleagues on the bench in that case, especially V.D. Tulzapurkar and A. Varadarajan, would dissent, but they went along with him and the judgment was unanimous.[169] Desai said that he was very pro-labour and pro-tenant in his decisions.[170] He supported the supersession of Justices Shelat, Hegde and Grover in 1973,[171] and said that there was no going back to decisions like *Golak Nath, Bank Nationalization* and *Privy Purses*.[172]

Justice M.P. Thakkar[173] said that he was ideologically very close to Desai, and agreed that he was an activist, though he did not use that term.[174] He too favoured the supersession of the three judges in 1973.[175]

When Justice G.L. Oza was asked why he accepted a Supreme Court judgeship, he said that the Supreme Court has the power not merely to prevent the government from doing something, but to compel it to do something, a clear reference to judicial activism.[176] Oza was a judge appointed to the court by Chief Justice Bhagwati.[177]

Justice D.P. Madon considered himself a closet judicial activist.[178] He said that his judgment in the case of *Central Inland Water Transport Corporation Ltd v. Brojo Nath Ganguly*[179] contained an endorsement in favour of judicial activism. In this case, the Supreme Court held that a government company, the Central Inland Water Transport Corporation Limited, was a part of the 'State' under Article 12 of the Constitution, even though it was not actually the government itself. This essentially meant that a person aggrieved by the corporation's actions could file a writ petition against it, which is a much quicker remedy instead of filing a cumbersome civil suit. The court also held that an unconscionable term contained in an employment contract between the corporation and its employees could be found to violate Article 14 of the Constitution for being arbitrary and discriminatory. While arriving at these conclusions, Justice Madon held that the 'law exists to serve the needs of the society'.[180] Likewise, Justice Goswami said that since the 1970s, even conservative judges like himself, who came to the Supreme Court, had moved to the left, and been supportive of progressive decisions.[181]

Interestingly, Justice Khanna himself did not subscribe to the Bhagwati school of judicial activism. Khanna believed that the Supreme Court of the 1980s decided cases which tilted in favour of the government under the cover of 'high-sounding words like social justice'. Khanna thought that the Supreme Court's judgments at this time had the effect of '[unsettling] settled principles and [diluting] or [undoing] the dicta laid down in . . . earlier cases'.[182] He was critical of 'leftist leaning' pro-labour judges who ruled in favour of employees 'who were guilty of glaring acts of insubordination and indiscipline'.[183]

In 1983, Justice Tulzapurkar also thought that the court had gone too far in favour of insubordinate employees. Though he made it clear to Gadbois that he was not opposed, in principle, to judicial activism, he said that the activism had got out of hand. He gave the illustration of a case which came before the Supreme Court involving a bus conductor. The bus conductor had been convicted of fraud for taking money from passengers but not issuing tickets.[184] Activist judges at the Supreme Court rewarded him (or those like him) by giving him back pay and damages. Justice Tulzapurkar said that the activism at the court started with Krishna Iyer. Activism involved concern for the poor and downtrodden, but in a manner which stretched the law. He said that landlord–tenant and labour–management disputes were the two broad areas of disagreement in the Supreme Court at that time.[185]

Justice A.P. Sen, on the other hand, was definitely not an activist. He did not approve of how Justice Bhagwati brought the due process clause of the American Constitution into Indian constitutional law despite the fact that the framers of our Constitution had rejected it.[186] Sen described himself as a 'complete misfit' at the Supreme Court in the 1980s. He was brought up in the old traditions of the judicial role, and could not keep pace with the expansive legal interpretations of his activist colleagues. He felt that matters of policy were best left to the government. He told Gadbois about his dissent in *Rajendra Prasad v. State of Uttar Pradesh*,[187] where he disagreed with the view of two activist judges, Krishna Iyer and D.A. Desai. Iyer and Desai had refused to sentence a criminal to death because they were morally opposed to the death penalty. Rejecting this view, Sen wrote that the 'humanistic approach should not obscure our sense of realities'. Sen told Gadbois that he did not have 'the creative spirit' of his activist brethren, and that his colleagues disliked him for this. He believed that judges were interpreters of law, not makers of it. He was very critical of D.A. Desai's statement, made at an Indo-East German seminar, where he had said, 'I propose to remain in the system, corrode it and refill it with new elements so that the system can render justice.'[188] He was critical of Justice Bhagwati for projecting his own theories in cases, and thought that public interest litigation (PIL) would ruin the Supreme Court. PILs, he thought, made the court a parallel government.[189]

Sen was not alone. Justice Kailasam was very critical of activist judges, of lawmaking by judges and PILs.[190] Justice Varadarajan agreed that he viewed things differently from his colleagues like Bhagwati and Desai.[191] He thought that some of his colleagues were more interested in peddling their own political and social philosophies (e.g., pro-labour, pro-tenant) than dispensing impartial justice.[192] Justice Pathak considered himself to be in the centrist category. He was very critical of the procedural innovations of his activist colleagues, like converting letters into writ petitions.[193]

The older generation of retired judges was highly critical of the activists.[194] Justice S.K. Das, who retired from the court in September 1963, said that judges should not be populists; they should not play to the gallery and give speeches to various audiences.[195] Das was particularly critical of Desai. Das said that on one occasion, Desai had an argument with a judge he was hearing a case with and abruptly left the bench, refusing to sit with that judge again.[196] He said that public interest litigation was really 'publicity interest litigation'.[197] Justice Sarkar, who retired from the court in June 1966, said that the judges of the 1980s were interested in publicity-mongering.[198] Justice Hidayatullah, who retired in December 1970, said that in his time, the arrears of cases were less because the court did not 'accept postcards' as writ petitions.[199] He said that political ideology played too large a role in decision-making in the 1980s; that judges were asking themselves what the right thing to do was, not what could be legally done in a case. Hidayatullah was opposed to judicial legislation and said that activism must not mean a rampage by the judges.[200] In fact, Hidayatullah spoke out in public against the activists. In a lecture he delivered in the early 1980s, he said that relaxing the rules of procedure would result in 'the annihilation of all procedure'. 'There are many ways of skinning a cat,' he said. 'You can do it quietly or you can do it ostentatiously.'[201]

Many judges who belonged to the older generation were critical of Bhagwati and Krishna Iyer. For instance, Justice Grover was critical of Justice Bhagwati for marking PIL cases for himself, by converting letters he got as the head of the Legal Aid Committee into writ petitions.[202] It was, after all, the function of the chief justice of India, as the master of the roster, to assign cases to the different judges of the court. Echoes of such disagreements can be heard at the court even today. Similarly, Justice Dua, who retired in October 1972, said that judges like Krishna Iyer made their own ideologies clear in their judgments, and tended to be too emotional. He disagreed with Krishna Iyer's style.[203]

Several judges belonging to the older generation criticized the generation of the 1980s for making public speeches. For instance, Justice G.K. Mitter said that when a judge makes a public speech on issues which might come before him in court, it indicates that he will not keep an open mind in that case.[204] When asked to compare the court in the 1980s with the court during his time, Justice P. Jaganmohan Reddy, who served at the court between 1969 and 1975, said, 'We didn't hawk our judgments'; and that some judges in the newer generation wrote judgments to get press coverage.[205]

In fact, some judges of the older generation were even otherwise critical of the newer judges. They said that the new judges were passing orders first and giving reasons later, whereas the lower courts needed guidance in the form of reasons immediately.[206] Justice Grover had been injured by a deranged man with a knife at the Supreme Court a month after his appointment, but he returned to work around a week later.[207] He was unhappy about how judges in the 1980s, by contrast, went abroad while the court was in session. He said that the older judges were more conscious of their duties. He also felt that the newer judges wanted to write separate opinions in the big cases, while in his time, only one judgment was written (like in the *Bank Nationalization* case), which all the judges on the bench helped in writing.[208]

By the same token, the activists were very critical of the older generation of judges, their predecessors. The poster boy of the older judges was Justice Hidayatullah, whom many of the new activist judges of the 1980s criticized. Hidayatullah had studied at Cambridge and belonged to the old British legal tradition. By contrast, said the activist Justice D.A. Desai, the newer generation of Indian judges had studied at smaller law colleges in India and were more socially conscious. He said that judges like Hidayatullah went to private clubs, played cards, had drinks, and were very modern and elitist.[209] Perhaps this was a little unfair, because Desai's description of Hidayatullah could also fit one of Desai's own activist colleagues from Bombay at the Supreme Court in the 1980s. Another activist judge, Chinnappa Reddy, said that judges like Hidayatullah were, during the freedom movement, like spectators at a cricket match. They had only been interested in rising up the ladder in the legal profession, and had taken no part in the freedom struggle. He believed that while those like Hidayatullah were not in touch with the ordinary Indian, the newer generation of judges knew what the people wanted and were more conscious of India's problems. Reddy proudly believed that while earlier judges of the Supreme Court used to copy British judges, his generation of Supreme Court judges had surpassed their British counterparts, especially in the field of administrative law.[210] He was glad that judges in his time had moved away from 'traditional and Anglo-Saxon jurisprudence'.[211] Reddy believed that after 1980, Supreme Court judges realized that the court had 'a role other than that of a mere arbiter of disputes', though he agreed that 'like all new converts the court has sometimes gone [too] far'.[212]

The absence of a foreign education was something that differentiated the earlier generation of Supreme Court judges from the later ones. About 50 per cent of the judges who served at the Supreme Court between 1950 and 1967 had received some part of their education in England.[213] There was a significant decline in the number of judges who were educated abroad thereafter.[214] This was partly[215] because the Reserve Bank of India had a policy, after Independence, not to grant approval for foreign exchange to Indian students who wished to go to London to get called to the bar, though one could get foreign exchange to get a foreign law degree.[216] Also, after Independence, the costs of going to England solely to get called to the bar exceeded the benefits; barristers ceased to enjoy their colonial-era privileges at the bar in India, and the process of getting called to the bar did not significantly enhance a person's substantive knowledge of law.[217]

Justice Hidayatullah, on the other hand, believed that while the judges of the later generation were no different from the earlier ones in terms of their ability and competence (he referred, in particular, to Justices Chandrachud and Bhagwati), they probably suffered from an inferiority complex on account of not having studied in England. He felt that they lacked self-confidence and were not imbued with English common law traditions.[218] He was particularly 'galled', however, by 'the opprobrious way in which some judges' in the 1980s referred to 'their predecessors' who had an 'English University education', by saying that they had an 'Oxbridge mentality'. He said that sitting judges of the 1980s referred to the work of the older generation of judges (like himself) as 'judicial feudalism', 'forensic colonialism' and 'robed populism'. 'These harsh remarks come very badly,' he said, 'from judges with well-known crimson populist pronouncements.' He said that the older generation of judges, unlike the present generation, did not have any 'feelings of inadequacy'.[219]

In turn, the newer judges lampooned the earlier generation for being completely out of touch with the real India. In 1983, D.A. Desai said that the days of the Oxford judges were over. Criticizing Justice Hidayatullah in particular, Desai said that him and his other Oxbridge-type colleagues looked only towards Privy Council judgments and cosmopolitan jurisprudence. He said that even though early judges like Harilal J. Kania and Subba Rao were educated entirely in India, their orientation was nonetheless western.[220] He felt that after India got its own Constitution in January 1950, Supreme Court judges should have consciously moved away from English jurisprudence, and should not have continued citing Privy Council judgments.[221] Justice Varadarajan could not understand why Indian judgments cited so much foreign law.[222]

However, even after 1980, foreign cases continued to be cited by Supreme Court judges. One judge was critical of Justice Krishna Iyer, an activist judge who belonged more to Desai's school than Hidayatullah's, for citing too many American sources.[223] When Gadbois visited Justice M.N.R. Venkatachaliah, who was appointed to the Supreme Court in October 1987, he noticed photographs of American judges, Benjamin Cardozo and Oliver Wendell Holmes, in his study (Venkatachaliah referred to a third photograph of another American judge, Learned Hand, though Gadbois did not see it there). Venkatachaliah confessed to Gadbois that he had read and reread Cardozo's classic book, *The Nature of the Judicial Process*, and said that every evening he read a letter exchanged between Holmes and British jurist Sir Frederick Pollock, published in a popular volume. He actually told Gadbois that he thought that American and English judges were of a higher quality than Indian ones, not merely in terms of their command over the English language, but also in terms of their thought processes.[224] In the notes of his interview with another judge, Gadbois recorded, 'All Indian judges seem to speak highly of English judges who were here.' 'I detect a note of inferiority complex,'[225] he added.

Bhagwati–Pathak

When the chief justice of India retires, the President of India is not required, under the Constitution, to consult him on who his successor ought to be.[226] However, it was sometimes the practice for the retiring chief justice to name his successor.[227] By Bhagwati's time, it seems, the chief justice was supposed to formally consent to his successor's appointment.[228] After retiring from office, Chief Justice Bhagwati was succeeded, according to the seniority convention, by Chief Justice R.S. Pathak (1924–2007). However, Bhagwati, an activist judge, did not like Pathak, who was known for his conservative views, and wanted to have him superseded. There were two rumours about whom Bhagwati was thinking about superseding Pathak with.

The first was that Bhagwati wanted Justice Ranga Nath Misra to supersede Pathak.[229] This would have meant the supersession of not merely Pathak, but also Justices E.S. Venkataramiah and Sabyasachi Mukharji, both of whom were in line to become chief justices of India according to the seniority convention. Misra would have served as chief justice of India for a term of nearly five years. Though this did not materialize, Misra, who was otherwise not in line to become the chief justice of India, eventually got to serve in that office for a little over a year because Chief Justice Sabyasachi Mukharji died in office in September 1990. Misra would have otherwise, in the natural scheme of things, retired during the chief justiceship of Sabyasachi Mukharji.

The second (and the better-known) rumour was that Bhagwati wanted to supersede Pathak with a direct appointment from the bar: Attorney General K. Parasaran. It was this version which was reported in the May 1986 issue of the *India Today* magazine.[230] Bhagwati said that this story was absolutely false.[231] However, Pathak believed this story to be true, and said that the government did not take Bhagwati's suggestion seriously.[232] Pathak believed that Law Minister Asoke Sen, as a formality, wrote Chief Justice Bhagwati a letter asking him if the government could proceed with appointing Pathak to the chief justiceship, but that Bhagwati never responded to it.[233] An article which was published in December 1986 in *India Today*, said Pathak, largely recorded the correct facts.[234] The article said that Bhagwati was eventually summoned by President Giani Zail Singh and asked whether Pathak was a suitable successor, and it was only then that Bhagwati concurred with Pathak's appointment. Eventually, Pathak learnt, about a month before Bhagwati retired, that he would be the next chief justice of India.[235]

However, Bhagwati had a different version of events. He said that Law Minister Asoke Sen wrote to him on 16 October 1986, and asked for his views on Pathak. On 22 October 1986,

Bhagwati verbally told Sen that he had no objection to Pathak's appointment. On 3 November 1986, at a bar council function where the prime minister, Bhagwati and Pathak were all present, the prime minister asked Bhagwati about Pathak's suitability, and Bhagwati once again said that they should go ahead with Pathak's appointment.[236] However, Pathak was correct to say that Bhagwati never wrote a formal letter recommending Pathak's appointment, which is what President Giani Zail Singh found missing in the file. The story of Bhagwati having been summoned was therefore correct. Gadbois recorded that Bhagwati had a poor opinion of Law Minister Asoke Sen and had some harsh things to say about him, which are not being reproduced here.

It was also clear that Bhagwati did not like Pathak. Bhagwati sarcastically said that Pathak wrote very few judgments, was lazy and not a leader.[237] To be fair, this was not a view held by Bhagwati alone. Other judges felt that Pathak gave one the impression that he was so distinguished, that he came from such a prominent family, that the chief justiceship was owed to him.[238]

Bhagwati and Pathak battled each other on who should hold the chairmanship of the Legal Aid Committee after Bhagwati's retirement. Bhagwati wanted to hold on to the position after his retirement, but Pathak did not let him as he thought that a sitting judge should hold that post.[239] Decades later, Bhagwati was still bitter about this. In his autobiography, he wrote that he expected, owing to his 'zeal and commitment to realize legal aid for all citizens', that he would be able to continue as the chairman of the Legal Aid Committee. 'However,' wrote Bhagwati, 'Justice Pathak, who succeeded me as the Chief Justice of India, insisted that he should be appointed Chairman and the Government of India yielded to his pressure and appointed him as the Chairman . . . even though he had no commitment to the legal aid programme.' Annoyed by this, Bhagwati further wrote,

'This decision, according to me, was taken in order to benefit the holder of the office [of] CJI rather than to help the impoverished people of the country to realise their basic Human Rights.'[240]

Ahmadi–Kuldip Singh

Justices A.M. Ahmadi (born 1932) and Kuldip Singh (born 1932) were both appointed to the Supreme Court of India on 14 December 1988. Ahmadi had been a judge of the Gujarat High Court, while Kuldip Singh was appointed directly from the bar, i.e. Singh had not served as a high court judge, though he had been offered a high court judgeship in the past and had turned it down.[241] According to an unwritten convention prevalent at the time, when a bar judge like Singh and a high court judge like Ahmadi were appointed to the Supreme Court on the same day, the bar judge would get seniority over the other. In other words, Kuldip Singh, being appointed directly from the bar, should have, according to this convention, been considered senior to Ahmadi. This was important because Singh was officially around two months older than Ahmadi,[242] and both were younger than Justice Venkatachaliah, who would retire as the chief justice of India in October 1994. Accordingly, if Singh were considered senior to Ahmadi, he would get to serve as the chief justice of India from October 1994 until he retired in December 1996, and Ahmadi would thereafter serve as the chief justice of India for only a few months in 1997. On the other hand, if Ahmadi were considered senior to Singh, then he would serve as the chief justice of India from 1994 until 1997, while Singh would not get to serve as the chief justice at all (since he would retire during Ahmadi's term).

In August 1988, a few months before his appointment to the Supreme Court, Justice Kuldip Singh received a phone call from Chief Justice Pathak, who informed him that he was being appointed to the court. He was told by Pathak that he would be sworn in first, that he would be senior to Ahmadi. However, the government changed the order of the swearing-in ceremony, and Ahmadi was sworn in first. Justice M.P. Thakkar, a retired Supreme Court judge from Gujarat, was influential in determining the order of seniority in favour of Justice Ahmadi. Both Justice Pathak and Singh believed that Thakkar may have played a role in determining Ahmadi's seniority over Singh.[243] Singh was very bitter about this and considered withdrawing his consent to becoming a Supreme Court judge, but Chief Justice Pathak persuaded him not to do so. In fact, as a judge deciding the *Second Judges* case,[244] Justice Singh made a tacit reference to his situation, stating the following in his judgment:

> When Judges are appointed to the Supreme Court from two sources, and they take oath on the same day, no one knows how the inter-se seniority is fixed. On an earlier occasion [an] appointee from the Bar was placed senior but on a later occasion the process was reversed.[245]

Ironically, Singh was actually born on 26 April 1932, but his father simply recorded all birthdates as 1 January, which is why his official birthdate was 1 January 1932.[246] In other words, Singh was actually younger than Ahmadi (who was born on 25 March 1932), and ought to have served as the chief justice of India.[247]

Both Ahmadi and Singh had been appointed to the Supreme Court at least in part because of their religions—Ahmadi was a Muslim and Singh a Sikh.[248] However, Singh informed Gadbois that Ahmadi was not really a Muslim; he belonged to a sect of Islam which Muslims did not really consider as being a part of their religion.[249]

2

Disagreement without Dissent

We have seen in the previous chapter that judges of the Supreme Court have had some very public, professional and petty rivalries. Yet, it is quite surprising that despite all of this, when the court actually sits down to decide cases and deliver judgments, there are very few dissents which are penned by the judges. The near-absence of dissent at the Supreme Court of India is puzzling. Why are there so few dissents if there are often interpersonal disagreements at the court? This chapter explores some of the answers which judges in the 1980s gave when they were asked about the disinclination of Indian judges towards dissent. Among other reasons, they said that they were overworked and did not have enough time to write dissenting judgments, a theme which will be explored in greater detail in the next chapter. They said that they preferred to speak in one voice, like the Privy Council did in the colonial era, so that lower courts would not get confused about the law laid down by the Supreme Court. They also said that the size of the two-judge bench compelled compromise, that the chief justice constructed benches to minimize dissent, and that there was a preference against dissent in order to preserve the collegiality of the court. Many of these reasons perhaps still remain true today.

There is a great deal of international scholarly debate about whether judges should be allowed to deliver dissenting and concurring judgments. Judges in civil law countries in continental Europe, barring a few exceptions, are not permitted to dissent. But the debate about the benefits or drawbacks of dissent focuses on whether allowing judges to dissent weakens the authority and legitimacy of the court. By contrast, many Indian Supreme Court judges in the 1980s thought of dissent from the standpoint of their own workload, of ensuring that the lower courts understood what they were saying, and not from the point of view of the public image of the court. We will also see that the Supreme Court of India follows a system of delivering judgments which straddles the divide between the old civil law and common law traditions. As in civil law countries like Germany, Supreme Court judges in India dissent from the majority judgment only in extreme cases, out of a sense of loyalty to the institution, preferring to go along with the majority even when they may slightly disagree with it. Judgments of the Supreme Court of India are not delivered 'per curiam', or for the court as in civil law countries, anonymously and unanimously, but they are also not delivered 'in seriatim', with each judge writing a separate judgment, as in English common law courts.

Benches and Dissents

The Supreme Court today has a sanctioned strength of thirty-one judges, including the chief justice. Courts like the US Supreme Court (nine), high court of Australia (seven), Supreme Court of New Zealand (five) and the UK Supreme Court (twelve[1]), have significantly fewer judges. Many Supreme Courts in different parts of the world sit 'en banc', meaning all the members sit together and decide every case. The Supreme Courts of the US, Canada and New Zealand, and the high court of Australia, are examples of this system.[2] By contrast, there are many Supreme Courts whose members break up into smaller panels or divisions in order to decide cases, e.g., the UK Supreme Court, the German Federal Constitutional Court and the Supreme Court of Ireland.[3] The Supreme Court of India follows the latter system, and sits in smaller panels called 'benches'. Each bench consists, typically, of two, three or five judges, sometimes more. The largest-ever bench consisted of thirteen judges, and decided one of India's most famous constitutional cases, *Kesavananda Bharati v. State of Kerala*,[4] also known as the *Basic Structure* case, where the court held that the Constitution has certain essential features or a 'basic structure' which Parliament cannot amend. The chief justice of the Supreme Court gets to decide which judge sits with whom on the court. He has the power to compose benches and to assign cases to different benches.

Cases are decided by a majority vote at the Supreme Court. This means that if a bench consists of, say, five judges, the outcome of the case will be decided by a majority of at least three judges to two.[5] Broadly speaking, there are three kinds of judgments that can be authored at the Supreme Court: a 'majority' judgment, a 'concurring' judgment and a 'dissenting' judgment. The majority judgment, quite simply, is the judgment with which the majority of the judges on the bench agree. A concurring judgment is a separate judgment written by a judge who agrees with the majority but decides to write his own reasons in support of the outcome of the case. A dissenting judgment is a separate judgment written by a judge who disagrees with the view taken by the majority. So, for example, in an important case called *Bangalore Water Supply & Sewerage Board v. A. Rajappa*[6] a bench of seven judges of the Supreme Court decided the meaning of the word 'industry' under the Industrial Disputes Act, 1947. Justice Krishna Iyer wrote a judgment, and Justices P.N. Bhagwati and D.A. Desai agreed with that judgment without writing a separate judgment of their own. Chief Justice M. Hameedullah Beg and Justice Y.V. Chandrachud each wrote a separate concurring judgment, agreeing with the conclusions of Justice Krishna Iyer, but on their own reasoning. Justice Krishna Iyer's judgment therefore became the majority judgment. Justice Jaswant Singh wrote a partially dissenting judgment, with which Justice V.D. Tulzapurkar agreed.

It is not always easy to tell the difference between a concurring and dissenting judgment. Sometimes, judges write concurring judgments which are, really, veiled dissents. In fact, Justice Krishna Iyer admitted that he used to write concurring judgments which were actually dissents, and acknowledged that he was criticized for doing so by a well-known scholar of the day.[7] Judgments can also be partly concurring and partly dissenting. At times, it is hard to tell what the majority view adopted by the court in a case is altogether. Consider, for example, that in one of the earliest constitutional cases, *A.K. Gopalan v. State of Madras*,[8] all the six judges of the Supreme Court wrote a separate judgment, and Attorney General Motilal C. Setalvad believed that there was 'bewildering conflict' among the six judgments,[9] making it hard for anyone to understand what the Supreme Court had actually held in that case.

We have seen in the previous chapter that there are some fantastic professional (and sometimes petty) rivalries among the judges of the Supreme Court. One would have guessed that these disagreements among the judges would have translated into a large number of dissenting judgments. Surprisingly, however, the numbers tell a different story. Between 1950 and 1967, dissenting judgments were written in only 8 per cent of the cases decided by the court.[10] 'The typical Supreme Court judgment,' wrote George H. Gadbois, Jr. in an article published in the *Economic and Political Weekly* in 1970, 'is a unanimous one, and is characterised by a single judgment or opinion—the judgment of the Court.'[11]

A bench of five or more judges is called a 'constitution bench'. It is so called because a case involving 'a substantial question of law as to the interpretation of [the] Constitution' has to be decided by a bench of no less than five judges under the Constitution.[12] Among all the cases decided by constitution benches between 1950 and 2009, dissenting judgments were recorded in only 11 per cent[13] of the cases.[14] In cases involving the right to free speech decided by the Supreme Court, regardless of bench size, between 1950 and 2011, dissenting judgments were written in only 10.2 per cent of the cases.[15] In such cases, there has been a decline in the rate of dissent—while more dissents were recorded in the early years of the court when benches of larger strength were constituted, fewer dissents were recorded in later years (barring the 1970s) when benches convened in smaller sizes.[16] Justice K. Subba Rao was one of the great dissenters of the court in its early years.

Even the rate at which judges write concurring judgments in the Supreme Court of India is generally low. Only about 12 per cent of the cases decided by constitution benches between 1950 and 2009 had concurring judgments.[17] In free speech cases decided by the court between 1950 and 2011, separate concurring opinions were recorded in only 15.8 per cent cases.[18] In other words, it is not as though there is a high rate of

dissenting judgments which could pass off as concurrences at
the Supreme Court either.

The low rate of dissent in the Supreme Court is consistent
with how colonial courts functioned in British India. Out of
the 411 cases decided by benches of two or more judges of the
Bombay High Court, sampled between 1866 and 1944, only
three cases had dissenting judgments written in them.[19] Judges
were also institutionally discouraged from dissenting in the
colonial period. Until 1927, when the two judges in a division
bench (i.e. a bench consisting of two judges) disagreed, the
view taken by the senior judge prevailed.[20] The appointments
of temporary or 'acting' judges[21] who served in the Bombay
High Court would sometimes not be confirmed by the chief
justice if they disagreed with him in a case. Thus, an acting
judge of the Bombay High Court during the colonial period,
by the name of George Clifford Whitworth, was not confirmed
because he disagreed with Chief Justice Lawrence Jenkins in a
case. This also happened with acting judges D.D. Nanavati and
A.C. Wild, who disagreed with Chief Justice Sir John Beaumont
of the Bombay High Court during the colonial era.[22] However,
starting in around the 1920s, there was a sudden spurt of
concurring opinions at the Bombay High Court, such that
between 33 and 42 per cent cases had concurring judgments
in them thereafter, a sign that judgment writing was probably
becoming less collaborative among the judges.[23] The low rate
of concurring judgments at the Supreme Court therefore sets
itself apart from this trend.

The rate of dissent at the Supreme Court of India is very low
in comparison with some other countries. In the US Supreme
Court, between 1946 and 2009, only about 30 per cent of the
cases were unanimous; dissents were recorded in the remaining
cases.[24] The US Supreme Court may be an outlier for the

number of dissents it produces, but even other Supreme Courts around the world have a higher rate of dissent than India. Between 1970 and 2010, about 58.9 per cent of the decisions of the Australian High Court, 75.6 per cent of the decisions of the Canadian Supreme Court, and 81.2 per cent of the decisions of the UK House of Lords/Supreme Court were unanimous.[25] The rate of dissent in India is comparable with a civil law country like Germany, where the constitutional court has a dissent rate of around 6 per cent.[26] It is also comparable with South Africa where, during that period, 90.9 per cent judgments were unanimous.

An interesting question therefore arises: Why is it that the rate of dissent in the Supreme Court of India is so low, especially given the fact that there are otherwise such strong disagreements among the personalities of the court?

Rarest of the Rare

The broad sense one gets is that dissent is generally frowned upon at the Supreme Court,[27] and dissents get written only in the rarest of cases involving irreconcilable conflict. Chief Justice M. Hidayatullah admitted to 'ragging' two of his colleagues who dissented from his view in the very first case they heard together, because he was responsible for bringing them to the court.[28] However, he did feel reassured by their independence.[29] Justice P.B. Gajendragadkar, known for his pro-labour leanings, once wrote a draft judgment with which his colleague, Justice N.H. Bhagwati, disagreed. Bhagwati suggested that Gajendragadkar make some changes to the judgment in order to secure Bhagwati's agreement to sign off on it. Gajendragadkar refused to change a word of his draft. Bhagwati signed the judgment anyway, since another judge

on the bench, Justice S.K. Das, had also agreed to sign it, and
Bhagwati did not want to dissent.[30] In February 1983, a bench
of two judges had said that in a death penalty case if the person
convicted is not executed within two years, then the sentence
automatically stands commuted to life imprisonment.[31] Shortly
after this judgment was delivered,[32] it was overruled by a bench
of three judges of the court.[33] Justice A. Varadarajan believed
that if the two judges who had delivered the judgment in the
earlier case had sat with the three judges who decided the later
case, even they would have been convinced to be a part of the
majority in the later case.[34]

Justice H.R. Khanna, arguably one of the greatest dissenters
of all time at the Supreme Court, who disagreed with the
majority view in the *Habeas Corpus* case,[35] admitted that he
did not dissent in one of the early cases he heard in the court
even though he disagreed with the view of the majority.[36] The
Supreme Court's judgment in that case[37] had the effect of raising
car prices. Although he 'did not feel happy with the view they
took', Khanna agreed with the judgment of the majority because
he 'did not think it proper to strike a discordant note at the
very beginning' of his judgeship at the Supreme Court.[38] 'The
atmosphere in court' at the time, noted Khanna, 'was of general
cordiality.'[39] This, of course, did not stop Justice Khanna from
dissenting in the *Habeas Corpus* case, where a majority of the
judges of the bench held that the right to seek the writ of habeas
corpus and to challenge arbitrary arrest and detention could
be suspended during an Emergency. Dissent at the Supreme
Court, then, seems to be reserved for the most egregious and
exceptional circumstances.

'I did not believe in writing separate or dissenting
judgments for nothing,' wrote Justice P.N. Shinghal in a letter to
Gadbois. 'So if I have written dissents,' he continued, 'they were

necessary to place my irreconcilable views on record.'[40] Justice A.C. Gupta was critical of his colleagues who were eager, in big cases, to write separate judgments. He pointed out that Justice E.S. Venkataramiah wrote a judgment of over 300 pages in the *Judges* case.[41] Justice Krishna Iyer felt that writing a dissent gained little, and did not serve much purpose. He stressed that the whole court was very congenial, 'delightfully united', and there was a 'happy sense of cooperation' prevalent at the time.[42] He believed that divided decisions were not as good as unanimous ones.[43] In fact, who is writing the majority judgment for the court also matters. Justice P. Jaganmohan Reddy believed that the majority judgment of the Supreme Court in the *Bank Nationalization* case[44] should not have been written by Justice J.C. Shah because Shah had delivered the judgment in an earlier case in which the court had taken a seemingly contrary view. He felt that somebody else should have written the majority judgment or even a concurring judgment.[45] The majority judgment of Shah was extensively discussed by the judges prior to being delivered, and several passages were removed and added by other judges.[46] The court wrote one judgment in order to achieve clarity and avoid contradictions.[47]

Many judges apart from Justices Khanna and Krishna Iyer saw an atmosphere of collegiality at the court. Since the very inception of the court, judges met in the morning in the chamber of the chief justice, where they discussed 'all subjects, politics not excluded'.[48] Perhaps designed to ensure that judges would get to court on time through social pressure, this was one tradition which possibly came from the Bombay High Court, where judges in the colonial period would meet in the chamber of the chief justice prior to the commencement of the court in the morning. In fact, several traditions at the Supreme Court came from Bombay, because the Supreme Court's first chief justice (Harilal J. Kania), attorney general (Motilal C. Setalvad) and solicitor general (C.K. Daphtary) were all from Bombay.[49] The morning meeting was not a very long one, and lasted about ten minutes or so.[50] Judges would discuss things like the special leave petitions, the arrears, and their own poor working conditions and salaries.[51] Some complained that the judges of the court did not meet each other enough.[52] Today, Supreme Court judges still meet each other in the morning, though in a common room and not in the chief justice's chamber. They also get together for a weekly lunch.[53]

As the chief justice of India in 1954, M.C. Mahajan said that his colleagues gave him 'complete cooperation and affection'. He noted that he and his colleagues '[r]arely, if ever . . . differed or wrote dissenting judgments'. Though they 'freely criticised each [other's] views', they 'ultimately reached . . . unanimous decisions' in most cases, being 'on the best of terms with one another'.[54] He also called the first eight judges of the Supreme Court 'a very cohesive and friendly team'.[55] In fact, some judges wrote judgments for other judges. Justice Rajagopala Ayyangar said that he wrote a few judgments for Chief Justice B.P. Sinha, which were then published as Sinha's judgments.[56] Hidayatullah said that Justice J.C. Shah finished judgments that Sinha had started writing as well. One could tell that this had happened, said Hidayatullah, when the early part of the judgment had a word like 'aforesaid' (one of Sinha's favourite words) and the later part had the word 'manifestly' (which Shah was known to use).[57] Interestingly, Sinha's judgments in at least two cases[58] used the word 'aforesaid' in their early parts and 'manifestly' in the later parts. Shah sat with Sinha in those cases but did not officially write any judgment.

This rule of dissenting only in the most extreme cases is similar to the rule of institutional loyalty prevalent in civil law countries like Germany, where dissenting judges at the Federal Constitutional Court 'choose not to publish their dissents or even to be identified as dissenters partly out of a sense of institutional loyalty' to their brethren, and where 'personalized dissenting opinions' are considered 'proper only when prompted by deep personal convictions'.[59] By contrast, some judges in England hold the view that a dissent should be written when a judge simply believes that the majority got it wrong.[60] Likewise, in the US Supreme Court dissents which are written in harsh and vituperative terms do not seem to affect the atmosphere of collegiality in the court.[61] Justice Elena Kagan, who frequently disagreed with the late Justice Antonin Scalia, went hunting with him.[62]

Many judges of the Supreme Court of India said that even though there were several disagreements at the court, there was just not enough time to articulate them.[63] Justice Chandrachud said that it was very common for judges to disagree with as much as half of an entire judgment written by a colleague, but to not write dissenting judgments expressing that disagreement because there was simply no time to do so. He mentioned that Justice Bhagwati in his judgments would cite Sri Aurobindo or Sanskrit sources, and many of the other judges on the bench would have no idea what he was talking about; so it was hard to disagree with something they did not understand. There was a lot of disagreement, he said, but little dissent.[64] This actually accords with the view taken by Richard Posner and others who have argued that there is a negative correlation between the workload of the court and the rate of dissent.[65] In simple words, the more work there is at the court, the more cumbersome it is for judges to write dissenting judgments. The docket explosion of the Supreme Court is therefore clearly responsible, at least in part, for the lack of dissent at the court.

Others said that there were few dissents because the court's judges wanted to speak, as far as possible, in one voice, to make the law less uncertain, so that the lower courts could understand and apply the law laid down by the Supreme Court. In fact, in the early years, the Supreme Court seemed to follow the practice of the House of Lords in delivering judgments seriatim. We have seen that in *Gopalan*'s case, the six judges of the court delivered six separate judgments, creating confusion about what the law was. Justice Gajendragadkar said that in the early years, there was an unfriendly atmosphere at the Supreme Court, and each judge wanted to write his own judgment, which was invariably 'long, elaborate, repetitive [and] concurrent'.[66] It was Chief Justice S.R. Das, whose term as such began in 1956, who brought judges together 'with his tact and ability', and concurring judgments gradually ceased to be written in the court. This was much like what Chief Justice John Marshall did at the US Supreme Court, as we will see later on.

The Law Commission, in its 14th report in 1958,[67] asked itself whether it would be better for the Supreme Court to write a single judgment as was done in the Privy Council. It noted that in the early years, there were a large number of dissents and concurring judgments which led to uncertainty in the law. However, it felt reassured by the fact that the court had, more recently, favoured a single judgment in the 'large majority of the cases'. The Law Commission was obviously referring to the practice started under Chief Justice S.R. Das. It therefore recommended that judges should feel free to write dissenting or concurring judgments wherever they felt it necessary to do so.

Justice S. Murtaza Fazal Ali said that unanimous judgments were preferred at the Supreme Court so as not to confuse the high courts.[68] Justice Varadarajan said that the near-absence of dissent at the court had nothing to do with lack of time. He said that Supreme Court judges felt that lower courts could handle unanimous decisions better.[69] Justice Krishna Iyer believed that the Privy Council was the model Indian judges had followed,[70] and the Privy Council, until 1966,[71] did not allow dissent. This was also what Chief Justice Sinha wrote in his autobiography.[72]

However, trying to ensure certainty in the law is not a very convincing reason for frowning upon dissenting judgments. This is for at least two reasons. Firstly, the Supreme Court of India today is a polyvocal court, which speaks in different voices.[73] It is not really one court, but many courts, on account of the fact that it sits in different benches. The law laid down by one bench sometimes conflicts with that laid down by another bench of coordinate strength. This renders the law uncertain. If the court is really interested in ensuring certainty in law, then it should convene in larger panels and then render unanimous judgments. Secondly, the motivation of ensuring certainty in the law explains why concurring judgments, not dissents, should not be written. If there are many concurring judgments, then it is certainly hard for lower courts to figure out which of those judgments contains the majority view of the court. However, if a pure dissenting judgment is written by a judge (i.e. a judgment which does not partly concur with the majority judgment), the lower court can safely ignore it, because it forms no part of the majority judgment. A dissent therefore does not really render the law uncertain.[74]

Some judges thought that there was a lack of dissent because the quality of judges in the court had declined.[75] Justice Fazal Ali, for instance, said that the calibre of judges in the Supreme Court was now lower than before, that many were not qualified to dissent.[76]

However, interestingly, many said that the formation of benches by the chief justice had a lot to do with the absence of dissent at the Supreme Court. Justice Tulzapurkar, for example, said that benches were often constructed by the chief justice in an effort to minimize dissent. If both the judges on a two-judge bench disagreed, the case would have to be referred to a larger bench, which would cause delays. In order to avoid this, said Justice Tulzapurkar, the chief justice made bench assignments to minimize confrontation. For example, he said that he was very seldom made to sit with Justices Bhagwati and Desai (except in a few tax matters), with whom he would tend to disagree more.[77] Justice K.S. Hegde said that he had no doubt that the chief justice does indeed influence the outcomes of cases by constructing benches in a certain manner. This is why, Hegde felt, there ought to be a permanent constitution bench, both in order to avoid chief justices influencing the outcomes of cases, and in order to ensure a consistent interpretation of the law.[78] Justice Bhagwati said that Chief Justices Subba Rao and Gajendragadkar used to stack benches more than any other chief justices of India. He referred to Gajendragadkar as a 'shrewd' man, who was pro-government, and said that Gajendragadkar was seldom in the minority.[79] Chief Justice Chandrachud said that in order to get over these kinds of problems, he composed benches in 'politically important cases' which consisted of the most senior judges of the court, so that he could avoid criticism from the bar and the general public, that he was influencing the outcome of the case by stacking benches in a certain way.[80] Accordingly, in the contentious *Judges* case,[81] Chandrachud constituted a bench consisting of the seven most senior judges of the Supreme Court excluding himself (since he had been involved in the transfers), and excluding three judges who recused themselves because they had been transferred during the Emergency.[82] This was despite the fact that he could have easily kept his rival, Bhagwati, who later caused him significant embarrassment in the case, off the bench. Chandrachud felt that his role, as the chief justice of India, of assigning cases to judges was an 'awkward' one. Justice R.S. Pathak said that, as the chief justice, he found it difficult to set up the bench for hearing the case against Mrs Indira Gandhi's assassins, because there were very few Supreme Court judges who had experience in criminal trials.[83] Justice Krishna Iyer said that since it was known that he held views against the death penalty, he was not put on a bench hearing a death penalty appeal. However, he also said that even judges who were known to have supported the death penalty were kept off that bench. He said that the chief justice avoided assigning any judges to that case who had known opinions on the death penalty.[84] Likewise, Chief Justice B.P. Sinha knew that Justice Gajendragadkar had pro-labour leanings, so he put him on the labour bench with Justice K.N. Wanchoo, who was not pro-labour in his views.[85]

In fact, the chief justice is rarely in dissent in cases. While composing a bench of judges who are to sit with him to hear a case, the chief justice might select judges who are likely to agree with him. As a puisne judge, Justice Subba Rao was, according to Gadbois, 'the greatest dissenter in the history of the Supreme Court'.[86] He dissented forty-eight times during his nine-year term at the court, more than anyone else in the court's history until then,[87] and perhaps even since then. But during his nine-and-a-half-month tenure as the chief justice of India, he did not dissent even once in seventy-seven reported decisions.[88] When Gadbois met Subba Rao and asked him why this was so, Subba Rao said that as the chief justice of India, he was the one who picked the judges who sat with him on the bench.[89] Justice Hidayatullah was obviously referring to Subba Rao when he wrote, in his autobiography, of a chief justice who 'had the largest number of dissents when he was a puisne judge but was never in a dissenting minority after he became Chief Justice'.[90] Hidayatullah also said that another chief justice never wrote a dissent himself, and was in the minority in only one case.[91] Even according to more recent data, the chief justice has participated in 77 per cent of the 1532 cases decided by constitution benches between 1950 and 2009, and has dissented in only ten such cases.[92]

Judges might also hesitate to disagree with the chief justice for fear that they will not be assigned to another important constitution bench if they do so, quite similar to the fear that 'acting' judges had at the Bombay High Court of not being made permanent, as we have seen above. Justice Hidayatullah felt frustrated by the fact that Chief Justice Sinha did not put him on any constitution bench case. He was stuck doing 'mostly tax or criminal cases', and regretted that all his 'study of Constitutional law was not to be put to use'.[93] Justice A.P. Sen felt frustrated by the fact that his ten-year-long tenure at the court had been wasted because Chief Justice Chandrachud had not put him on a constitution bench.[94]

Sometime during Justice C.A. Vaidialingam's tenure at the court, i.e. 1966–73, the minimum number of judges who could hear a case was reduced from three to two, in order to ensure a quicker disposal of cases and to get rid of arrears,[95] though two-judge benches had been constituted even in the 1950s in order to dispose of cases quicker.[96] However, some judges of the Supreme Court complained that the two-judge benches forced compromise and stifled dissent. Justice Pathak, for instance, was critical of two-judge benches, and said that they compelled compromise. He believed that a bench should not have less than three judges on it.[97] If there was disagreement between the judges of a two-judge bench, then the case had to be referred to a larger bench.[98] Justice A.P. Sen said that there was little one could do on a two-judge bench, but agree with one's colleague.[99]

Justice Hidayatullah attributed his numerous dissents in the Supreme Court to the fact that he did not discuss cases with his colleagues. He believed that if he had discussed each case with his brethren, 'as was frequently done by the others', he might have been able to persuade the majority to vote with him. Instead, he was content to write his judgment and to leave it to his colleagues whether to accept his point of view or not.[100]

Is the Absence of Dissent Bad?

There is a great deal of debate about whether individualistic behaviour, like concurring and dissenting judgments, is good for a judicial system.

Judges of ordinary[101] courts in civil law countries are typically not allowed to publicly express any dissenting or concurring opinion. European civil law countries usually follow rules of unanimity and anonymity. Decisions are unanimous—there is no concurring or dissenting opinion; and they are anonymous—nobody knows who the author of the opinion was.[102] These are often referred to as per curiam opinions, or opinions for the court,[103] and are sometimes seen in common law countries as well.[104] The idea behind this practice is that the law should only have one correct interpretation, and that is the image which must be conveyed to the public through a single opinion.[105] However, judges of most constitutional courts (as distinguished from ordinary courts) in Europe are now allowed to write dissenting opinions.[106] Even so, constitutional courts there do not publish how many judges voted for or against a decision, or identify how each of the judges voted.[107]

By contrast, judgments of the English common law courts, like the erstwhile House of Lords, are delivered seriatim. [108] In other words, each judge writes a separate judgment, and all the judgments are set out in order of the judges' seniority. Strangely, the Privy Council, until 1966, followed a practice similar to the civil law tradition of having only one judgment delivered for the court.[109] Similarly, in criminal cases, the Court of Appeal in the UK is prohibited from delivering more than one judgment, unless the presiding judge permits otherwise.[110] The idea is that a dissenting judgment is like rubbing salt into a wound for a convict.[111]

The Privy Council decided cases by majority, and once the case was decided it was expressed on behalf of all the judges, even those who might have privately dissented from the view taken by the majority. In fact, during the colonial period, M.R. Jayakar, a Bombay lawyer who was a judge of the Privy Council, once disagreed with the view taken by the majority of the judges of the court in a case involving Hindu law. However, Jayakar was then asked to write the judgment, without expressing his disagreement with the view taken by the court.[112] The idea was that the Privy Council was technically only giving 'advice' to the Crown, so it was thought to be a better idea for that advice to be expressed in the form of a single opinion.[113] The Privy Council was also laying down the law for people who Englishmen considered their inferiors in the far colonies of the British Empire. It was therefore thought better to express opinions in one voice so that the court would appear more legitimate to the people of the colonies who might not be familiar with the workings of the metropole.[114]

The US Supreme Court follows a middle path between the seriatim and per curiam approaches.[115] A single-majority judgment is announced for the court, and judges can decide to

dissociate themselves from that judgment, to varying degrees.[116]
The US Supreme Court initially followed a mixed system of
delivering opinions. Some opinions were delivered seriatim,
others by the court. Dissenting judgments were issued from
the very inception of the court.[117] However, the fourth chief
justice, John Marshall, insisted that he alone should deliver a
unanimous opinion of the court for himself and for the rest
of his colleagues.[118] His opinions would say: 'Marshall, C.J.,
delivered the opinion of the Court.'[119] Marshall was criticized
by President Thomas Jefferson, who wanted judges' opinions
on the Supreme Court to be known, so that they could be
impeached if necessary.[120] The first real dissent from a judgment
of the court was delivered in 1806.[121] Today, the court delivers
a judgment with which justices agree or disagree at differing
levels. This often results in quite a complicated judgment. For
instance, in one case, the US Supreme Court's judgment began
as follows:

> O'CONNOR, J., delivered the opinion of the Court with
> respect to Parts I, II-B, and V, in which BRENNAN,
> MARSHALL, STEVENS, and SCALIA, JJ., joined, and with
> respect to Parts III and IV, in which all participating Members
> joined, and an opinion with respect to Part II-A, in which
> STEVENS and SCALIA, JJ., joined. BRENNAN, J., filed an
> opinion concurring in part and concurring in the judgment,
> in which MARSHALL, J., joined. REHNQUIST, C.J., filed an
> opinion concurring in part and dissenting in part, in which
> WHITE and BLACKMUN, JJ., joined. KENNEDY, J., took
> no part in the consideration or decision of the case.[122]

The Supreme Court of India also follows an approach which
falls between the civil law and common law traditions. Unlike

the civil law tradition, there is no anonymity here. Judges identify the judgment they have authored or voted to go along with. Likewise, there is no enforced unanimity. Judges are free to write dissenting or concurring opinions, although, as we have seen above, this is generally frowned upon. On the other hand, unlike the common law tradition, judgments are mostly not delivered seriatim in the Supreme Court of India. A judge has the freedom to accept the view taken by another judge without writing his own judgment.

There are several merits and demerits to each system. The argument most often made against a system which allows dissent is that it weakens the legitimacy of the court in the eyes of the public.[123] Governments in southern states in the US did not want to enforce a judgment of the US Supreme Court which called for the desegregation of schools at which black and white children studied separately. For this reason, in the desegregation judgments handed down by the US Supreme Court in particular, the fact that the court wrote unanimous opinions was a powerful signal to the executive governments in the southern states.[124] Another factor in favour of the anonymity system is that if the author of the judgment is unknown, then a judge might not be attacked for writing the judgment, thus making him or her more independent.[125] For example, Justice Harry Blackmun, the author of the US Supreme Court's judgment in *Roe v. Wade*,[126] in which the court held that the right to privacy includes a woman's right to have an abortion, was constantly attacked for his opinion, even though it was delivered by a 7-2 majority.[127] Abortion was, and remains, a hotly contested issue in the US. By contrast, the judges Gadbois spoke to mostly said that they did not dissent either to ensure that the court's judgments were clear to the lower courts, or because there was no time to do so.

On the other hand, there are several arguments which can be made in favour of a system which allows separate dissenting judgments. The most important among these is that a dissenting judgment has the potential to impact tomorrow's law: The dissenting judgment of today can very well become tomorrow's majority judgment.[128] Chief Justice Charles Evans Hughes famously wrote, 'A dissent in a court of last resort is an appeal to the brooding spirit of the law, to the intelligence of a future day, when a later decision may possibly correct the error into which the dissenting judge believes the court to have been betrayed.'[129] Identifying how judges vote in cases makes them accountable for their views.[130] Since a dissenting or concurring judgment may point out flaws in the majority judgment and vice versa, it also ensures that judgments are written more carefully.[131] According to Justice Ruth Bader Ginsburg of the US Supreme Court, less attention is paid to judgments that are delivered per curiam; they may be drafted by law clerks and not edited properly.[132] Supreme Court judges in India, on the other hand, do not dissent every time they believe that the majority is wrong, but only in those cases where they have a strong feeling against the view of the majority. Collegiality and clarity take precedence over the correctness of the view being taken, except in the most egregious of cases.

3

Special Leave, a Special Burden

When a judge is elevated to the Supreme Court, the first challenge he faces is the task of reading and preparing for the daunting onslaught of a species of cases called 'special leave petitions' (SLPs). The new Supreme Court judge comes relatively unprepared for this kind of case, because it does not exist at the high courts. Most Supreme Court judges told Gadbois that the work of dealing with SLPs was absolutely overwhelming and it drained the fun out of being a judge. The Supreme Court inherited the Privy Council's powers to entertain such petitions, but the Privy Council was not flooded with SLPs, at least in part because it was located in the far metropole, in London, and filing an SLP was costly and cumbersome. By contrast, since filing an SLP is relatively simple and inexpensive in New Delhi, the Supreme Court now spends around 40 per cent of its productive time (i.e. two out of five working days every week) dealing with admissions of SLPs, which are still exponentially choking the court's docket. The Supreme Court is to be partly blamed for this, because it is more liberal in admitting SLPs than the Privy Council was or the Supreme Courts of other countries are. Yet, many judges said that the judiciary is helpless to institute any serious reforms to the system in the face of the powerful Supreme Court Bar which has vested interests in ensuring that things remain as they are. People often complain that the standards of the judiciary have fallen, that judges today are not what they used to be in the 1950s or 1960s.[1] However, this chapter helps explain why this may be so. If the quality of judgments is indeed lower today, it is because judges are overwhelmingly overworked; because the SLP system leaves them with little time to revise their own draft judgments, to read, or to do anything else; and because they are virtually unable to institute any reforms against the wishes of the powerful bar.

Origins of the SLP

Before the Constitution came into force in 1950, a litigant who lost his case at a high court had limited options for filing an appeal at the Privy Council. In civil cases, there were, essentially, two kinds of appeals which could be filed at the Privy Council: an appeal by right, or an appeal by special leave. A person had the right to file an appeal before the Privy Council in a civil case if the following conditions were met: (i) the value of the subject matter had to typically be Rs 10,000 or more[2] (also, if the court whose decision was being appealed had affirmed the decision of the lower court, then the case had to involve 'some substantial question of law'[3]), and this had to be certified by the court whose decision was being appealed against[4]; or (ii) the court whose decision was being appealed against had to provide a certificate that the case was otherwise fit for appeal.[5] In short, in order to file an appeal as a matter of right before the Privy Council in a civil case, a losing litigant had to petition the court whose decision was being appealed against (usually the high court) for a certificate. If the certificate was granted by the court, the litigant had to deposit some security for costs with the court, and then his appeal would be admitted by the court and transferred to the Privy Council.[6]

Alternatively, a losing litigant in a civil case could petition the Privy Council itself for 'special leave' to appeal to it.[7] In criminal cases, there was, for the most part, no right of appeal before the Privy Council.[8] A losing litigant in a criminal case, therefore, had no option but to file a petition for special leave to appeal before the Privy Council. But special leave petitions could be filed before the Privy Council in civil cases as well. The 'special leave' route of filing an appeal before the Privy Council was unpredictable. As Bakshi Tek Chand,[9] a former judge of the Lahore High Court, said in the Constituent Assembly— while debating the provisions of the Constitution dealing with appeals to the Supreme Court—anyone who examined the cases of the Privy Council would not be able to find or extract any consistent rule as to when the Privy Council would grant leave and when it would not.[10] In some cases, he said, the Privy Council would refuse, and in other identical cases, it would grant special leave to appeal. Most of the petitions for special leave filed before the Privy Council (Tek Chand believed the statistic to be 99 per cent) were dismissed. Tek Chand noted that in criminal cases, the Privy Council granted leave to appeal only in exceptional cases, in cases where there had been a violation of 'the principles of natural justice'.[11] The phrase 'natural justice', noted Tek Chand, was 'vague and undefined', and did not 'cover substantial and serious errors of law or even [a] miscarriage of justice'.[12]

Apart from appeals to the Privy Council, from around 1937 onwards,[13] a litigant who lost a case, whether civil or criminal, at a high court, could appeal to the newly established Federal

Court in New Delhi if the high court certified that the case involved 'a substantial question of law as to the interpretation of' the Constitution (i.e. the Government of India Act, 1935, or any rules made under it).[14] In short, the Federal Court had the power to hear appeals only in constitutional cases.

When the Constitution of independent India was enacted in 1950, it blended together the pre-existing law on appeals to the Privy Council and Federal Court with some modifications. Accordingly, like at the Federal Court, the new Supreme Court had the power to hear appeals of cases, whether civil or criminal, involving, according to either the high court or Supreme Court, 'a substantial question of law as to the interpretation of this Constitution'.[15] Likewise, in civil cases, a right was given to appeal to the Supreme Court if the high court certified: (a) that the amount of the subject matter was Rs 20,000 (up from Rs 10,000 earlier)[16]; or (b) that the case was otherwise fit for appeal to the Supreme Court.[17] In 1973[18] and 1979,[19] the provision dealing with the right of appeal in civil cases was amended in order to make it more difficult to file appeals. No longer would it be sufficient if the case merely involved stakes of more than Rs 20,000. After these amendments, a litigant could only file an appeal in civil cases if the high court certified that the case involved 'a substantial question of law of general importance' and, in the opinion of the high court, that question needed to be decided by the Supreme Court.

However, a right of appeal was also conferred before the Supreme Court in some limited criminal cases,[20] though there had been no such right before the Privy Council.[21] Now, a final decision of a high court in a criminal case could be appealed against if the high court: (i) had, on appeal, reversed an order of acquittal and sentenced the accused to death; (ii) had transferred to itself a trial pending before a subordinate court and sentenced the accused to death; (iii) had certified that the case was fit for appeal.

Similarly, the jurisdiction of the Privy Council to grant special leave to appeal was conferred on the Supreme Court as well.[22] The original provision in the draft Constitution which gave the Supreme Court the power to grant special leave to appeal only applied against a 'judgment, decree or final order',[23] i.e. not against interlocutory proceedings. However, in October 1949, T.T. Krishnamachari[24] introduced an amendment which completely replaced that provision, and allowed special leave petitions to be filed against any 'judgment, decree, determination, sentence or order'.[25] His amendment was passed without any substantial or meaningful debate.[26] However, in the colonial period, the Privy Council too had exercised the power to grant special leave to appeal against interlocutory orders.[27] Even so, thanks to Krishnamachari's amendment, SLPs could now theoretically be filed at the Supreme Court against the most inconsequential of orders, involving interlocutory proceedings.

Even prior to Krishnamachari's amendment, many members of the Constituent Assembly had noted, some with concern, others with pride, that this provision gave incredibly wide powers of appeal to the Supreme Court. Sir Alladi Krishnaswami Ayyar said that the Supreme Court had 'wider jurisdiction than any superior court in any part of the world'.[28] B.R. Ambedkar,[29] K.M. Munshi[30] and Tek Chand[31] said that the jurisdiction of the Privy Council in special leave cases was essentially vested in the Supreme Court by this provision.[32] While Pandit Thakur Das Bhargava[33] believed that the provision was too wide,[34] Sir Alladi was happy about this; he thought that the provision would not fetter the Supreme Court in exercising appellate jurisdiction in criminal cases as the Privy Council had done.[35]

A Docket Explosion

When a litigant loses his case at a high court, he has the option of filing a petition in the Supreme Court known as a 'special leave petition'. By filing this petition, under Article 136 of the Constitution, a litigant who has lost his case before a high court essentially seeks 'special leave' from the Supreme Court for filing an appeal against the decision of the high court. Like such petitions which were filed before the Privy Council, this process is highly discretionary. Motilal C. Setalvad openly likened the process of getting an SLP admitted by the Supreme Court to a gamble; he was able to get an SLP admitted where a virtually identical SLP had been dismissed a few days earlier.[36] If the petition is successful, then the litigant is allowed to actually appeal against the decision of the high court. If not, the high court's decision stands. Article 136 was a residuary provision. It allowed the Supreme Court, obviously in exceptional cases (though this was not specified in the provision), to grant 'special leave' to a litigant to appeal against any order (whether it was final or not), if the litigant filing the appeal did not have a right to file an appeal.

However, SLPs under Article 136 soon became the most preferred and exclusive choice of filing an appeal before the Supreme Court. Justice Mehr Chand Mahajan, who served in the court between 1950 and 1954, noted that the right to grant special leave 'had been very widely phrased in the Constitution', and the court was 'soon flooded with applications for special leave to appeal wherever a litigant could afford the high cost of such a proceeding in the Supreme Court'. Troublingly, he found that '[s]ome of these applications were so frivolous' that he was able to dispose of 'about a dozen of them at one sitting'.[37] He constituted a bench to sit over the court's vacation, the first time this had happened, in order to clear all the arrears for his successor.[38] After taking over as the chief justice of India in late 1959, B.P. Sinha estimated that it would take the Supreme Court two and a half years to clear all its pending cases, if it did not take any new cases at all.[39]

It was not only the Supreme Court which was facing a docket explosion. In a speech made in September 1957, Prime Minister Nehru spoke with some alarm about the 1.64 lakh cases that were pending in the courts. The problem of arrears was one which troubled him a great deal. He believed that increasing the strength of judges would not solve the problem. He thought that the 'more the Judges, more the work, more the litigation, more the arrears'.[40] In December 1958, Nehru wrote that he had recently been 'much troubled . . . by the long delays of the Law and how in some of the High Courts of India many appeals are not disposed of for ten years or more'; a matter, thought Nehru, which deserved 'the urgent attention of all of us and more especially of lawyers'.[41]

Available statistics[42] on the filing of cases before the court suggest that the court's workload is ominously on the rise, and has been so for several decades. About 1215 new cases were instituted in the court in 1950, and the figure steadily rose to 14,501 in 1977. Then, all of a sudden, there was an explosion of cases the following year, 1978, when as many as 20,840 new cases were instituted in the Supreme Court. This figure reached its peak of 55,902 cases in 1983 and, after showing some signs of decline, rose again to 70,352 in 2008. In 2016, which is the last full year for which data is available as this book is being written, the court saw 79,244 new cases being filed. The actual work done by the court has also substantially increased. The court disposed of 525 cases in 1950, which rose to 10,395 cases in 1977. The following year, as the docket exploded, the work done by the court increased substantially as well, with 17,095 cases disposed of by the Supreme Court in 1978. A record 45,824 cases were disposed of by the court in 1983, rising to 67,459 cases in 2008. In 2016, as many as 75,979 cases were disposed of by the court.

The number of judges at the Supreme Court has also increased, in order to keep up with the increase in the court's docket. The court began, in 1950, with a maximum sanctioned strength of eight judges (including the chief justice), but its strength increased to eleven in 1956, fourteen in 1960, eighteen in 1977, twenty-six in 1986 and thirty-one in 2009.[43] However, the statistical history of the court has shown us that while increasing the strength of judges might help reduce arrears, it is not a long-term strategy to make the functioning of the court more efficient and it cannot eliminate arrears altogether. Some more far-reaching institutional reforms may be necessary in order to stem the tide of SLPs (e.g., doing away with an oral hearing for SLPs, imposing costs when an SLP is dismissed in limine, etc.). By increasing the number of judges, the court was able to increase the number of cases disposed of, but it was not able to keep pace with the high number of cases which were being filed each year. So while there were only 690 cases pending on the court's docket in 1950, the number of outstanding cases reached its peak in 1990, with 1,09,277 cases pending at the end of that year. This figure has commendably been brought down over the years, but there were, as of 2016, still 62,537 cases pending at the end of the year. One scholar has surmised that it would take the court three full years to clear all its arrears if it stopped accepting new cases altogether.[44]

The statistics set out above don't really tell us what proportion of the court's instituted and disposed of cases were attributable to SLPs. After all, a wide variety of cases can be filed before the Supreme Court apart from SLPs—writ petitions, transfer petitions, statutory appeals, etc.[45] However, the sense one gets is that the lion's share of these cases comes to the court as SLPs.[46] Consider that by 1958 alone, out of the 794 criminal appeals which were pending at the Supreme Court, 548 were SLPs.[47] Today, certificates of appeal granted by the high court have nearly disappeared.

By contrast, in the entire history of colonial India leading up to 1949, the Privy Council handed down only about 2500 judgments in Indian appeals.[48] Though appeals from India constituted the highest number of appeals to the Privy Council in comparison with any other dominion or colony—whether 'white-settler' (like Australia or Canada) or otherwise[49]—the proportion of Indian appeals dealt with by the Privy Council was minuscule in comparison with the volume of SLPs which the Supreme Court would have to wrap its hands around later on. In fact, a few years after the Constitution came into force, a high court chief justice noted that the Supreme Court was granting leave to appeal 'very liberally', more so than the Privy Council where special leave petitions, especially in criminal cases, were seldom admitted.[50] During the colonial period, the Bombay High Court more often cited its own judgments as authorities than judgments of the Privy Council, partly because there were not enough precedents generated by the Privy Council on every point of law as there are Supreme Court judgments today.[51]

Initially, the Supreme Court took note of the tests applied by the Privy Council in deciding whether or not to admit an SLP. In one of the earliest cases involving Article 136,[52] the Supreme Court held that the provision conferred a 'wide discretionary power' on the court, one which was to be 'exercised sparingly and in exceptional cases only', 'where special circumstances are shown to exist'. Akin to a test laid down by the Privy Council for granting leave in criminal cases, the court in that case held that, generally speaking, it would not grant special leave unless it were shown that 'exceptional and special circumstances exist, that substantial and grave injustice has been done and that the case in question presents features of sufficient gravity to warrant a review of the decision appealed against'. However, this soon changed. Of the 291 SLPs filed in labour matters before the Supreme Court in 1956, for instance, the court admitted as many as 257.[53] In 1958, the Law Commission noted that the court had strayed from the test it had laid down for admission of SLPs, at least in criminal cases.[54] It also found that the number of SLPs filed at the court was increasing, and the manner in which the court was granting leave to appeal had 'considerably shaken the prestige of the High Courts as the highest courts of criminal appeal in the States'.[55] It counselled the Supreme Court to restrict admitting SLPs in criminal matters to 'cases of grave and real miscarriage of justice'.[56]

More recently, Nick Robinson pointed out that since 1996, the Supreme Court admitted between 15 and 26 per cent of the cases instituted before it,[57] whereas the US Supreme Court approximately admits less than 1 per cent of the cases filed before it.[58] At the same time, one cannot lose sight of the fact that the Privy Council was located in London. This made it far more difficult and expensive for Indian litigants to file petitions for special leave.[59] One of the arguments made in 1921 in the Central Legislative Assembly by Dr Hari Singh Gour to set up a Supreme Court in colonial India was that it was far too expensive to file an appeal before the Privy Council.[60] Since the Supreme Court is located in New Delhi, which makes it comparatively less expensive,[61] the filing of special leave petitions has resulted in an explosion of the court's docket. In fact, recent scholarship suggests that cases come to the Supreme Court most often from the northern states, which are more geographically proximate to the court, and from affluent states like Maharashtra.[62]

The Overburdened Judge

In the early years, the Supreme Court was certainly in favour of admitting SLPs rather than dismissing them. When judges like P.B. Gajendragadkar and M. Hidayatullah were appointed to the court in the late 1950s, they found that there was a strange convention prevalent at the court: Even if only one judge on the bench thought that there was some merit in an SLP, then it would be admitted, even if all the others disagreed.[63] The reason behind this convention was that some judges might not have been able to read or grasp all cases, so each case had to be given a good chance of being admitted.[64] Gajendragadkar found this practice quite strange, and the convention was restricted during his tenure at the court.[65] However, the admission of SLPs remained quite liberal.

When Justice Hidayatullah arrived at the Supreme Court in December 1958, Mondays at the court were known as 'admissions days'. On Mondays, the court only decided whether or not to admit SLPs and miscellaneous matters.[66] On his first day in court, a Monday, Justice Hidayatullah was sitting on a constitution bench (i.e. a bench of five or more judges) which was hearing SLPs for admission. Late on Sunday night, Hidayatullah had found on his bed a huge bundle of papers, some thirty to thirty-five SLPs, running into a thousand pages, and he was expected to have read them by the following morning. Justice Vivian Bose, with whom Hidayatullah was staying at the time, advised him only to read the later cases, and to skim through the earlier ones, because most of his colleagues would not have been able to read the later cases, and he could control the conversation then.[67]

By Chief Justice Y.V. Chandrachud's tenure in the late 1970s and early 1980s, on admissions day (every Monday), about seven or eight benches were constituted, each having to hear about thirty cases,[68] though some SLPs were heard on other days as well.[69] Sometime in the late 1970s, probably during the chief justiceship of Chandrachud, Fridays at the Supreme Court got earmarked for SLPs as well. Even today, Mondays and Fridays are reserved for SLPs and miscellaneous matters. In other words, two out of the court's five working days, i.e. 40 per cent of the court's productive time, is spent on SLP admissions. As a puisne judge, Chandrachud had requested Chief Justice A.N. Ray to set apart some more time for admissions cases, but Ray had refused, saying that he would not change any of the court's traditions while he was the chief justice.[70] Of course, the irony of this might not have been lost on Chandrachud, as Ray had been instrumental in altering one of the greatest traditions of the Supreme Court, the seniority convention in the matter of appointing the chief justice of India.

Justice P.S. Kailasam, who served at the court in the late 1970s, guessed that about 280 SLPs were each heard on Mondays and Fridays every week, and about half of them were admitted. The rate at which cases were instituted was about six times higher than the rate at which cases were disposed of by the court, guessed Kailasam.[71] Justice A.P. Sen believed that each judge was dealing with forty to fifty cases each on Mondays and Fridays, apart from hearing SLPs on other days as well, making a total of approximately 150 SLPs every week at the Supreme Court.[72]

Additionally, because of the large volume of pending cases, judges might not actually get to decide the SLPs which they

agreed to admit. Justice M.P. Thakkar felt frustrated by the fact
that though he would serve a term of five and a half years at the
Supreme Court, he would not get a chance to decide most of the
SLPs that he had admitted, since it took a long time, on account
of the case arrears, for SLPs to come up for final disposal.[73]
In short, reform-minded judges like Thakkar did not get the
opportunity to make much of a difference because they were
essentially deciding cases admitted by others.[74]

Many judges said that the burden of dealing with these
SLPs was incredibly taxing. '[The] Supreme Court will kill
you,' said Justice P. Jaganmohan Reddy.[75] 'The work there
is killing,' he said, '[y]ou have to be in good health.' He
said that several judges were not in good health when they
arrived at the Supreme Court; judges like P. Govinda Menon,
P. Satyanarayana Raju and S.C. Roy eventually died in office.
Justice N.L. Untwalia said that he was not in good health
during his years at the Supreme Court, that he had suffered
a heart attack in 1976.[76] Justice D.P. Madon found it difficult
to adjust to Delhi partly because he had to leave his long-
time physician behind in Bombay and find a new one in the
capital.[77] He also missed the social and cultural life of Bombay,
saying that Delhi just wasn't the city that Bombay was. Apart
from the workload, some judges found it a little difficult to get
used to the weather,[78] dust and allergies in Delhi.[79]

In addition to everything else, Justice Sabyasachi Mukharji
found it hard to socially adjust to Delhi (he had lived in the same
house in Calcutta for about fifty years). Judges of the Calcutta
High Court also had to specialize in a particular field of law,
whereas Supreme Court judges had to be generalists. Before
getting to the Supreme Court, he had hardly ever dealt with a
criminal case, but once there, he had to familiarize himself with
that branch of law.[80]

Many judges felt that most SLPs were a waste of time, that several SLPs which were admitted were not important enough to come to the Supreme Court (though there was no consensus on what kinds of cases ought to be admitted), and that admissions days were frenzied and chaotic.[81] Dealing with them gave Supreme Court judges time to do little else. Justices A.C. Gupta and A. Varadarajan felt that they had no leisure, no time to read, once they got to the Supreme Court.[82] Gupta recalled the words of one of his retiring colleagues who had said that Indian Supreme Court judges 'are the most ignorant judges on earth' because they have no time to read once at the court.[83] 'My Saturdays, Sundays, Tuesdays and Wednesdays were always mortgaged for homework on SLPs,' said Gupta.[84] Justice A.P. Sen felt frustrated by the fact that during his long tenure at the Supreme Court, he hardly wrote a handful of judgments of which he could be proud. The SLPs did not leave him with enough time. 'I am mentally fatigued,' he said to Gadbois. On the last day of court in May 1983, he delivered an eighty-eight-page judgment, the last twenty pages of which had been dictated on the last day of the court's term.[85] He did not feel proud of having written that judgment.[86] At times, he wrote reported judgments without even revising them.[87] Justice Madon's wife referred to Thursdays at the court as 'Black Thursdays', because of the sheer amount of cases which her husband had to read in order to get ready for Friday.[88] Often, judges felt overwhelmed by the SLP because there was nothing like it in the high courts.[89]

Several reasons were offered to Gadbois by the judges about why so many SLPs were admitted by the court. Justices P.N. Bhagwati and R.S. Pathak felt that the court was constrained to admit many SLPs against decisions of high courts because there had been a general fall in the standards of decision-making at the high courts,[90] which perhaps, in turn, had a lot to do with the fact that judges at these courts were overworked and underpaid. Justice R.N. Misra said that the Supreme Court's judges were conscious of the fact that they were in a court of last resort—since the Supreme Court was the final court, its judges had a greater responsibility towards the litigating public.[91] It was perhaps for this reason that so many SLPs were admitted by the court.

Many judges complained that they did not get adequate assistance when they reached the Supreme Court, in the form of law clerks or competent staff.[92] Some judges complained that the staff at the Supreme Court was less competent than at their own high courts.[93] For example, Justice M.H. Kania said that the Bombay stenographers were more qualified than those at the Supreme Court.[94] Justice S. Natarajan said that stenos at the Madras High Court even proofread judgments and corrected errors in drafts, which they did not do at the Supreme Court.[95] At the US Supreme Court, brilliant law students are selected, after they graduate, to be law clerks for Supreme Court justices, and they spend a year or two with them. Among other tasks, they assist in writing the opinions of the court. In India, law clerks are a relatively recent phenomenon, and they had not got to the court when the interviews were conducted, in the 1980s.[96] Justice A.N. Grover said that there were no law clerks in the Supreme Court at that time for two reasons: (i) because Indian law schools did not turn out high-quality law graduates (this, of course, was before the advent of the National Law Schools in India); and (ii) because of a fear that law clerks would be pressured by litigants or their own kin to influence the outcomes of cases, or that the litigating public would have the perception that law clerks were trying to influence cases.[97] On the other hand, Justice Bhagwati felt that law clerks were needed at the court.[98] Justice Pathak thought that young law graduates would be too academic, and therefore not very useful as law clerks. He would have preferred to have a senior district judge work as a law clerk for him.[99]

Ad hoc and Acting Judges

The Constitution gives the chief justice of India (with the previous consent of the President) the power to appoint high court judges as ad hoc Supreme Court judges.[100] However, this power has been exercised very rarely. For instance, it was used between August and December in 1950, when a special bench of the Supreme Court was set up temporarily in Hyderabad, consisting of Supreme Court judge Mahajan and two ad hoc judges who were really Hyderabad High Court judges, to hear cases which had been transferred from the Privy Council of Hyderabad to the Supreme Court.[101] However, high court judges are rarely appointed as ad hoc Supreme Court judges to clear case arrears.

Similarly, though the Constitution enables the chief justice of India (with the previous consent of the President) to appoint retired Supreme Court judges as acting Supreme Court judges,[102] this power is now rarely exercised. Initially, retired judges were appointed as acting Supreme Court judges in order to relieve the pressure on the court. For instance, after C.A. Vaidialingam and I.D. Dua retired in 1972, they were brought back as acting judges on a bench with the newly appointed Justice A. Alagiriswami, while the *Basic Structure* case was being heard over six months.[103] These appointments have now ceased not merely because they are unpopular with high court judges,[104] but also because retired judges have no interest in returning to the court and sitting as junior judges.[105] Once retired judges

come back as acting judges, they lose their seniority at the
court. The bench Vaidialingam and Dua sat on with Justice
Alagiriswami should have been presided over by Alagiriswami,
though he was actually the most junior judge among the three.
However, Alagiriswami graciously allowed Vaidialingam to
preside over the bench.[106] Chief Justice Bhagwati wanted Justice
A.N. Sen to stay on as an acting judge after he (i.e. Sen) retired in
September 1985, but Sen was not interested.[107] The government
gets in the way of such appointments as well. In August 1989,
Chief Justice E.S. Venkataramiah tried to appoint three retired
Supreme Court judges (G.L. Oza, M.M. Dutt and Natarajan) as
acting judges, but the 'Law Minister slept over the matter and
there was [a] change of Government'.[108] Venkataramiah had
informed the law minister that the health of these judges was
'quite sound' and 'their reasoning faculties are quite sharp'. He
had also written to the law minister that he 'would be distressed
to note that the Court would be losing their services when they
are needed most'.[109]

Bullying by the Bar

Many judges said that while it was possible to reform the
SLP system in order to make things more efficient and less
burdensome, the bar (i.e. lawyers who practise at the Supreme
Court) would not tolerate any changes to the system. The SLPs
heard on Mondays and Fridays constitute the bread-and-butter
work of the Supreme Court Bar. Each case takes only a few
minutes,[110] at the most, to be heard, which enables lawyers to
take up dozens of cases each Monday and Friday. Any change
to this system would affect the earnings of the Supreme Court
Bar. For instance, the Supreme Court could theoretically decide
not to grant an oral hearing for SLPs, which is essentially

the practice in the US Supreme Court. There, petitions for certiorari or 'cert petitions', as they are called,[111] do not get an oral hearing. The justices of the US Supreme Court 'pool' together the thousands of petitions which are filed each year and, with the aid of their law clerks, select a small sample of cases, which get a time-bound oral hearing. The rest of the cases are unceremoniously rejected. For instance, in 2010, nearly 8000 cases were filed at the US Supreme Court, but only eighty-six were admitted for hearing.[112] The Indian Supreme Court Bar would be substantially affected by this, and would never permit this to happen.

Several judges said that Supreme Court judges essentially got bullied by the bar, and they were not able to institute reform against the wishes of the bar. For instance, Justice P. Jaganmohan Reddy felt that the bar would not tolerate any changes to the present SLP system.[113] In 1978, he had recommended to Chief Justice Chandrachud that ad hoc benches of the Supreme Court be set up in five different regions in India for reducing civil and criminal appeals, but Chandrachud had told him that Supreme Court lawyers would not accept this decision.[114] Justice R.S. Sarkaria felt that judges were afraid of the bar, and were scared to make changes to the SLP system.[115] Justice A.C. Gupta attributed this to weak leadership.[116] He said judges who served as chief justices of India did not have the courage to stand up to the bar. An incident that occurred at the court during the tenure of Justice Kailasam, who served between 1977 and 1980, is instructive. Noted lawyer L.M. Singhvi was arguing an SLP for admission before Kailasam, who saw no merit in it and dismissed it. He must have said something harsh to Singhvi. Apparently, this angered Singhvi, who snapped and said that he would not appear before any bench which had Kailasam on it. Singhvi apparently also called a bar association meeting about this. Six judges of the Supreme Court (Kailasam, P.N. Shinghal, Untwalia, A.P. Sen, A.D. Koshal and V.D. Tulzapurkar) threatened to resign if something was not done about this. Chief Justice Chandrachud called a meeting of the judges to resolve the problem. A compromise was struck, though it is unclear what that was. With hindsight, Kailasam was disappointed with Chief Justice Chandrachud. He said that Chandrachud was 'too soft', and he could not deal with trouble.[117]

Chief Justice Chandrachud had also obtained permission from the President to institute some reforms in SLPs. The court had decided that SLPs filed against decisions of single high court judges would be heard by a single Supreme Court judge. This would free up more judges, since at the time, all SLPs were heard by benches consisting of at least two judges. However, Chandrachud did not implement this change. Though his successors, Bhagwati and Pathak, were critical of him for failing to do so, they too were not able to institute this change. Justice Chinnappa Reddy believed that they were unable to do so because they feared opposition from the bar.[118] In 1982, Chief Justice Chandrachud issued a circular that a small category of cases would be disposed of without a hearing. The Supreme Court Bar threatened to go on strike, the chairperson of the bar association declined Chandrachud's invitation to meet him about this, and the reform proposal was dropped.[119] While retiring from the court, one of Chief Justice Chandrachud's few regrets was that he was unable to 'speed up the course of justice'. '[O]ur whole system is so hidebound,' he said, 'that it is difficult to introduce innovations.'[120] Similarly, Chief Justice Satish Chandra of the Allahabad High Court had instituted several practices to eliminate delays in hearing cases. The Allahabad Bar went on strike, in protest, and Chandra was eventually transferred.[121] 'The Bar won,' wrote scholar Upendra Baxi about this incident.[122]

Justice A.P. Sen believed that the bar was 'insolent' towards the judiciary. He felt, rightly or wrongly, that leading lawyers looked down on judges, and found their meagre pay packets 'laughable' in comparison with their own.[123] This could very well have been an inferiority complex harboured by some judges against members of the bar. Justice Thakkar too emphasized that what some advocates made in one day, Supreme Court judges made in six months. He felt that he could not approach Chief Justice Chandrachud with any suggestions for reform, for those would simply be filed away and ignored.[124] He too said that some judges were afraid of the bar, that they tried to please senior advocates. He believed that the bar had vested interests in perpetuating some of the worst features of the Supreme Court (e.g., lengthy oral arguments). The bar was powerful and vocal, he said, and could smear a judge with criticism and rumours.[125]

Indeed, much of this accords with what Marc Galanter and Robinson have written about the 'grand advocates' of the Supreme Court.[126] Supreme Court judges serve in office for short periods of time, but advocates practise at the court longer, and consider themselves to be more a part of the institution than even the judges.

Justice Bhagwati believed that oral arguments could not be done away with entirely, and they were needed because Indian lawyers did not write good briefs.[127] Kania too agreed that most SLPs were poorly written.[128] However, Bhagwati felt that limits on oral arguments were necessary,[129] but lawyers would not allow judges to limit oral arguments to a certain time frame.[130] Many judges felt that an enormous amount of time was wasted on oral arguments. Justice Sarkaria evoked the example of the famous case of *Bachan Singh v. State of Punjab*,[131] involving the question of whether the death penalty was constitutionally valid. In that case, he said, the advocates for the petitioners and interveners, including R.K. Garg, presented oral arguments for around thirty days in court.[132] The government's lawyers presented their case in just about an hour. Over that entire period of time, Justice Sarkaria took down only one and a half pages of notes. He believed that the nearly unlimited time which was given for presenting oral arguments in that case was absurd. He also believed that this was because judges were afraid of the bar.[133] Justice A.C. Gupta was critical of his colleagues who interrupted lawyers' arguments in order to express their own views,[134] which probably slowed things down even further.

Justice Bhagwati thought that the Supreme Court's jurisdiction should be split up between two courts: a court of appeal, below the Supreme Court, to deal with ordinary appeals like SLPs, and a permanent constitution bench consisting of the court's five, seven or nine most senior judges, to deal with constitutional cases.[135] He was opposed to the increase in the number of judges at the Supreme Court from eighteen to twenty-six which occurred around 1986,[136] and wanted the work of the court to be split up in this manner instead. However, the government did not show much interest.

4

Decliners

This chapter looks at the reasons why those who were offered judgeships at the Supreme Court or at high courts declined those offers. We will see that several lawyers who were offered judgeships typically turned them down because the salary of judges was very low, which was not substantially offset by the other perks and benefits offered as remuneration to judges. Many lawyers did not accept high court judgeships in the 1980s because of the transfer of judges policy, under which they could be arbitrarily transferred away from their homes to other states on the whims of the government. We will see that, surprisingly, many high court judges also turned down offers to be elevated to the Supreme Court. In the initial years, chief justices of prestigious high courts like the ones at Bombay and Calcutta preferred to remain in these positions rather than become junior judges of the Supreme Court. However, this reason later ceased to be valid, especially because of the 'transfer of chief justices policy' (which continues to remain intact today), under which a person can no longer serve as the chief justice of his own high court (i.e. the high court in which he was first appointed a judge). Other high court judges turned down offers to come to the Supreme Court because of ego tussles involving seniority: judges junior to them had been appointed to the Supreme Court ahead of them. Others refused on account of problems of social adjustment.

Many of the factors for declining judgeships discussed in this chapter continue to be relevant today. We will see that judges' salaries, even now, despite a recent increment, are low in comparison with what lawyers earn at the bar. Though puisne judges are no longer transferred on the whims of the government, the 'transfer of chief justices policy' virtually ensures that no high court chief justice will now refuse an offer to be elevated to the Supreme Court. Above everything else, this chapter tells us about the rise of the prestige of the Supreme Court, accompanied by a dilution of the status of the high courts.[1] In 1949, Chief Justice M.C. Chagla of the Bombay High Court declined an offer to become a puisne judge at the Supreme Court, because being a Bombay High Court chief justice was more prestigious, back then, than becoming a junior Supreme Court judge. This is no longer true. The status of the high courts has, over the years, been diluted, while that of the Supreme Court has risen by leaps and bounds. The Law Commission of India, in its famous 14th report prepared in 1958, had feared that there would be a fall in the 'prestige' of the high courts. Those fears have largely been realized.[2]

Structure of the Judiciary

Broadly speaking, there are three tiers or levels of courts in India. The topmost rung of the hierarchy is, of course, occupied by the Supreme Court of India. Beneath the Supreme Court, each state has a high court,[3] but Punjab and Haryana in the north, Maharashtra and Goa in the west, and

Assam, Nagaland, Mizoram and Arunachal Pradesh in the north-east, respectively share one high court between them.[4] Beneath the high courts sits a complex web of subordinate courts which exercise civil or criminal powers, and original or appellate powers.[5] Each state has its own different system of subordinate courts.[6] Recruitments to these courts also vary from state to state. In Maharashtra, depending on the court in question,[7] judges of subordinate courts may be recruited by competitive examination, promotion, or direct appointment from the bar.[8] Only a quarter of the district judges, who are the most senior civil judges in the hierarchy of the subordinate judiciary, can be selected directly from the bar, while the rest are appointed by promoting them from lower courts. This changes at the high court. At the Bombay High Court, the informal rule which has historically been followed is that two-thirds of the judges of the high court are appointed directly from the bar (in the colonial period, only a third of the court's judges belonged to the Indian Civil Service [ICS]).[9] There is at present no application or test for this method of recruitment. In other words, advocates practising at the bar of the Bombay High Court are invited by the chief justice to accept a judgeship at the court. If they say yes, and if all else goes well, then they are appointed judges. The remaining one-third of the high court's judges are recruited by promotions from the subordinate judiciary. Even the Law Commission in its 14th report said that the 'Bar must remain . . . the main recruiting ground for the High Court Bench'.[10]

At the Supreme Court, on the other hand, a very tiny proportion of judges is recruited directly from the bar. In fact, there was no bar appointment at the Supreme Court during two entire decades—the 1950s and the 2000s. There was only one appointment made to the Supreme Court directly from the bar in every decade for four decades: the 1960s, 1970s, 1980s and 1990s. In more recent times, however, three judges[11] (out of the court's sanctioned strength of thirty-one judges) were appointed directly from the bar, and a fourth[12] may soon be appointed as this book goes to press. The remaining Supreme Court judges are appointed by promoting high court judges (in recent times, usually high court chief justices[13]).

There is no formal application or examination for being appointed to the Supreme Court. It is the President of India who officially appoints Supreme Court and high court judges. However, the common perception is that prior to the 1970s, the interference of the government in judicial appointments, though not completely absent, was minimal.[14] It is commonly believed that at that time, the chief justice of India (sometimes in consultation with some of his colleagues either in the Supreme Court or the high courts) controlled the process of appointing judges to the Supreme Court and high courts. The chief justice submitted names to the President who, it is often believed, accepted the nominations. In the next chapter, we will examine in greater detail whether these commonly held perceptions about judicial appointments are actually true.

After the 1970s, the Indira Gandhi government started interfering in judicial appointments. In the 1990s, the Supreme Court set up the present 'collegium' system of appointing judges. According to this regime, for appointing Supreme Court judges, the chief justice of India and his four most senior colleagues at the court constitute a body called the 'collegium'.[15] The collegium submits names for appointment to the President. The nomination is virtually binding on the President.[16] For appointing high court judges, the collegium consists of the chief justice of India and the two most senior judges of the Supreme Court.[17]

Lawyers Who Declined

It was common for busy, successful lawyers, who were offered the opportunity to become judges of the Supreme Court or high courts, to politely decline those offers, though there were, of course, exceptions. Chief Justice B.P. Sinha offered a judgeship to Law Minister Asoke Sen, sometime prior to March 1960. Sen was around forty-five years old at the time, and would have served an enormous twenty-year term at the Supreme Court, approximately ten of which would have been as the chief justice of India. Sen told Sinha that he needed to think about the offer. Sinha even ran the offer past Prime Minister Nehru who, in turn, asked Home Minister G.B. Pant for his opinion. However, it is not clear why this appointment fell through.[18] Thereafter, one of India's best-known lawyers, Nani A. Palkhivala, was offered a direct Supreme Court judgeship around 1963 or 1964.[19] Had he accepted, he might have become the chief justice of India between 1971 and 1985,[20] which is far longer than the term served by any chief justice of India to date. However, he declined.[21] Another noted advocate, Lal Narain Sinha (who had been the advocate general of Bihar and had appeared in *Golak Nath's* case[22]), was offered a Supreme Court judgeship three times, but he declined.[23] Justice Hardayal Hardy, a judge of the Delhi High Court, declined a seat in the Supreme Court (offered to him by Law Minister H.R. Gokhale) because he wanted to practise in the Supreme Court after his retirement, having spent all the money he had earned as a lawyer during his high court judgeship.[24] It was after Hardy's refusal to go to the Supreme Court that H.R. Khanna was appointed to the court.[25] Thereafter, Chief Justice Y.V. Chandrachud offered four lawyers, Fali S. Nariman, K. Parasaran (who held the positions of advocate general of Tamil Nadu, solicitor general of India and attorney general of India[26]), S.N. Kacker (who had been the advocate general of Uttar Pradesh and solicitor general of India[27]) and K.K. Venugopal (who currently holds the position of the attorney general of India as this book is being written), direct appointments to the Supreme Court, but they declined.[28] Justice A.P. Sen said that Chief Justice Chandrachud and his two most senior colleagues, Justices P.N. Bhagwati and Krishna Iyer, met the lawyers when the offer was made to them. He also said that Justice Krishna Iyer was rude to one of the lawyers, Kacker. Sen believed that Kacker was scholarly and would have been a great asset to the Supreme Court. He thought that accepting a judgeship would have been beneficial to Kacker, because he was, according to Justice Sen, in bad health.[29] On hearing this, Gadbois noted down, 'Interesting point, others think it [a] good idea for [a] sinking advocate to become [a] judge!'

One of the primary reasons why lawyers declined those offers was because of the low salaries paid to judges in India.[30] In 1966, Fali Nariman was offered a judgeship of the Bombay High Court by Chief Justice S.P. Kotval, at the young age of thirty-eight. Kotval had taken special permission from the chief justice of India, J.C. Shah, for appointing Nariman at such a young age. However, Nariman declined the offer for financial reasons. The monthly salary of a high court judge at the time was only Rs 3500, which was insufficient for him to support his family, including his wife, two children and grandmother.[31] In the 1980s, when he was fifty-three, Nariman was offered a judgeship of the Supreme Court by Chief Justice Chandrachud. Had he accepted, he would have possibly gone on to become the chief justice of India for around nine years.[32] However, once again, he declined.[33] Justice D.P. Madon agreed that the low salary was one of the reasons why he was unable, as the chief justice of the Bombay High Court, to convince top lawyers to join the ranks of judges.[34] Justice S. Natarajan said that it was difficult to recruit good lawyers for judgeships at the Madras High Court because of the poor judicial salary, even though lawyers' earnings in Madras were not as high as in Bombay or Calcutta.[35] In fact, the Law Commission in its 14th report recorded that the home minister of India had said in Parliament that 'attempts made to secure the appointment of distinguished advocates to the Supreme Court had not succeeded', because 'successful lawyers earn a considerable amount, and if you want suitable and competent, impartial and able Judges, to man the Supreme Court, then their salaries should have some relation to the earnings of the successful lawyers'.[36]

Judges' Salaries and Benefits

The salaries of high court and Supreme Court judges have, in independent India, been kept very low. Ironically, salaries paid to judges were actually quite handsome during the colonial period. In 1935, for instance, the chief justice of the Bombay High Court earned a higher salary than the chief justice of the US Supreme Court.[37] In the late nineteenth century, the chief justice of the Calcutta High Court earned an annual salary of Rs 72,000 per annum, which was higher than the salary of a puisne judge in England or that of the chief justice of any other British colonial court.[38] Towards the end of the colonial period, the chief justice of the Federal Court earned a salary of Rs 7000 per month,[39] a Federal Court judge earned a salary of Rs 5500 per month,[40] a high court chief justice typically earned between Rs 5000 and 6000 per month,[41] while a high court judge earned Rs 4000 per month.[42]

Judges' salaries were kept stagnant for a long time during the British Raj. As a consequence, a Bombay High Court judge earned the same salary in the 1890s as he did in the 1920s.[43] However, once the Constitution of independent India came into being, salaries of judges were actually reduced instead of being increased.[44] In 1950, the salary of the chief justice of the Supreme Court was lowered to Rs 5000 per month,[45] salaries of Supreme Court judges and high court chief justices (who are compensated the same because they are considered to be at the same level) were reduced to Rs 4000 per month, and those of high court judges were reduced to Rs 3500 per month.[46] This was less than what Indian judges were paid in British India.

One of the hallmarks of an independent judiciary is that judges' salaries must not be altered to their detriment once they assume office. The law of British India prohibited the salaries of judges from being reduced once they were appointed to office.[47] However, ironically, the Constitution of independent India did not (and continues not to) give the same guarantee to our judges. In other words, the salary of a Supreme Court or high court judge can theoretically be reduced after he/she has assumed office, which can technically be used to penalize judges for deciding cases against the government.[48]

In November 1948, Prime Minister Nehru was worried that the low salaries of high court judges would prevent competent advocates from being appointed as judges of the East Punjab High Court. Nehru had been alerted that attempts were being made by followers of Master Tara Singh to 'capture the High Court', and appoint a Sikh as its chief justice. Tara Singh made fiery speeches advocating the creation of a separate Sikh state (even hinting at secession); the government was unhappy about the consequent communal disharmony between Hindus and Sikhs at this time.[49] The low salary of high court judges, thought Nehru, would result in 'some Sikhs' getting high court judgeships 'for political reasons', 'even though they might not be competent'.[50] That month, the chief justice of the Federal Court, Harilal J. Kania, met Nehru at a party at the American Embassy and told him that 'the quality of the judges would suffer greatly' on account of the proposed reduction in judges' salaries. Nehru thought that the best way to 'meet this difficulty' was 'not to raise the proposed salaries but to provide other amenities' for the judges, like 'a free house or a free car, or a car allowance'.[51] In Nehru's correspondence with Home Minister Sardar Vallabhbhai Patel, the subject of low judicial salaries often recurred.[52] Even in 1980, Justice K.S. Hegde said that the quality of judges had gone down because of low salaries.[53]

Over time, the salaries of Supreme Court judges have rarely been increased. Between 1950 and 1985, salaries of Supreme Court and high court judges remained the same.[54] This meant, to put it into perspective, that a chief justice of India who retired from the Supreme Court in 1985 was paid less money per month than the chief justice of the Calcutta High Court in 1893, nearly a hundred years earlier. By contrast, the cost of living in India kept going up. There was high inflation in India in the 1960s, 1970s and even 1980s. For instance, inflation reached 13.3 per cent in 1964, 28.6 per cent in 1974 (though it dropped to -7.6 per cent in 1976, and rose again to 8.3 per cent in 1977), and 11.8 per cent in 1983.[55] In fact, Justice R.B. Misra said that lawyers refused judgeships because inflation had made the value of the judges' salaries very low, and because the earnings of lawyers had substantially risen over the years.[56] The Law Commission in its 14th report in 1958 found that the salaries of high court judges were not low in places other than Bombay and Calcutta because lawyers there (except those who had an inter-state practice) did not earn substantially more than what a judge did. Thus, it did not recommend an increase in salaries,[57] though it noted that even then, there was 'undoubtedly a feeling among the members of the Bar that the present salary of High Court Judges [is] too low to attract the members of the Bar in the front rank to judgeships'.[58] However, the cost of living went up substantially thereafter, and it is conceivable that lawyers' earnings in other cities went up as well.

India's lengthy Constitution contained unnecessary details like the precise amount of the salaries to be paid to Supreme Court and high court judges. Consequently, increasing judges' salaries initially required a constitutional amendment,[59] which was a cumbersome process.[60] The first enhancement of judicial salaries occurred by virtue of a constitutional amendment in 1986,[61] when the salary of the chief justice of India was increased to Rs 10,000 per month, that of Supreme Court judges and high court chief justices to Rs 9000 per month, and that of high court judges to Rs 8000 per month. However, this amendment also made it possible to change judges' salaries without amending the Constitution.[62] Thereafter, their salaries have been raised more frequently. Accordingly, salaries of the chief justice of India, Supreme Court judges/high court chief justices, and high court judges were increased in 1998 (with retrospective effect from 1996), to Rs 33,000, Rs 30,000 and Rs 26,000 respectively.[63] In 2009, the salaries of these judges were increased to Rs 1 lakh, Rs 90,000 and Rs 80,000 respectively. More recently, in 2018, salaries have been increased to Rs 2.80 lakh, Rs 2.50 lakh and Rs 2.25 lakh respectively.[64]

Historically, judges' salaries have been barely comparable with what lawyers earn at the bar, at least in some parts of India.[65] In 1949, for instance, Prime Minister Nehru was constrained to instruct all ministries and departments of his government not to overspend on lawyers. 'In one recent case,' noted Nehru, 'twelve hundred rupees a day were fixed, in addition to some other payment' for a lawyer's fees. To put that into perspective, the lawyer Nehru was referring to had earned a third of a high court judge's monthly salary in one day. Lawyers' fees paid by the government, said Nehru, must henceforth be 'normal and reasonable', and a 'bigger fee' could only be paid if approved by a minister with information conveyed to Nehru himself.[66] Nehru, at times, had unconcealed disdain for lawyers. As he wrote to Home Minister K.N. Katju in June 1952, 'I am tired of your lawyers and legal [opinions],' adding, '[i]f lawyers have their way, this world would become petrified and dead.'[67] In October 1955, Nehru made a speech at the chief ministers' conference in which he said that a 'very competent lawyer may get as much as five times the salary of a High Court Judge'.[68] At that conference, both G.B. Pant and Morarji Desai said that there were many cases where competent lawyers had refused to serve as judges. To this, Nehru said that if lawyers elevated to the bench were not paid 'decently', then 'third-rate men' would be appointed as judges. Nehru was arguing against a proposal for reducing salaries of high court judges below Rs 3500 per month.[69]

Until the recent increase in judges' salaries in 2018, the basic salary drawn by even the chief justice of the Supreme Court of India, who is the highest-paid judge in the country, was lower than what a fresh graduate of a law school earned in his first year at some of the country's top law firms. In 2016, fresh law graduates were drawing maximum salaries of Rs 18.2 lakh per annum, and a lawyer with only six years of experience could draw a maximum salary of Rs 65 lakh per annum.[70] Even after the increase in 2018, judges' salaries are barely comparable with what a relatively junior lawyer can earn at the bar (at least in the bigger cities), and all this pales in comparison with what leading advocates charge at the bar. In 2015, it was estimated that an advocate who declined both a high court and a Supreme Court judgeship, charged between Rs 11 lakh and Rs 15 lakh per appearance at the Supreme Court, which is nearly half the present annual salary of the chief justice of India, for appearing in court on just one occasion in a case.[71]

This is also less than what many other countries pay their judges, even if one takes into account the cost of living in those countries. In 2018, the chief justice of the US Supreme Court annually earns about \$2,67,000 (approximately Rs 1.72 crore), and associate justices about \$2,55,300 (approximately Rs 1.65 crore).[72] In the UK, in 2016, the lord chief justice of England and Wales earned £2,49,583 (approximately Rs 2.09 crore) per annum, lord justices of appeal earned £2,04,695 (approximately Rs 1.71 crore) per annum, and puisne high court judges earned £1,79,768 (approximately Rs 1.16 crore) per annum.[73] In Singapore, in 2017, the chief justice earned an annual pensionable salary of 3,47,400 Singapore dollars (approximately Rs 1.60 crore), judges of appeal earned 2,53,200 Singapore dollars annually (approximately Rs 1.17 crore), and judges of the Supreme Court earned 2,34,600 Singapore dollars annually (Rs 1.09 crore).[74] Even if one considers the higher cost of living in these countries, these salaries are still quite competitive in comparison with those offered in India until the 2018 enhancement.

Apart from the bare salaries, other perks have been given to judges from time to time as well. Today, judges are statutorily entitled, during their tenure in office, to a rent-free furnished[75] official residence,[76] a travel allowance (including 'leave travel concession', giving judges return airfare for visiting any place in India covering themselves, their spouses and dependent members of their families, a certain number of times per year),[77] sumptuary allowance,[78] dearness allowance,[79] facilities for medical treatment,[80] free water and electricity.[81] After retiring, judges can draw a pension[82] (sums drawn towards pension have been increased from time to time), and they get facilities for medical treatment[83] for themselves and their families.

The size of a retired judge's pension typically depends on the number of years that he/she has spent in service; the higher the number of years, the higher the pension.[84] In fact, as a result of an amendment made to the law in 2005, lawyers appointed directly to the Supreme Court are considered as having put in ten years of judicial service on the date of their appointment, so as to enhance their pensions and make it more attractive to accept a direct Supreme Court appointment.[85] The maximum pension which can be drawn by a judge is half the annual salary of the post at which that judge retired (in the early years, it was about one third of the annual salary).[86]

In 1976, judges were given a small monthly conveyance allowance, but they had to purchase and maintain their own 'motor cars'.[87] However, in 1986, judges were given not only a 'staff car' but also 150 (later 200[88]) litres of free fuel per month.[89] Initially, the perks enjoyed by judges like rent-free accommodation and travel allowance were taxable. Many early judges of the Supreme Court were quite annoyed about this. For example, Justice M. Hidayatullah got a house at 2, Teen Murti Marg in Delhi as an official residence. However, he had to pay a tax on the house and the furniture in it, which was 'almost equal to the rent' for the house. 'The provision in the Constitution' which said that Supreme Court judges would get free accommodation, thought Hidayatullah, 'appeared to be an eye-wash'.[90] Justice Hegde said that the additional allowances given to judges were taxable and resulted in judges getting taxed at the rate of 65 per cent.[91] However, after 1980, these were slowly taken out of their taxable incomes.[92] Even so, their salaries and pensions were still taxable.[93] In the early years, the monthly salary of Rs 3500 paid to a high court judge was reduced to less than Rs 1200 after payment of taxes.[94]

There are several other perks offered to judges. For example, Supreme Court judges who travel abroad for conferences are fully funded by the government, which includes first-class airfare; they can use special 'VIP'[95] lounges at airports; they get to hire a relatively large battalion of staff to work at home and in the office; they have access to government-run guest houses called 'circuit houses' for subsidized stay throughout the country; they get the benefit of a police escort while travelling intercity, etc. However, judges still have to pay, for example, for the education of their children; these and other expenses tend to make the perks offered to judges seem insufficient. Many of the perks also disappear once judges retire, though retired Supreme Court judges (who are barred from formally practising law after retirement), especially in the larger commercial cities, can earn large sums of money in arbitrations and chamber practice, and retired high court judges can practise at the Supreme Court. Justice Bhagwati said that even at the end of twenty-six years as a judge, he didn't own a house. He commuted half his pension in lump sum in order to buy a house at Greater Kailash II in New Delhi.[96]

Of course, not all advocates earn the same high fees uniformly across the country. At the chief ministers' conference in October 1955, P. Govinda Menon, the chief minister of the state of Travancore-Cochin,[97] said that the highest-paid lawyer in his state made no more than Rs 2500 per month, because there were no zamindars (i.e. landlords) or big businesses there. He therefore opined that a salary of Rs 3500 per month for high court judges was quite extravagant there.[98] Even today, it is doubtful whether the leading advocates at, say, the Jharkhand High Court or Tripura High Court command the same fee as top advocates like Harish Salve or Abhishek Manu Singhvi do at the Supreme Court in New Delhi. There may be regional variations in advocates' earnings, and there is a general lack of data available on what lawyers earn in smaller cities. The cost of living in larger cities like Mumbai and Delhi may also be much higher than in smaller towns. Therefore, it is difficult to say whether the salaries of judges today are inadequate in high courts located in smaller cities. However, it is clear that judicial salaries in larger cities like Delhi and Mumbai are still inadequate in comparison with front-ranking lawyers' earnings at the bar in those places.

Further, the low salary is not the only reason why lawyers say no to offers of judgeship. There are multiple other reasons as well. Justice A.N. Sen, for example, told Gadbois that lawyers had greater freedom than judges,[99] and they enjoyed more independence at the bar, which is why they turned down offers of judgeship. After all, top lawyers had the ability to be selective in the work they did, whereas judges had to hear all cases they were assigned, whether they were interesting or dull. In fact, many lawyers declined judgeship offers because the Indira Gandhi government was bullying judges and making them less independent. There was a scheme in place at the time called the 'transfer of judges policy', under which judges of high courts could be transferred to other high courts, virtually on the whim of the executive government. Many lawyers declined a high court judgeship because they did not want to be transferred out of the city which they considered to be their home. When Justice Madon was the chief justice of the Bombay High Court in the early 1980s, he found it difficult to persuade first-rank advocates to accept judgeships. He said that though the low salary was a factor, the main reason was the fear of transfers. He said that Bombay was a very attractive place to live and work, and few would want to be transferred elsewhere.[100] Likewise, when he was the chief justice of the Calcutta High Court between December 1979 and January 1981, Justice A.N. Sen said that ten members of the bar turned down judgeship offers partly because the government was (perhaps deliberately) taking too much time to make the appointments and was even turning down some of their names, which was humiliating.[101] Similarly, Justice Balakrishna Eradi said that as the chief justice of the Kerala High Court, he (and at least one of his successors, Chief Justice V.S. Malimath) faced long delays in filling vacancies because of lack of cooperation on the part of the communist government which was in power in the state.[102] Justice A.P. Sen believed that Soli Sorabjee, a prominent Supreme Court advocate, would have accepted an offer of judgeship to the Supreme Court, but the government would not have given its consent to appoint him,[103] perhaps because it thought that he was too independent.

Justice R.B. Misra told Gadbois that the prestige of judges had gone down, that they no longer got the respect that they used to, which is why not many lawyers wanted to become judges.[104] Some lawyers, however, had other personal reasons for declining judgeships. H.M. Seervai, who was the advocate general of Maharashtra and India's foremost constitutional law scholar, was offered a judgeship both of the high court and the Supreme Court.[105] Had he accepted, he would have possibly been the chief justice of India for five and a half years. However, he declined for 'personal reasons' and 'for reasons that had to do with his book, *Constitutional Law of India: A Critical Commentary*'.[106] He thought that he would have a greater impact on the development of the law by writing his book than by becoming a judge. Likewise, Justice A.P. Sen believed that Kacker declined an offer to become a Supreme Court judge because of a rivalry he had with Justice R.S. Pathak.[107] Kacker's name had earlier been suggested for appointment to the Allahabad High Court, but it was rumoured that his name was torpedoed by G.S. Pathak, vice president of India, and R.S. Pathak's father, so that his own son could be appointed. Now,

Kacker did not want to accept a Supreme Court judgeship because he would be junior to Pathak.[108]

Of course, not every lawyer who is offered a judgeship refuses the offer. Many accept. Those who accepted offers to take up a judgeship at a high court said that they did so out of a sense of duty, because tradition requires that you do not say no when you are asked to be a judge, or because they were not enjoying being lawyers.[109] For example, Justice A.M. Ahmadi gave Gadbois three reasons why he accepted a judgeship in the subordinate judiciary in Gujarat. Firstly, he said that it was a part of his family background, since his father was a judicial service man. Secondly, he said that he was invited to be a judge in the subordinate judiciary by the chief justice (J.M. Shelat), and the tradition was that ordinarily one did not decline such an offer. Thirdly, he accepted the offer because of the job satisfaction of being a judge, in order to be of service to the nation and to litigants. He was critical of lawyers who turned down such offers and then criticized the judiciary for not being good enough.[110] Similarly, when Leila Seth was offered a judgeship of the Delhi High Court by Chief Justice T.V.R. Tatachari, she accepted and said that she had been 'brought up never to refuse an honour when offered',[111] though she did not apply the same rule earlier when she declined an offer of judgeship at the Patna High Court, because there was nothing that her husband could do in Patna.[112]

Some accepted judgeship because being a judge was less stressful than being a lawyer. Justice G.K. Mitter took up a high court judgeship in November 1952 because he was concerned about his health; his father, mother and brother had high blood pressure, and he wanted less stress. 'In those days,' said Justice Mitter, 'judges had less work.'[113] Justice M.M. Dutt accepted a judgeship of the Calcutta High Court in September 1969 because he felt he was slowing down as a lawyer, and because judges get a pension which lawyers do not.[114] Justice S.C. Roy, who had been in indifferent health all his life,[115] agreed to accept a direct appointment to the Supreme Court in 1971 (he had previously been an advocate at the Calcutta High Court) because he thought that being a judge would be easier on his health.[116] However, Roy had his own masseur who came to him every day in Calcutta, but he had to do without him in Delhi. Unfortunately, he passed away only a few months after he was appointed to the Supreme Court. Though Justice M.H. Kania initially hesitated to accept a judgeship of the Bombay High Court in November 1969 because it involved a big loss of income, he eventually accepted it at least partly because he thought he would have better hours as a judge. As a lawyer, Kania did not get back home until after 8 p.m., and his wife liked the idea of him being able to return home earlier as a judge.[117]

Supreme, but No Thanks

It is not only lawyers who have declined offers of judgeship. High court judges have also, at times, rejected offers to be elevated to the Supreme Court. In the early years, many high court chief justices declined offers of elevation to the Supreme Court because they thought that their own posts were far more prestigious than that of a junior Supreme Court judge. In fact, when the Federal Court was set up under the Government of India Act, 1935 (prior to that time, there was no court akin to a Supreme Court in British India; there were only provincial high courts like the Bombay High Court), though the retirement age of high court judges was sixty years,[118] the retirement age of Federal Court judges was fixed at sixty-five years.[119] This gap between the retirement ages of Federal Court and high court judges was specifically designed in order to encourage high court judges to agree to come to the Federal Court.[120] It was anticipated that high court judges would refuse to go to the Federal Court because high courts had far greater antiquity and status than the new Federal Court (a court which did not even have its own building).[121] On account of the retirement age gap, high court judges who agreed to go to the Federal Court would get an extra five years in service. Even after the Constitution of independent India came into being, in 1950, this gap in retirement ages continued[122] (though in 1963,[123] the retirement age of high court judges was increased to sixty-two). Today, Supreme Court judges still retire at the age of sixty-five, while high court judges retire at sixty-two.[124] The age of retirement was increased from sixty to sixty-two, and not sixty-five, because Prime Minister Nehru's cabinet was worried that if the retirement age were increased to sixty-five, it would become difficult to find judges for the Supreme Court.[125]

In 1949, the chief justice of the Federal Court of India, Harilal Kania, offered a Supreme Court seat to Chief Justice Chagla of the Bombay High Court.[126] In their correspondence, Kania even explained to Chagla that if he accepted the offer before the Constitution came into being in January 1950, Chagla would get the higher British-era salary of Federal Court judges, and not the lower salary under the Constitution. Kania assured Chagla that, 'in the ordinary course', Chagla would succeed Kania as the chief justice when he retired[127] (though Kania eventually died in office in 1951, several years prior to his retirement in 1955). However, Chagla declined the offer because he thought he was 'doing more useful work as Chief Justice of Bombay' than what he would be doing as a puisne judge of the Supreme Court.[128] Among others, Chagla consulted Attorney General Motilal C. Setalvad, who agreed that Chagla should not accept a puisne judgeship of the Supreme Court, but that he should accept the chief justiceship of the Supreme Court directly, if it were offered to him after Kania retired.[129] In other words, Chagla, who held the prestigious post of the chief justice of the Bombay High Court, did not want to become a junior judge at the Supreme Court.

Chief Justice Hidayatullah believed that chief justices of prestigious high courts did not want to accept Supreme Court judgeships because they did not want to become junior Supreme Court judges.[130] Though they are compensated the same, the perks and benefits which chief justices of some high courts get, even today, are more impressive than those enjoyed by junior Supreme Court judges. Similarly, when Justice Chandrachud was offered a seat at the Supreme Court, he and his wife were not too anxious to go there. Chandrachud was on the threshold of becoming the chief justice of the Bombay High Court, which was a very prestigious post. He felt that the Bombay High Court was the most distinguished court in India, having produced the Supreme Court's best advocates, like Seervai, Palkhivala, Nariman, Sorabjee, etc.[131] This reason does not apply to puisne judges of high courts.[132]

Many other high court chief justices declined offers to be elevated to the Supreme Court. P.V. Rajamannar, the chief justice of the Madras High Court, did not accept an offer of being elevated to the Supreme Court not only because his father was ill and he needed to look after him, but also because he was holding the glamorous post of the chief justice of the Madras High Court, the first Indian to have done so, which he held for thirteen years.[133]

Chief Justice Satish Chandra of the Allahabad High Court was offered a seat at the Supreme Court by Chief Justice Chandrachud three times between 1979 and 1980, but he too wanted to stay on at the Allahabad High Court.[134] It was because Chandra declined, and Chandrachud's next choice, Justice Yasoda Nandan, was rejected by the government, that R.B. Misra was appointed from the Allahabad High Court to the Supreme Court in January 1981.[135] Justice Misra himself was well aware of the fact that he was the third choice from the Allahabad High Court.[136] He said that high court chief justices with long tenures declined offers to come to the Supreme Court, and their salaries were the same as those of Supreme Court judges.

Interestingly, while he was still a puisne judge, in May 1977, Satish Chandra had sent the President of India a letter resigning from the Allahabad High Court, effective from a future date. He resigned because he was very resentful of the fact that Justice D.M. Chandrashekar who was transferred to the Allahabad High Court became its chief justice in 1977.[137] In July 1977, before the anticipated date of his resignation, he withdrew his letter. A petition was filed in the Allahabad High Court challenging Chandra's continuance in office. A bench of three judges of the Allahabad High Court (one of whom was Justice R.B. Misra) held against Chandra. However, their decision was reversed by the Supreme Court,[138] which held that Chandra's resignation could be withdrawn. In the notes of his interview with Justice R.B. Misra, Gadbois wrote that Misra informed him that Chandra was related, by marriage, to Law Minister Shanti Bhushan[139] (Chandra was Bhushan's brother-in-law[140]), perhaps hinting that Chandra was offered a Supreme Court seat during the Janata Party's regime because of Shanti Bhushan. However, eventually, after serving as the chief justice of the Allahabad High Court, between 1978 and 1983,[141] Chandra was transferred to the Calcutta High Court, where he served as the chief justice between 1983 and 1986.[142]

Similarly, in 1980, the chief justice of the Madras High Court, M.M. Ismail,[143] was offered a seat at the Supreme Court by Chief Justice Chandrachud, but he declined because he wanted to stay on in Madras as the chief justice.[144] He was the first Muslim chief justice of the Madras High Court.[145] Eventually, however, Ismail was transferred by the government to the Kerala High Court, but instead of moving to Kerala, he resigned in July 1981.[146] Similarly, Chief Justice Chandrashekar of the Karnataka High Court was offered a Supreme Court seat several times, but he declined.[147]

Sometimes, judges of high courts do not accept judgeships at the Supreme Court because of difficulties of social adjustment, typically problems associated with relocating to Delhi. Some have elderly parents to look after and daughters to be married, all of which is harder to do in a relatively alien city far from home.[148] Chief Justice Chandrachud said that a Supreme Court judge who came from the Kerala High Court in January 1981 had a hard time finding a suitable husband for his daughter in Delhi.[149] Likewise, Justice Syed Sarwar Ali, of the Patna High Court, was offered a Supreme Court seat by Chief Justice Chandrachud in 1981.[150] However, he turned it down because he was going through some difficulties in his personal life (he was having marital problems,[151] and he wanted to be close to his daughter[152] [who eventually became a Patna High Court judge herself[153]], and he had to look after his land[154]). Eventually, Sarwar Ali did not accept a transfer out of Patna, even to another high court as the chief justice, and retired as the most senior judge of the Patna High Court, after having served as the acting chief justice of that court.[155] The Law Commission in its 14th report noted that a high court judge 'may well prefer to continue to be where he is which would probably be his home town with a family house and family connections'.[156] It recommended making it a 'condition of service or a well-established convention' that it should be the duty of a high court judge to accept a Supreme Court judgeship if offered.[157] However, in his interview notes, Gadbois recorded that one chief justice of India told him that a high court chief justice was offered a seat at the Supreme Court, but he refused to come because he was a man of doubtful integrity and stood to profit more by remaining at his own high court than by coming to Delhi.[158]

Some judges do not go to the Supreme Court because judges junior to them were appointed to the court first. This happened with P.B. Chakravartti who served as the Calcutta High Court chief justice between 1952 and 1958, the court's first Indian chief justice who replaced Chief Justice Sir Arthur Trevor Harries.[159] When he was first offered a seat at the Supreme Court, he asked for more time because he was building a house. However, a judge junior to him, A.K. Sarkar, was appointed to the Supreme Court in March 1957, after which Chakravartti refused to go to the Supreme Court.[160]

Similarly, another Calcutta High Court chief justice, S.P. Mitra, who served as such between 1972 and 1979,[161] was offered a judgeship of the Supreme Court by Chief Justice S.M. Sikri. Prior to joining the bench, Mitra had been a member of the Bengal Legislative Assembly between 1952 and 1957, and a minister in the government of West Bengal in 1956 during the Congress regime there.[162] He became a judge of the Calcutta High Court immediately after serving a five-year term as a member of the Legislative Assembly of West Bengal, in 1957, and was appointed the chief justice of the high court in 1972.[163] When he was offered a Supreme Court judgeship, Mitra was around fifty-five, and was in line for the chief justiceship of the Supreme Court of India for a long time, until around December 1982.[164] Mitra accepted the offer, but asked that his appointment be delayed. Then, Justice Chandrachud's appointment was notified on 14 August 1972, and he was sworn in on 28 August, which meant that Mitra would not become the chief justice if he went to the Supreme Court, since Chandrachud was younger than him. Thereafter, Mitra declined the offer to move to the Supreme Court.[165] Had Mitra been appointed before Chandrachud, the latter would have served as the chief justice of India between 1982 and 1985, for less than three years, whereas he eventually served for a term of more than seven years as such. Eventually, after Mitra retired from the high court, he accepted a seat in the Rajya Sabha.[166]

Likewise, V.S. Malimath, who had served as the chief justice of both the Karnataka and Kerala High Courts, declined an offer to be elevated to the Supreme Court. He was offered a seat at the Supreme Court in 1988, but he refused to accept because judges junior to him like Justices E.S. Venkataramiah and M.N.R. Venkatachaliah (both from the Karnataka High Court, which was also Malimath's parent high court) were already in the court.[167]

The Rising Prestige of the Supreme Court

One gets the sense that today it is very unlikely that a high court judge or chief justice would refuse a seat in the Supreme Court. Many judges of the Supreme Court, appointed more recently among all the interviewees, said that they would never even dream of turning down a Supreme Court judgeship. Many said that the Supreme Court was a court of greater status and prestige than the high court, a judgeship there was a glamorous post, and moving to the Supreme Court was considered to be a promotion.[168]

For instance, before getting to the Supreme Court, Justice G.L. Oza was the chief justice of the Madhya Pradesh High

Court. Even so, he accepted a seat in the Supreme Court (he was appointed in October 1985) because he felt that there was a greater scope to make a change there.[169] On the other hand, though Justice M.P. Thakkar thought he could have achieved more as the chief justice of the Gujarat High Court (a post he held until he was elevated to the Supreme Court in March 1983), than as a junior Supreme Court judge, he accepted a Supreme Court seat because he felt it was a 'call of Duty', and that it was an honour to serve in that court.[170] When Justice K.N. Saikia was asked whether he considered declining the offer of a Supreme Court seat because he was going to serve for a very short while, he emphatically said no, adding that it was 'a great honor' to serve at the Supreme Court, something he had dreamed of doing, and that the 'period of time doesn't matter'.[171] Justice Venkatachaliah said that he accepted the Supreme Court judgeship on account of 'subconscious vanity'.[172] Interestingly, the sons of both L.N. Sinha[173] and Fali S. Nariman, who themselves had declined judgeship offers, became judges of the Supreme Court.

Justice D.N. Sinha was accused by some Supreme Court judges of having unsuccessfully 'canvassed' for a Supreme Court appointment for a long time,[174] despite the fact that he held the prestigious post of the chief justice of the Calcutta High Court between 1966 and 1970.[175] Chief Justice S.P. Kotval of the Bombay High Court, who served as such between 1966 and 1972, was just plain unlucky. His name had been recommended for appointment to the Supreme Court (along with the name of Chief Justice M.S. Menon of the Kerala High Court) by Chief Justice Hidayatullah before the latter retired.[176] Thereafter, the new chief justice of India, J.C. Shah (who did not know about the Kotval and Menon recommendations made by Hidayatullah[177]) wanted Kotval to be elevated along with Justice Bhagwati to the Supreme Court.[178] However, as we have seen in a previous chapter, Shah's recommendation never went through. Nothing further seems to have happened on Justice Kotval's elevation to the Supreme Court thereafter. Either Chief Justice Sikri, who followed Hidayatullah and Shah, withdrew the names of Kotval and Menon[179], or the government refused to appoint them.[180]

Some judges agreed to go to the Supreme Court because of financial incentives. For example, several high court judges moved to the Supreme Court because it gave them three more years in office,[181] and consequently a higher pension.[182] For Justice A. Varadarajan, this was the 'driving factor' of moving to the Supreme Court in December 1980.[183] Justice Oza needed the higher pension in order to educate two of his sons.[184] Justice Hidayatullah had told the 14th Law Commission that both high court and Supreme Court judges should retire at the same age and get the same pay, which would prevent high court judges from canvassing for Supreme Court judgeships and 'burning the tracks' to Delhi.[185]

The 'transfer of judges policy' introduced by the Indira Gandhi government was another reason why many judges agreed to go to the Supreme Court. Justice Sabyasachi Mukharji accepted a seat in the Supreme Court, even though he would have been able to serve as the chief justice of the Calcutta High Court for about seven years, because he was worried that he would get transferred out of Calcutta.[186] Likewise, Justice M.H. Kania went to the Supreme Court in order to avoid getting transferred from the Bombay High Court to another court.[187] Even today, a person typically cannot serve as the permanent chief justice of his own court, and chief justices come to a high court from the outside. Since a judge today cannot become the chief justice of his own high court, he/she prefers to go to the Supreme Court instead of remaining the chief justice of some high court which is not where his/her home is.

5

The Fictional Concurrence of
the Chief Justice

This chapter discusses the process which was followed for appointing judges to the Supreme Court between 1950 and 1989. We will see that even in the early decades, between 1950 and 1971, there were several instances where the executive government, either the Union home minister or the chief minister of a state, succeeded in appointing a judicial candidate against the wishes of the chief justice of India or the high court chief justice. However, during those years, the chief justice of India or the high court chief justice would eventually agree to compromise with the executive and sign off on the appointments which were initiated by the government. A fiction would thereby be maintained, in theory, that all judicial appointments had been made with the concurrence of the chief justice of India and the high court chief justices. We will see that thereafter, between 1971 and 1989, the same fiction was preserved, and even when the executive government named judges against the wishes of the chief justice of India, the appointment was typically made with the fictional concurrence of the latter.

However, we will also see that the process of appointing judges changed in the year 1971 in three ways. Firstly, whenever a judicial appointment was made by the executive government against the wishes of the chief justice in the 1950–71 period, it was typically motivated not by ideology but by considerations of political patronage or to ensure communal or regional representation. In other words, in the two decades from 1950 onwards, the judicial nominees of the government were not appointed because they had an ideology which meshed with its political philosophy but because it wanted to dole out political favours, or to ensure that certain regions or communities were represented in the Supreme Court. This differed from executive influence in judicial appointments after 1971, when the ideology of judges began to be openly discussed, and the government started actively looking for 'committed' or favourable judges. Secondly, the extent of executive interference in judicial appointments from 1950–71 was limited, whereas it was far more comprehensive in the period thereafter. Thirdly, judicial appointments between 1950 and 1971 were not accompanied by a sustained attempt to intimidate the judiciary through supersessions and transfers.

This chapter will then conclude by discussing how today's collegium system, put in place in the 1990s after the *Second Judges* case,[1] changed the process of appointing judges in two ways: firstly, by removing the 'primacy' of the chief justice of India over his senior colleagues and, secondly, by transforming the fiction of the 'concurrence' of the chief justice of India in judicial appointments into reality. However, while the collegium system has enhanced the independence of the judiciary substantially, it has not been able to fully guarantee judicial independence since the government can still award employment to retired Supreme Court judges.

Pre-1950

Judicial Appointments in Colonial India

The Government of India Act, 1935, which was the last Constitution of British India, said that Federal Court and high court judges were to be appointed by 'His Majesty by warrant'.[2] There was no formal provision for the queen or king in England to consult any judge while making judicial appointments. In practice, however, chief justices of high courts were usually consulted before a judicial appointment was made. The governor of a province, after consulting the chief justice of the high court, gave his recommendation to the governor general of India, who advised the king in England, through his secretary of state in London, about whom to appoint to the high court.[3] Accordingly, two features of the colonial judicial appointments process were noteworthy. Firstly, the opinion of the chief justice of the high court was not binding on the crown, though it might have been entitled to great weight.[4] Secondly, elected politicians like the prime minister (which is what chief ministers were called before the Constitution came into being) or the home minister of a state, were not formally consulted in the process of appointing judges.[5]

Prior to Independence, Indian politicians had played virtually no role in appointing judges. For example, in May 1947, only a few months before India became independent, the prime minister of the central provinces, R.S. Shukla, wrote a letter to Vallabhbhai Patel recommending that Justice Vivian Bose be made the chief justice of the Nagpur High Court because he had 'made a mark in giving independent judgments in 1942'. Shukla did not want a judge from the ICS to be appointed to the chief justiceship of the high court.[6] Patel wrote back to Shukla and said, 'We shall do our best.'[7] However, a few weeks later, when Shukla wrote to Patel to express his disappointment over the fact that an ICS judge had been appointed to the chief justiceship of the Nagpur High Court,[8] Patel wrote back saying that he had found out about the appointment for the first time from Shukla's letter.[9]

Judicial Appointments and the Constituent Assembly

In May 1947, the ad hoc committee on the Supreme Court, constituted within the Constituent Assembly with some very eminent members on it,[10] was worried about the President of India having 'unfettered discretion' in making judicial appointments. It recommended that the President's powers be circumscribed by a kind of Privy Council, a panel of eleven members, consisting of high court chief justices, some members of both the houses of the Central Legislature and a few law officers of the Union.[11] It suggested two alternative methods for appointing judges. The first method was that the President, in consultation with the chief justice of India, would recommend a name and that name would then have to be approved by at least seven of the eleven panel members. Alternatively, the panel itself would suggest three names, out of which the President, in consultation with the chief justice of India, would select one. The chief justice of India was not to be consulted when the President was considering whom to appoint to the post of the chief justice of India.[12]

Both the Union and Provincial Constitution Committees of the Constituent Assembly, which were tasked with drafting the Union and Provincial parts of the Constitution, rejected the ad hoc committee's idea of setting up a Privy Council for appointing judges. On 10 June 1947, at a joint meeting of both the committees, it was agreed that high court judges would be 'appointed by the President of the Union in consultation with the Chief Justice of the Supreme Court and the Governor and the Chief Justice of the Province concerned'.[13] The following day, the Union Constitution Committee agreed that 'the President should appoint the judges of the Supreme Court after consulting the Chief Justice of the Supreme Court and such other judges of the Supreme Court and of other High Courts as may be necessary for the purpose'.[14] By October 1947, the draft Constitution clarified that the chief justice of India was always to be consulted except when the President was considering whom to appoint as the next chief justice of India, and, similarly, high court chief justices were always to be consulted except while appointing the next high court chief justice.[15]

In the meantime, in August 1947, Home Minister Patel was annoyed by the fact that he was not properly consulted over the appointment of M.C. Chagla to the chief justiceship of the Bombay High Court. On 11 August 1947, days before India became independent, Governor General Louis Mountbatten wrote a letter to Patel, asking him for his opinion on Chagla's suitability.[16] The announcement had to be made prior to 15 August, the day India was to become independent. Patel was unhappy about the fact that Chagla, who would become the first Indian chief justice of the Bombay High Court, would supersede an ICS judge, K.C. Sen. On 14 August, the eve of independence, he wrote a letter[17] to Mountbatten and said that in the 'absence of papers to show why Mr. Sen is proposed to be superseded', it was difficult for him to give his opinion. He wrote that he only agreed to the proposal to appoint Chagla because there was not much time, and Nehru had already agreed to the appointment. He hinted in his letter to Mountbatten that the appointment had been made even before his concurrence was obtained. The same day, Patel also wrote a letter to Nehru, expressing his disappointment over how he was not properly consulted over Chagla's appointment. 'I should have personally preferred to have looked more into the merits of the case,' he wrote, 'but since you had already agreed to the appointment, I had no alternative but to concur.'[18]

The Memorandum of Procedure

Thereafter, the home ministry issued a memorandum of procedure on 4 November 1947.[19] This memorandum, for the first time, said that the chief minister of a state, acting in consultation with his home minister, and the home minister at the Centre, were to be involved in the judicial appointments process. This new procedure got many people worried. The chief justice of the Madras High Court, Sir Frederick Gentle, resigned from his position at least partly because of this new provision in the memorandum of procedure. The governor of Madras, Archibald Nye, supported him. Lord Mountbatten brought this issue up with Home Minister Patel, who maintained that the politicians had to be consulted.[20]

In December 1947, in the light of what had happened at the Madras High Court, the chief justice of India, Harilal J. Kania, wrote a letter to Prime Minister Nehru and asked him to revise the memorandum of procedure to ensure that the Supreme Court and high courts could directly be in touch with the President, instead of communicating with the home ministry, over judicial appointments.[21]

In February 1948, a dispute arose between Chief Justice Chagla of the Bombay High Court and Home Minister Patel over a judicial appointment. Chagla wrote to the prime minister of Bombay state, B.G. Kher, and informed him that when there had been a vacancy in the high court earlier, he had not pressed for the appointment of an acting judge whom he wanted because he 'found that there was a difference of opinion between the Government of India and the Provincial Government supported by the Chief Justice', i.e. because the central government did not agree with his recommendation. However, Chagla now wanted a man called Honawar to be appointed an acting judge of the Bombay High Court. He wrote that 'judicial appointments should not be influenced by political considerations and should not be dictated by the executive'.[22] When Kher conveyed this letter to him, Patel was incensed by Chagla's views. 'I do not know from where the Chief Justice got the idea that any question is involved of judicial appointments being influenced by political considerations or being dictated by the executive,' Patel wrote to Kher. 'We have also to safeguard individual officers against supersession on purely personal predilections,' he added.[23] Chagla seems to have lost that fight with Patel, because there is no record of a judge called Honawar having been appointed to the Bombay High Court.

This was not the only conflict between Chagla and Patel. Later that year, Patel read about Chagla's visit to the town of Jalgaon in Bombay state, in a newspaper called *Azad Hind* published in Ahmednagar. The newspaper apparently said that Chagla was entertained at an event at which alcohol was served. This annoyed Patel, since the Bombay government was pursuing a policy of prohibition (the Bombay Prohibition Act, which brought the policy into effect, came into force in June 1949). Patel complained about Chagla to Harilal Kania. In a letter he wrote to Kania in December 1948, Patel said that Chagla's conduct was 'most unfortunate', and that '[w]hatever the position of the Chief Justice of the High Court may be', he felt that Chagla's 'public conduct should be in keeping with Government policy on important matters like prohibition'.

'If this is not done,' wrote Patel, 'both the judiciary and the Government are bound to be brought into public ridicule.'[24]

The chief justice of India, on the other hand, was not much concerned by Patel's letter. He wrote back to Patel saying that the reporter who had written the story for the *Azad Hind* 'appears to be someone not familiar with an entertainment to dinner on the English style'. Kania also wondered whether the newspaper 'has some substantial circulation or is a local rag'. However, Kania told Patel that the Supreme Court did not exercise any supervisory powers over the high court, and that he had no 'voice in the regulation of the life of a provincial chief justice or a judge, outside his court hours'. 'I do not know therefore what I can do in the matter,' he wrote to Patel.[25] Patel wrote back to Kania and asked him to merely 'drop a hint' to Chagla when he next met him.[26] Kania responded evasively, saying that he would speak to Chagla, but that Chagla would be travelling to Europe when the court closed for the vacation, 'and, if so, I am unable to say when I shall see him'.[27]

In March 1948, Chief Justice of India Kania held a conference in Delhi of Federal Court judges and high court chief justices to 'consider the draft of the new Constitution of India in so far as it affects the judiciary and also to consider certain questions affecting the High Courts and the judiciary generally'.[28] At the conference, the judges expressed their dissatisfaction with how judicial appointments were being made in independent India.[29] They said that judges were being appointed not only on merit but also on 'political, communal and party considerations'. The executive government, said the judges, might conceivably recommend some lawyers for elevation to the bench because they would be 'co-operative' towards the government, or even because 'the Ministry wants to get rid of them as they might be inconvenient in the political sphere', i.e. some lawyers would be kicked upstairs as judges so as to remove them from politics. The provincial prime ministers, said the judges at the conference, were sometimes not even conveying the recommendations of the high court chief justices to the Centre. Importantly, the conference recommended that all appointments must be made with the 'concurrence' of the chief justice of India (i.e. the opinion of the chief justice of India must be binding on the President while making judicial appointments). The concurrence of the chief justice, said the judges at the conference, would be an important safeguard against 'political and party pressure at the highest level being brought to bear in the matter'. They believed that there was a convention that appointments were made with the concurrence of the chief justice of India. They assumed that since the President would be acting on the aid and advice of the council of ministers, the President's appointments would be made along political lines. They also suggested that high court chief justices be allowed to send their recommendations directly to the President, without going through the chief ministers.

The following month, in April 1948, Kania wrote to Patel that he was unhappy over the appointment of the chief justice of the newly established Assam High Court, R.F. Lodge. He said that it was a 'strange coincidence' that 'the first High Court inaugurated after the Independence Act' would have as its chief justice 'an English ICS' man.[30] Patel responded by saying that his appointment was necessary because 'the prejudice of the Assamese against the Bengali is so deep-rooted that apparently the Prime Minister of Assam felt that an ICS British judge would be better than a Bengali from the bar'. Patel also said that 'local talent' at the bar was 'of course not of the requisite standard'.[31]

Many controversies seemed to have arisen over appointments to the Madras High Court. For instance, Congress leader N.G. Ranga[32] wrote a letter to Patel in September 1948, complaining about the fact that all the recent appointments to the Madras High Court had been from the bar or ICS, and not from the non-ICS subordinate judiciary.[33] Patel responded by saying that 'in determining whether the best possible candidate has been nominated', the Government had to 'rely on the judgment of the [High Court] Chief Justice, the Provincial Premier and the Governor'. If the government got 'unanimous recommendations from these three authorities', then, 'unless a recommendation [was] manifestly improper', it would be 'impossible for [the Government] to set it aside'.[34]

In May 1949, B.R. Ambedkar defended in the Constituent Assembly the judicial appointments process envisioned in the draft Constitution. He rejected the suggestion that appointments should be made with the concurrence of the chief justice of India,[35] calling this a 'dangerous proposition'. He said that the concurrence argument seemed to 'rely implicitly both on the impartiality of the Chief Justice and the soundness of his judgment'. '[A]fter all,' said Ambedkar, 'the Chief Justice is a man with all the failings, all the sentiments and all the prejudices which we as common people have; and I think, to allow the Chief Justice practically a veto upon the appointment of judges is really to transfer the authority to the Chief Justice which we are not prepared to vest in the President or the Government of the day.'[36]

Ambedkar said that the Constitution '[steered] a middle course' between the UK and US systems of judicial appointments. In the UK, the executive government could appoint judges without any limitations, whereas in the US, some judicial appointments were subject to confirmation by the senate. Ambedkar felt that 'it would be dangerous to leave the appointments to be made by the President [of India], without any kind of reservation or limitation', as was done in the UK. Ambedkar believed that the US model of senate confirmation was unsuitable for India because not only was it 'cumbrous' but it also involved 'the possibility of the appointment being influenced by political pressure and political considerations'. In other words, the consultation between the President and the chief justice of India was not meant to be an empty formality. It was designed to be a check on an arbitrary exercise of power by the President.

Accordingly, the Constitution said that Supreme Court judges were to be appointed by the President of India after consulting such Supreme Court and high court judges as the President deemed necessary.[37] The chief justice of India always had to be consulted while appointing any Supreme Court judge other than the chief justice.[38] Similarly, the Constitution said that high court judges were to be appointed by the President, who was to consult the chief justice of India, the governor of the state concerned and (except while appointing the high court chief justice) the high court chief justice.[39]

Four Salient Constitutional Provisions

Under the Constitution, there were four features of the judicial appointments process which were particularly noteworthy.

Firstly, the President was not bound by the recommendations given by the chief justice of India or any other judge in the consultation process. This was despite the fact that the judges themselves (in an opinion expressed at the conference of Federal Court judges and high court chief justices) wanted to ensure that no judge was appointed without the 'concurrence' of the chief justice of India. Ambedkar believed that to require judicial appointments to be made with the concurrence of the chief justice of India would give too much power to one individual, who may not always be impartial or sound in his judgement.

Secondly, however, the consultation between the President and judges was not an empty exercise. It was designed to be a real check against the arbitrary exercise of power by the President. Ambedkar wanted the system to function differently from the UK, where there were no limits on the power of the executive government to appoint judges.

Thirdly, though the chief justice of India had to merely be consulted by the President, he was the most important judge in the judicial appointments process. The President could decide which of the other Supreme Court or high court judges he wanted to consult, but he had no option but to consult the chief justice of India in judicial appointments (except while deciding whom to appoint to the post of the chief justice of India itself). Similarly, the President had no option but to consult chief justices of high courts while making judicial appointments at their high courts (except to high court chief justiceships). We will see that later, the collegium system did away with this preponderant position of the chief justice of India by institutionally including senior Supreme Court judges in the judicial appointments process. However, the chief justice of India was not the only judge to be consulted in the process.[40]

Fourthly, the Constitution did not specifically say that the home minister or chief minister was to be involved in the process of appointing judges. In other words, the provisions of the November 1947 memorandum of procedure were not incorporated in the Constitution. However, it was presumed by the conference of Federal Court judges and chief justices that the President would act on the aid and advice of the council of ministers, and that therefore, politicians would have a role to play in the process.

From 1950 to 1971

In February 1950,[41] a revised memorandum of procedure for appointing judges was drawn up by the home ministry. This memorandum provided that when a permanent vacancy was likely to arise in a high court, the chief justice of the high court would communicate to the chief minister his recommendations for judges who could be appointed to that post. The chief minister would, in consultation with the governor of the state, forward the chief justice's recommendation to the home minister in the central government. The home minister, in turn, after consulting the prime minister and chief justice of India, would advise the President about whom to appoint.[42] All correspondence among these officials had to be in writing. In short, though the Constitution did not give any place to the home minister or chief minister in judicial appointments, the memorandum of procedure drawn up by the home ministry continued to give these politicians a role.

Harilal Kania's Losing Battle on Judicial Appointments

In the 1950s, the chief justice of India did not always get his way when it came to appointing judges.[43] In fact, the first chief justice of India, Harilal Kania, lost three distinct judicial appointment battles against the government, which are discussed below.

A few days before the Constitution came into force, on 23 January 1950, Nehru wrote some very anxious letters to Patel, saying that Chief Justice Kania should be asked to resign. Kania had written letters regarding certain appointments of judges at the Madras High Court. It is not clear what these letters contained, but upon reading them, Nehru was 'shocked'. He thought that the letters 'exhibited a mentality which is very far from being judicial and is totally unbecoming in any person holding a responsible position, more specially a judge of a supreme tribunal'.[44] In particular, Nehru was 'deeply shocked' by the attitude of Kania towards Justice Basheer Ahmed Sayeed, an additional judge of the Madras High Court. Nehru and Patel wanted him to be made permanent, but Kania objected. Once again, it is not clear what Kania's reasons were, but Nehru felt they confirmed his 'opinion that Chief Justice Kania's approach is completely unjudicial and indeed improper'. Nehru also felt that Kania's work, in the past, had not been 'up to the standard . . . necessary for such a high position'. 'In view of these facts,' wrote Nehru to Patel, 'we should ask Chief Justice Kania to resign. It would be a great risk to make him the permanent Chief Justice of the Supreme Court of India.'[45]

Patel, who was not one for superseding judges (as we have seen with Chagla and Sen at the Bombay High Court), wanted to retain Kania. He wrote to Governor General C. Rajagopalachari on 23 January and said, 'Jawaharlal is naturally upset, but I am sure you will agree that we must allow the storm to blow over.'[46] He then wrote Nehru a letter on the same day and told him that he had informed Kania that rejecting Sayeed's appointment would be perceived as being communal. 'To some extent,' he wrote, 'such indiscretions on the part of a man in the position of a Chief Justice of India have to be tolerated. Any other attitude would render us liable to be charged with interference with the judiciary.' 'After all,' he continued, 'asking Chief Justice Kania to resign does not mean that he would resign.' Patel told Nehru that he was 'fully conscious' of Kania's faults but 'on the whole, I think I have been able to manage him'. He said that this was the only time that Kania had been this assertive and, in the past, he had generally deferred to Patel's views. 'He is sensitive on certain points,' wrote Patel, '[h]e is even liable to become petty-minded and persist in his attitude; but that, unfortunately, is a trait not uncommon with some heads of the judiciary who feel that they have the sole monopoly of upholding its independence, integrity and purity.' Patel advised Nehru against discussing this matter in the cabinet. He hoped that Nehru would 'allow the breeze to pass over'.[47]

Eventually, Patel was able to convince Kania to defer to his views, and Sayeed was made a permanent judge of the Madras High Court.[48] It therefore appears that Kania, though initially opposed to Sayeed's appointment, did sign off on the views of Nehru and Patel in making him permanent in the court. In other words, though Kania did not want Sayeed to be appointed, he eventually compromised with the government, and the appointment went through with his concurrence.

Thereafter, in November 1950, a dispute arose between Chief Justice Kania and the chief minister of Madras, P.S. Kumaraswami Raja, over the appointment of a judge to the Madras High Court. Raja, the chief justice of the Madras High Court, P.V. Rajamannar and the governor of Madras unanimously wanted to appoint an ICS judge called Koman to the high court. Home Minister Patel thought that Koman's 'record on paper' was 'unimpressive', but he wrote to Nehru that the three constitutional functionaries of Madras had 'specifically said that he is the best candidate available'.[49] Koman was also backed by two former chief justices of the Madras High Court.[50] However, Kania had recommended two names for appointment instead, one of whom was a man called Umamaheshwaran. Raja rejected these two names citing the following reasons: '(a) lack of character; (b) insufficient practice and lack of recent familiarity with judicial work; (c) likelihood of unfavourable public reactions.'[51]

However, Kania refused to yield. Raja then wrote a strongly worded letter to Patel, supporting Koman. Patel responded by telling Raja that his letter was too strong for the official file. Patel accordingly drafted a letter for Raja, and asked him to sign it and send it back so that it could go into the file, for Kania's comments. However, Patel also wrote to Raja, 'I do not think we can contest the right of the Chief Justice [of India] to make suggestions if he feels that a particular person would be suitable in preference to one already suggested by you, even though with the concurrence of the [High Court] Chief Justice and the Governor.' After all, 'if all that he is expected to do is to register his approval to the proposal made by the State Government', wrote Patel to Raja, 'it is quite pointless for him to be consulted and certainly the Constitution would not have provided for a mere formality to be observed'.[52] Kania, however, took umbrage even to Raja's watered-down letter which had been drafted by Patel.[53] It is unclear whether Koman was eventually appointed to the court. However, on 26 November 1953 (i.e. a few years after Kania's death), a judge called K. Umamaheswaran was appointed to the Madras High Court.[54] It therefore appears that Kania did not succeed in getting Umamaheshwaran to the court during his lifetime (Kania died in harness in November 1951, around a year after this episode).

Thereafter, both Nehru and Patel wanted K.N. Wanchoo, an Allahabad High Court judge (and later, the Supreme Court chief justice), to move to the Rajasthan High Court as its chief justice.[55] This was because they wanted a judge from a 'Part A' state like Bihar to go to a 'Part B' state in order to improve standards there.[56] However, the acting chief justice of the Rajasthan High Court, Naval Kishore, wanted the appointment for himself.[57] In a long note, Kania supported Naval Kishore. Even President Rajendra Prasad agreed with Kania. However, around February 1950, V. Shankar, the private secretary to the deputy prime minister, spoke to Kania about appointing Wanchoo to the post.[58] V.P. Menon, a prominent bureaucrat who had worked closely with Patel in integrating the princely states into India, then went to Kania and tried to persuade him about Wanchoo. Initially, Menon thought that he had succeeded in doing so. On 19 July 1950, Menon wrote a note indicating that Kania had consented to the transfer of Wanchoo as the chief justice. However, on 4 November 1950, Kania wrote a note reiterating his objection to Wanchoo's transfer to Rajasthan. Menon then went back to Kania and tried to persuade him once again. This time Kania said he would consent to the appointment of Wanchoo as the chief justice of the Rajasthan High Court if the appointment were made on a provisional basis. However, Patel told Kania that such a provisional appointment could not be made. Finally, Kania relented, and agreed to Wanchoo's appointment.

Nehru and Patel had a major disagreement about how Kania was forced into submission on the matter. 'The Chief Justice of India finally surrendered,' wrote Nehru in a note dated 21 November 1950.[59] Nehru was also annoyed that bureaucrats like Shankar were involved in discussions with the chief justice of India over judicial appointments, and complained to Patel about the 'casual procedure adopted in this matter'.[60] Patel, who was miffed with Nehru's letter, who was not feeling very well at the time, and who had a difficult relationship with Nehru even apart from this issue, wrote a letter to Nehru in December 1950 and said, 'I am . . . sorry that you have referred to the final concurrence of the Chief Justice of India as a surrender.' Referring to the incident involving Basheer Ahmed Sayeed, Patel added, '[y]ou know how determined and persistent the Chief Justice is. He is the last man to yield to pressure.' Patel said that Kania had a low opinion of ICS judges, which is why he did not like Wanchoo, an ICS judge. To say that he had 'surrendered', wrote Patel to Nehru, would be unfair to Kania.[61] Patel ended his letter with the following terse words: 'Receiving from you and writing in reply long letters is a new experience to me. Frankly speaking, I do not relish it.' Eventually, Wanchoo was appointed the chief justice of the Rajasthan High Court on 2 January 1951, during Kania's tenure as the chief justice of India,[62] while Naval Kishore retired as a puisne judge of that court in November 1951.[63]

Kania and Nehru also duelled over the pre-Constitution removal of an Allahabad High Court judge. In 1947, serious charges of judicial misconduct were levelled against a judge of the Allahabad High Court, Shiva Prasad Sinha. It had been alleged that he had been 'actuated by corrupt motives' in deciding some cases. Sinha was summoned to Prime Minister Nehru's residence in December 1947, where Nehru and the premier of the United Provinces, G.B. Pant, asked him to either immediately resign or face an inquiry. Sinha refused to resign. Accordingly, the Federal Court conducted an inquiry against Sinha and found him guilty. Following this, Governor General Rajagopalachari removed Sinha from the post of Allahabad High Court judge by order on 22 April 1949.[64] However, while passing its order in the inquiry proceedings, the Federal Court expressed its unhappiness over the fact that Sinha had been summoned by Nehru and Pant. In the concluding paragraph of its order, the Federal Court wrote that Sinha had been 'called upon to appear before certain executive authorities and was asked to resign his office or face an enquiry into his alleged misconduct'. This, said the Federal Court, was a procedure 'hardly consistent with the great dignity and prestige associated with the office of judge of a High Court' and was 'calculated to undermine the independence of the judiciary'. After the Constitution came into force, in February 1950, Nehru wrote to Kania, registering his protest against this paragraph of the Federal Court's order in Sinha's inquiry proceedings.[65]

Kania's Successors Defer to the Executive As Well

After Kania passed away, the executive government continued overruling his successor and other high court chief justices over some judicial appointments, all the while securing their notional concurrence.

For instance, the chief justice of the Patna High Court, David Ezra Reuben, wanted a district and sessions judge called H.K. Chaudhuri to be appointed to the high court. However, the chief minister and governor of the state of Bihar recommended the name of another district and sessions judge, Kamla Sahai, who was senior to Chaudhuri. The chief justice of India, M. Patanjali Sastri, was consulted on the matter. He said that on two previous occasions, he had opined that Sahai was not good enough for appointment to the high court and, consequently, he could not recommend Sahai for elevation. Even so, Sastri said that if, having regard to Sahai's seniority and general record of service, Sahai was appointed to the high court, he would not oppose it. The government took this to mean that Sastri had thereby 'practically agreed to the appointment'. Eventually, Chief Justice Reuben concurred in Sahai's appointment, but under protest, and Sahai was appointed to the Patna High Court in July 1953.[66]

Thereafter, the chief minister and governor of Andhra Pradesh, and the chief justice of the state's high court, recommended the name of an advocate, K. Bhimasankaram,[67] for appointment to the high court. M.C. Mahajan, the chief justice of India, objected to Bhimasankaram's appointment on the grounds that he was already fifty-four years old and had only a few years left in office. Mahajan also believed that he was a man of average ability, whose income from his law practice ranged between Rs 1000 and Rs 1500. 'The argument about age,' believed the home ministry, 'could hardly be accepted.' The home ministry also felt that 'if there was a better person getting a larger income and also able and willing, the Chief Justice of the High Court would have suggested the name'.[68] Bhimasankaram was consequently appointed in November 1954.

In 1954, when the Andhra Pradesh High Court was created, Justice K. Subba Rao, the most senior Andhra judge of the Madras High Court,[69] was made its chief justice. The chief justice of India, Mahajan, was unhappy about this, because it meant that a judge who was more senior to Subba Rao at the Madras High Court, Govinda Menon, had been superseded. However, Menon had apparently 'expressed his unwillingness to go to the Andhra Pradesh High Court'. Mahajan, however, was not aware of this. President Prasad therefore accepted the recommendations of Patel and Nehru, and appointed Subba Rao as the chief justice of the Andhra Pradesh High Court.[70]

In July 1957, when S.R. Das was the chief justice of India, another controversy arose concerning an appointment at the Andhra Pradesh High Court. The chief minister of Andhra Pradesh wanted to appoint a certain judge[71] to the high court. However, the chief justice did not want the chief minister's candidate to be appointed. Eventually, however, the chief justice was forced to consent to the appointment. President Prasad, in a letter to Home Minister Pant in July 1957, said he was unhappy that 'the Chief Minister should be so very insistent about his own views and not pay the attention that is due to the recommendation of the Chief Justice'. He hinted that the chief justice had acquiesced in the appointment of the chief minister's candidate, whereas, '[i]f there was to be any acquiescence . . . in a matter like this, it should rather be on the part of the Chief Minister to the Chief Justice than on the part of the Chief Justice in the suggestion of the Chief Minister'. Prasad said that 'if left to himself, the Chief Justice of Andhra High Court would have stuck to his first recommendation', and hinted that the chief justice of India was unhappy about the appointment. However, '[I]n view of the time that has elapsed and in view of the fact that we have not been able to induce the Chief Minister to change his views,' wrote Prasad, 'there is no other course open now.' Prasad made it very clear, however, that he was approving a recommendation which had been 'supported' by the chief minister and governor of Andhra Pradesh, and which had merely been 'acquiesced in' by the chief justice of the high court.[72]

Internal Disagreements within the Executive and Judiciary

Of course, it was not merely the chief justice of India or high court chief justices who disagreed with appointments proposed by members of the executive government. There were internal conflicts within the government as well. For example, when L.K. Jha's name was proposed for appointment to the chief justiceship of the Patna High Court, President Prasad thought that there were more deserving candidates. However, Prasad approved of the nomination after discussing the matter with the chief minister of Bihar. Prime Minister Nehru did not approve of the home ministry's recommendation for the appointment of M.C. Shah to the chief justiceship of the Saurashtra High Court, but he left the matter to be decided by President Prasad, and Prasad approved of the appointment.[73]

Likewise, there were internal disagreements within the judiciary over judicial appointments as well. In 1955, a disagreement arose between the chief justice of India and the Allahabad High Court chief justice over the appointment of V.G. Oak, who was a member of the subordinate judiciary.[74] In early 1955, the chief justice of the Allahabad High Court and the chief minister of the state wanted Oak to be superseded by a junior member of the State Judicial Service. However, the chief justice of India said that Oak should be appointed to the high court. Since Oak's name had been recommended by both the high court chief justice and the chief minister on three occasions in 1954, the appointment went through. Oak was appointed to the Allahabad High Court in March 1955[75] and later went on to become the court's chief justice.[76] Another such disagreement involved M. Sadasivayya, who was also a member of the subordinate judiciary. The chief justice of Mysore did not recommend him for appointment, though the chief minister and governor had suggested his name. The chief justice of India recommended him very strongly and said that the new chief justice of Mysore need not be consulted on the matter, since he had only recently been transferred there from the Calcutta High Court and would not be conversant with local affairs. Sadasivayya was accordingly appointed, and he too went on to become the chief justice of the Karnataka High Court.[77] Similarly, in 1955, Panchkari Sarkar was appointed a judge of the Calcutta High Court[78] despite the objections of P.B. Chakravartti, the chief justice of the Calcutta High Court. He had been recommended by the chief minister and the governor of the state. The previous chief justice of the high court, Sir Trevor Harries, had recommended him for appointment in 1951, though the appointment had not come through. When the chief justice of India was consulted about this, he said that the appointment should be made.[79]

Political Appointments at the Supreme Court

In the 1950s, apart from high court appointments, there were at least two judges who were appointed to the Supreme Court of India at least partly on the strength of their political connections. The first of them was Justice Govinda Menon, the Madras judge who had refused to go to Andhra Pradesh; he was appointed in September 1956. Many said that Menon's appointment was

M.N. Chandurkar, chief justice of the Bombay and Madras High Courts.
His name was recommended by Chief Justice Y.V. Chandrachud in 1985 for
elevation to the Supreme Court of India. Chandurkar's name was rejected
by the government merely because he had attended the funeral of RSS leader
M.S. Golwalkar and had said nice things about Golwalkar in a eulogy.

Nani Palkhivala, a famous advocate, was offered a direct Supreme Court
judgeship in 1963 or 1964. Had he accepted, he might have become the chief
justice of India between 1971 and 1985, which is, by far, longer than the term
served by any chief justice of India to date. However, he declined.

Fali S. Nariman (left) and Justice Y.V. Chandrachud. Nariman, a renowned advocate, was offered a judgeship of the Bombay High Court in the 1960s by Chief Justice S.P. Kotval, and of the Supreme Court of India in the 1980s by Chief Justice Chandrachud. He declined both offers.

Justice Y.V. Chandrachud (extreme left), Fali S. Nariman (second from left) and Justice M. Hidayatullah (extreme right).

Portraits of Harilal J. Kania, the first chief justice of the Supreme Court of India. Prime Minister Jawaharlal Nehru was so 'deeply shocked' by Kania's attitude towards Justice Basheer Ahmed Sayeed of the Madras High Court that he wrote to Sardar Vallabhbhai Patel, 'We should ask Chief Justice Kania to resign. It would be a great risk to make him the permanent Chief Justice of the Supreme Court of India.'

Justice M. Hidayatullah, who served as the chief justice of the Nagpur High Court and chief justice of the Supreme Court of India, was known by his nickname 'Haddi'. Hidayatullah criticized judicial activists and said that they would bring about 'the annihilation of all procedure'. The activists criticized him and said that he was like a spectator at a cricket match during the freedom movement.

George H. Gadbois, Jr., a professor in the department of political science at the University of Kentucky in the US. In the 1980s, Gadbois conducted over 116 interviews with more than sixty-six judges of the Supreme Court of India (nineteen of whom held the post of the chief justice of India), and others like senior lawyers, politicians, relatives of deceased judges, and court staff.

Chief Justice P.B. Gajendragadkar and his wife. Gajendragadkar was a pro-labour judge. Chief Justice S.R. Das said of him: 'His heart is literally bleeding for the under-dogs, and unless the bleeding can be stopped the under-dogs will very soon become top dogs.'

Justice J.C. Shah, chief justice of India. Chief Justice M. Hidayatullah believed that Justice Shah 'wrote a separate opinion every time I wrote what others considered a well-written Judgment'. 'I attributed this to jealousy,' wrote Justice Hidayatullah. However, Hidayatullah also believed that he 'saved' Shah from being superseded by the Indira Gandhi government.

IMPEACHMENT
of Shri J. C. Shah, Supreme Court Judge, by Parliament
Charges of dishonesty, falsehood etc , in judgment

Lawyer seeking Judge's favour makes false propaganda
against the noble-minded, patriotic victim Shri O. P. Gupta

On 15-5-1970 Two Hundred Members of Parliament gave
signed notice calling for the removal of Shri J. C. Shah, Supreme
Court Judge. The serious charges are that in giving judgment in
the matter of Shri Om Prakash Gupta the Judge has acted very
dishonstly, falsely and against law. A full enquiry against the
judge has been demanded. Every English-knowing person can get
copy of the notice from me or from Sori O. P. Gupta (7 Patel
Marg, Allahabad).

One Shri Vikram Chand Mahajan is a lawyer in the Supreme
Court and is also a member of the Lok Sabha. He has considered
this a good opportunity for gaining the judge's favour to increase
his practice and to get a judgeship. On 30-4-1970 suddenly, against
Parliamentary practice and in breech of the rules of Lok Sabha,
without giving a any notice of any purpose to the speaker
and despite the latter's attempt to top him, he made an entirely
false and baseless statement against he character of Shri O. P.
Gupta. A day before i.e. on 29. 4.1970 also Shri Mahajan had
tried to make this false statement, ut that day Smt. Sushila
Rohatgi was in the chair. She stopped Shri Mahajan with strict-
ness. Next day Shri Sri Chand Goyawas in the chair. He could
not stop that statement and remained tisfied by saying at the end
only that Shri Mahajan ought not to hve done so. The statement
was not even expunged from the ecord. Consequently Shri
Mahajan got it published in the who of India with his influence.
everal newspapers published even greater falsehoods than the
statement. According to the rules nothing can be stated in the Lok
Sabha against any person who can get no opportunity to clarify
the same there. Shri O. P. Gupta ent its full reply to every
newspaper and gave petition to the Hon'ble Speaker also, but not
a single word of his was printed by any newspaper. This is how
truth is being strangled ! This is h the reactionary big people
are using their influence to comm tyranny on the poor small
people ! !

I know Shri O. P. Gupta well. He is patriotic, highly intelli-
gent and of a very high character. He is First Class First, Gold
Medalist, Record Holder, M. Sc., B. c. (Hon.), LL. B. He succeeded in the I. C. S. competition in 193 and TOPPED in the whole
of India in I. A. S. Competition in 1956. For taking part in the
Salt Satyagrah of 1930 he was rusticate I from school and imprisoned.
He worked with martyrs like Sarda Bhagat Singh and Chandra

The first page of a scurrilous pamphlet supporting the impeachment of Justice
J.C. Shah because of some critical comments Shah made about a litigant in a case.

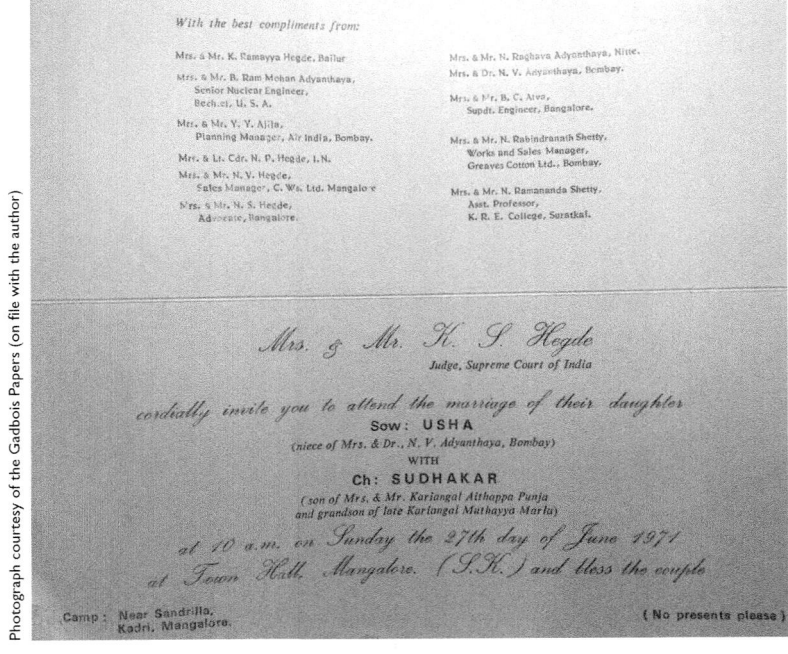

With the best compliments from:

Mrs. & Mr. K. Ramayya Hegde, Bailur

Mrs. & Mr. B. Ram Mohan Adyanthaya,
Senior Nuclear Engineer,
Bechtel, U. S. A.

Mrs. & Mr. Y. Y. Ajila,
Planning Manager, Air India, Bombay.

Mrs. & Lt. Cdr. N. P. Hegde, I.N.

Mrs. & Mr. N. V. Hegde,
Sales Manager, C. Ws. Ltd. Mangalore

Mrs. & Mr. N. S. Hegde,
Advocate, Bangalore.

Mrs. & Mr. N. Raghava Adyanthaya, Nitte.

Mrs. & Dr. N. V. Aayanthaya, Bombay.

Mrs. & Mr. B. C. Alva,
Supdt. Engineer, Bangalore.

Mrs. & Mr. N. Rabindranath Shetty,
Works and Sales Manager,
Greaves Cotton Ltd., Bombay.

Mrs. & Mr. N. Ramananda Shetty,
Asst. Professor,
K. R. E. College, Surathkal.

Mrs. & Mr. *K. S. Hegde*
Judge, Supreme Court of India

cordially invite you to attend the marriage of their daughter

Sow: USHA
(niece of Mrs. & Dr., N. V. Adyanthaya, Bombay)

WITH

Ch: SUDHAKAR
(son of Mrs. & Mr. Kariangal Aithappa Punja
and grandson of late Kariangal Mathayya Marla)

*at 10 a.m. on Sunday the 27th day of June 1971
at Town Hall, Mangalore. (S.K.) and bless the couple*

Camp : Near Sandrilla,
Kadri, Mangalore.

(No presents please)

A wedding invitation sent by Justice K.S. Hegde to Professor Gadbois,
inviting Gadbois to attend his daughter's wedding in June 1971.

V.D. TULZAPURKAR
JUDGE

SUPREME COURT OF INDIA
NEW DELHI

11, Tughlak Road,
New Delhi - 110011

May 3, 1983.

Dear Mr.Gadbois,

   I am in receipt of your last
letter written after you saw me in my
Chamber. It seems my attitude has
somewhat hurt you for which I am sorry.

   As desired I am returning your
pro forma containing my bio data. The
particulars in the pro forma are fairly
accurate. The additional information
which you wanted has been furnished on the
reverse of the pro forma, which I hope will
satisfy your requirements.

      With regards,

                  Yours sincerely,

                  3.5.83
                  (V.D.TULZAPURKAR)

Mr.George H.Gadbois, Jr.
Senior Research Fellow,
American Institute of Indian Studies,
12, Barakhamba Road,
New Delhi - 110001

A letter dated 3 May 1983 sent by Justice V.D. Tulzapurkar to Gadbois. Tulzapurkar initially refused to allow Gadbois to interview him, as he was weary of scholars like Upendra Baxi who had criticized him. However, thanks to the intervention of Justices P.K. Goswami and E.S. Venkataramiah, Tulzapurkar agreed to be interviewed by Gadbois in July 1983. The 'excellent' interview between them lasted two hours.

15 PANDITIA PLACE
CALCUTTA 29
(PIN 700 029)

14 May 1983

Dear Mr. Gadbois,

Yesterday I received your letter of 9 May and off prints of two articles written by you. I wonder why you felt hesitant about sending an article which contained "inferences about me". Any one who has occupied an office of importance in any country has met with impressive inferences and perhaps insinuations. One has to have a serene and strong mind not to be disturbed by criticism nor to feel flattered by praise. You have to treat both as impostors. Beyond this I cannot express my view.

You have said that there is a probability of your coming to Calcutta in the end of this month and you would like to meet me. There is just one word of caution. It is that I shall be away from home for about a fortnight as on 7 or 8 June is the date when I shall come back home after being away from about middle of next week.

With good wishes

Yours Sincerely
A. N. Ray

P.S. I thank you for sending the articles. I shall read them not without interest.

A handwritten letter sent by the reclusive Chief Justice A.N. Ray to Gadbois in May 1983. Ray became unpopular among many of his colleagues at the Supreme Court of India for superseding three senior judges, J.M. Shelat, K.S. Hegde and A.N. Grover. Gadbois wrote of his interview with Ray in 1983: 'He was very nervous, but tried to appear in control. Fed me mango and sweets.'

Justice O. Chinnappa Reddy

2, Motilal Nehru Marg
New Delhi. 110011

8.3.84

Dear Prof. Gadbois,

Thank you for your letter of Feb. 17. Your earlier letter has not reached me. I still feel that some of your enquiries (and mine here) serve no purpose. Your present query, I am afraid, is of that nature. You want to know whether I am a Christian or a Non-Brahmin-Hindu etc. I must say that I profess and practise no religion, my wife does not and my children do not.

My views on religion have been expressed by me in my judgment in S.P. Mittal vs Union of India (reported in 1983(1) S.C.R. 729) in which I have dissented from the majority on a particular question.

However, to keep the record straight I must say that my father was a faithful Roman Catholic and my mother and her family are all Hindus. Almost all our relatives are Hindus and the conversion of my father's ancestor doesn't seem to have made any difference to inter-marriages taking place as if that was any conversion. That is why, perhaps, no matter how we search and study. My father's family and my mother's family

belong to the same community known as the Reddi community (a caste). I refuse to be classified as belonging to any religion or any community. I prefer to be a human being and an Indian. I will certainly feel offended if you call me a Hindu or a Christian or a member of any caste.

If I may give some unsolicited advice, I would suggest that you read some of your judgments on social issues or find out what we have to say on national issues. Mean complete silence on our social background on whatever own origins are, about all of us belong to the socially elite classes and that is the very relevant background. As you know, not the acquisition of knowledge, wealth, status and other social symbols, human beings change their attitudes and judgments, no exception. My friend Justice Gangadhar Rao of the Andhra Pradesh High Court comes from a ... Brahmin landless family but today he is an atheist and an ardent follower of Socialism and Marxism. On the other hand my friend Mr. Justice Mukhtadar of our High Court, a believer and a follower in the human misery of past and present has now settled, fixed position on the religion of his forefathers. That is why I am afraid, our enquiry into the religion you think of a judge, whether Hindu, Muslim or Christian, is of no significance. That ... friend ... to indulge in which was ... too obvious to you from the diffidently yours

A handwritten letter sent by Justice O. Chinnappa Reddy to Gadbois in March 1984. Reddy wrote: 'I refuse to be classified as belonging to any religion or any community. I prefer to be a human being and an Indian. I will certainly feel offended if you call me a Hindu or a Christian or a member of any caste.' He also added: 'I must say that I profess and practise no religion, my wife does not and my children do not.' Reddy was ironically appointed to the Supreme Court of India on a Christian seat.

JUDGE, SUPREME COURT.
INDIA.

New Delhi, the 30th July, 1970.

Dear Dr. Gadbois,

I thank you for your letter of
the 23rd July and your kind words on my
address on Sovereignty. My wife and I
will be very grateful to you and Mrs. Gadbois
if both of you give us the pleasure of
having a cup of tea with us at 5 P.M. on
Saturday, the 8th August, 1970. I hope
the time and date will be suitable to you.
This will give both of us an opportunity
to know you and have a quite talk with
you.

Yours sincerely,

(J. M. Shelat)

Dr. George H. Gadbois,
9, Nizamuddin East,
New Delhi-13.

Gadbois shared an extensive correspondence with judges of the Supreme Court
of India. In this letter dated 30 July 1970, Justice J.M. Shelat invited Gadbois
and his wife over for a cup of tea. Little did any of them know at the time
that Shelat would be superseded around three years later.

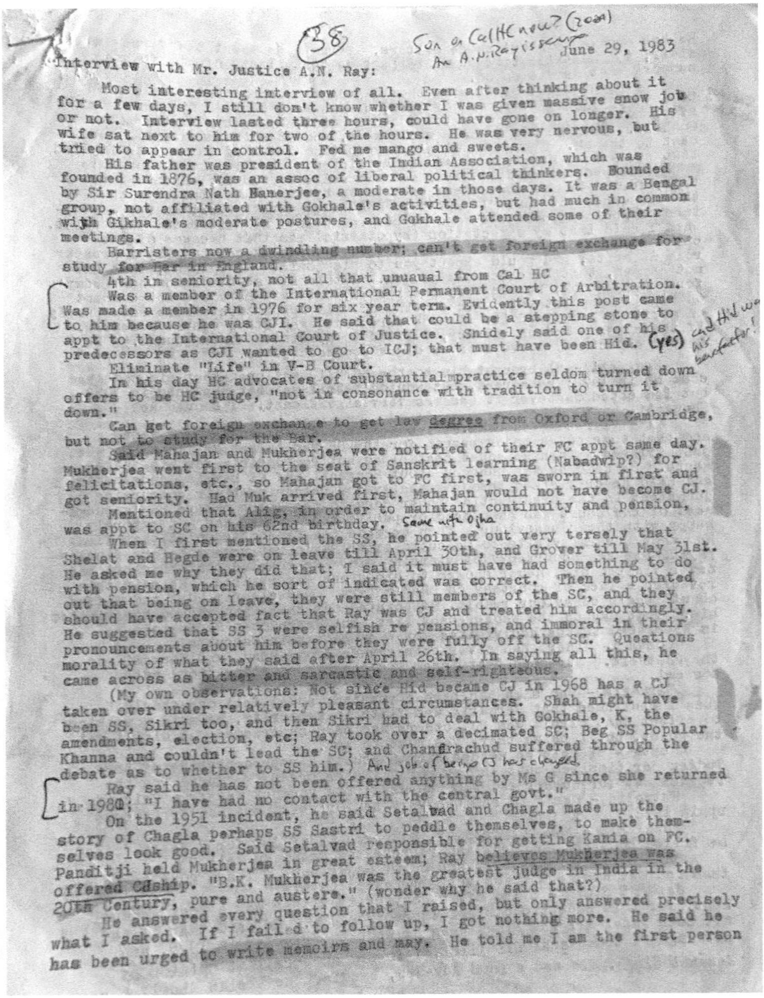

(38)   Sun on Cal(HC new? (2001)
An A.N.Ray issue?   June 29, 1983

Interview with Mr. Justice A.N. Ray:

Most interesting interview of all. Even after thinking about it for a few days, I still don't know whether I was given massive snow job or not. Interview lasted three hours, could have gone on longer. His wife sat next to him for two of the hours. He was very nervous, but tried to appear in control. Fed me mango and sweets.

His father was president of the Indian Association, which was founded in 1876, was an assoc of liberal political thinkers. Bounded by Sir Surendra Nath Banerjee, a moderate in those days. It was a Bengal group, not affiliated with Gokhale's activities, but had much in common with Gikhale's moderate postures, and Gokhale attended some of their meetings.

Barristers now a dwindling number; can't get foreign exchange for study for Bar in England.

4th in seniority, not all that unusual from Cal HC
Was a member of the International Permanent Court of Arbitration. Was made a member in 1976 for six year term. Evidently this post came to him because he was CJI. He said that could be a stepping stone to appt to the International Court of Justice. Snidely said one of his (yes) and HW w predecessors as CJI wanted to go to ICJ; that must have been Hid. his bro father!

Eliminate "Life" in V-B Court.
In his day HC advocates of substantial practice seldom turned down offers to be HC judge, "not in consonance with tradition to turn it down."

Can get foreign exchange to get law degree from Oxford or Cambridge, but not to study for the Bar.

Said Mahajan and Mukherjea were notified of their FC appt same day. Mukherjea went first to the seat of Sanskrit learning (Nabadwip?) for felicitations, etc., so Mahajan got to FC first, was sworn in first and got seniority. Had Muk arrived first, Mahajan would not have become CJ.

Mentioned that Alig, in order to maintain continuity and pension, was appt to SC on his 62nd birthday. Same with Ojha.

When I first mentioned the SS, he pointed out very tersely that Shelat and Hegde were on leave till April 30th, and Grover till May 31st. He asked me why they did that; I said it must have had something to do with pension, which he sort of indicated was correct. Then he pointed out that being on leave, they were still members of the SC, and they should have accepted fact that Ray was CJ and treated him accordingly. He suggested that SS 3 were selfish re pensions, and immoral in their pronouncements about him before they were fully off the SC. Questions morality of what they said after April 26th. In saying all this, he came across as bitter and sarcastic and self-righteous.

(My own observations: Not since Hid became CJ in 1968 has a CJ taken over under relatively pleasant circumstances. Shah might have been SS, Sikri too, and then Sikri had to deal with Gokhale, K, the amendments, election, etc; Ray took over a decimated SC; Beg SS Popular Khanna and couldn't lead the SC; and Chandrachud suffered through the debate as to whether to SS him.) And job of being CJ has changed.

Ray said he has not been offered anything by Ms G since she returned in 1980; "I have had no contact with the central govt."

On the 1951 incident, he said Setalvad and Chagla made up the story of Chagla perhaps SS Sastri to peddle themselves, to make themselves look good. Said Setalvad responsible for getting Kania on FC. Panditji held Mukherjea in great esteem; Ray believes Mukherjea was offered CJship. "B.K. Mukherjea was the greatest judge in India in the 20th Century, pure and austere." (wonder why he said that?)

He answered every question that I raised, but only answered precisely what I asked. If I failed to follow up, I got nothing more. He said he has been urged to write memoirs and may. He told me I am the first person

The first page of the typewritten notes of Gadbois's interview with Chief Justice A.N. Ray. Gadbois considered this as the '[m]ost interesting interview of all'. The interview 'lasted three hours' but 'could have gone on longer'. The highlighting and handwriting on each typewritten interview are of Gadbois himself.

not based on merit. Justice S.K. Das, for example, said that Menon's mental faculties were not too sharp, and he could not write a decent judgment.[80] Justice B.P. Sinha, on the other hand, thought very highly of Menon and said that he 'came from the Madras High Court with a great reputation as a distinguished Judge' and 'it was said in high quarters that he enjoyed the highest reputation as a great jurist'.[81] There appeared to be a broad consensus among the judges that Menon had been appointed to the Supreme Court because of his political patron, V.K. Krishna Menon,[82] who was, at the time, a Union minister without portfolio (he became the defence minister of India in 1957) and India's representative at the General Assembly of the United Nations.[83] Menon was also a good friend of Vice President S. Radhakrishnan. Menon's son was very defensive about this friendship, and was surprised that Gadbois knew about it.[84] However, the judges seemed to believe that Menon's patron was V.K. Krishna Menon and not Radhakrishnan.

The second of these judges was Justice J.L. Kapur. Many judges told Gadbois that Kapur came to the Supreme Court because of his long association with the Congress,[85] though Kapur's son, a judge himself, believed that while his father's Congress connections might have helped him get to the high court, they had no role to play in his elevation to the Supreme Court.[86] However, Kapur's son agreed that his father had a lot of clout in Delhi, and was even instrumental in the appointment of Justice H.R. Khanna to the Supreme Court.[87]

Though these appointments might have been politically motivated, it is important to bear in mind that Menon and Kapur were not appointed by the government because they had a philosophy which matched that of the government. It is not as though these judges were appointed by the government because it considered them to have views favourable to its policies. The worst that could be said of the government when it made these appointments was that it was doling out political patronage; handing out favours to friends and well-wishers. What S.R. Das, chief justice of India from 1956–59, said about high court appointments at this time is instructive: 'The Chief Minister holding a political office dependent on the goodwill of his party followers may well be induced to listen and give way to canvassing.'[88]

Likewise, in the 1950s, appointments were made to the Supreme Court on the basis of regional and communal considerations. In May 1947, K.N. Katju responded to a questionnaire issued to members of the Provincial Constitution Committee of the Constituent Assembly of India and said that while appointments to the high court bench ought to be made on the basis of 'merit', at the same time, 'adequate representation of the different communities [was] to be considered'.[89] In August 1959, President Prasad wrote a letter to Home Minister Pant observing that since Chief Justice S.R. Das was going to retire soon,[90] there would be a vacancy at the Supreme Court. 'As there is no Judge from Tamilnad in the Supreme Court at the present moment,'[91] he wrote, 'I would suggest that someone from that area should be appointed in the resulting vacancy.' Prasad wrote that he had no particular candidate in mind and 'due regard' would have to be given 'to the qualifications which are required for such appointments'. However, in his letter, Prasad, who was himself from the northern state of Bihar, reiterated to Pant, who was from the northern state of Uttar Pradesh, 'the desirability of having someone from Tamilnad for the ensuing vacancy in the Supreme Court'.[92]

Similarly, when Justice S. Fazl Ali, a Muslim judge, left the court in May 1952,[93] he was replaced with another Muslim judge, Ghulam Hasan, in September 1952.[94] Likewise, when

Hasan died holding office in November 1954, another Muslim judge, S.J. Imam, was eventually appointed in January 1955.

Appointments made to the Supreme Court in the 1950s also sought to preserve a broad regional balance between north and south India. Before N.C. Aiyar, a retired judge of the Madras High Court, was appointed as the seventh judge of the Supreme Court in September 1950, there was only one other judge from south India (M. Patanjali Sastri) at the court. Attorney General Motilal C. Setalvad, who had harsh (and sometimes unfair) things to say about some judges, could not figure out why Aiyar was appointed to the Supreme Court and said that this 'was, and will always remain, a mystery'.[95]

Appointments made along communal and regional lines in this manner were initiated at the behest of the government, not the chief justice of India.[96] This is evident not merely from the views of Katju and Prasad seen above, but also from the fact that several chief justices of India repudiated appointments made along communal lines. Chief Justice Sastri informed the Law Commission that 'unsatisfactory methods of selection' were being followed at the high courts, 'often influenced by political and other extraneous considerations'.[97] Chief Justice Mahajan said that appointments to the high courts were being made on '[n]arrow parochial considerations'.[98] Chief Justice S.R. Das[99] told the Law Commission that 'High Court appointments are not always made on merit but on extraneous considerations of community, caste, political affiliations, and likes and dislikes have a free play'.[100] Chief Justice Sinha also said that in one instance he had found that the 'recommendations of the Chief Minister were based on extraneous considerations like caste or creed of the proposed person'.[101]

However, Granville Austin was not impressed with these criticisms of judicial appointments made in the 1950s. He wrote in his book that '[f]inding hidden motives is a parlour game within the priesthood of the Indian legal community', and that these criticisms had to be considered with caution.[102] In fact, even when the appointments were made along political, regional or communal lines—at the behest of the executive government and against the better instincts of the chief justice of India— in most cases, such appointments had the 'concurrence' of the chief justice of India and the chief justice of the high court concerned.

The Law Commission Unearths a Fiction

In August 1957, the chairman of the 14th Law Commission, Attorney General Setalvad, sent Home Minister Pant a confidential letter containing an interim note prepared by four members of the Law Commission,[103] on how to deal with the 'accumulated arrears in the High Courts'.[104] This was before the Law Commission's 14th report was published in 1958. Paragraph 4 of the interim note said that senior members of the bar and judges had expressed an opinion that the recently made judicial selections had 'proceeded on no recognizable principle and [seemed] to have been made out of considerations of political expediency or regional or communal sentiment'. The interim note concluded by saying, 'We are strongly against the High Court being permitted to become a sort of communal museum in the name of the representation of this or that community or a particular class at the expense of efficiency and merit.'

This irked Pant, who wrote a letter marked 'secret' to Setalvad later that month,[105] in which he said that he had read paragraph 4 of the interim note 'with a feeling of bewilderment and concern'. He enclosed with his letter a table which showed that from 1955 (when Pant became the home minister) onwards, forty-one judges had been appointed to the high courts, and nearly all had been appointed with the concurrence of the chief justice of India, the chief justice of the high court, and the chief minister or governor of the state concerned.

Setalvad responded to Pant with his own secret letter that month, and said that the observations contained in the interim note were 'not confined to the period beginning with the year 1955'. He also quoted a reply given by the chief justice of India to a questionnaire issued by the Law Commission, to the effect that there were instances where the chief justice's recommendation on judicial appointments had been 'overruled' while that of the chief minister had prevailed. Therefore, in order to avoid 'the discomfiture and loss of prestige in having his nomination unceremoniously turned down', high court chief justices were, before making recommendations, trying 'to ascertain the views of the Chief Minister', so as to ensure that their recommendations would eventually go through.[106] In other words, Chief Justice S.R. Das had informed the Law Commission that high court chief justices were holding back appointments of truly meritorious and deserving judicial candidates, and only appointing those who were palatable to the executive government. Through this procedure of compromise, appointments were made with the theoretical concurrence of the high court chief justice.

In October 1957, the contents of the interim note relating to the unsatisfactory system of selecting judges were published by the newspaper *Statesman*. This annoyed Pant, who wrote to a member of the Law Commission and said that '[t]he wide publicity thus given to this matter is bound to cause considerable damage and prove harmful from the point of view of public confidence in the independence and efficiency of the judiciary in the country'.[107] Along with his letter, he enclosed another statement which showed that among the seventy high court judges appointed between 1950 and 1955, nearly all had been selected with the concurrence of the chief justice of India and the chief justices of the high courts. Pant found the reply of Chief Justice S.R. Das to the Law Commission's questionnaire hard to believe. He wrote, 'It is difficult for me to conceive that anyone occupying the eminent office of the Chief Justice can be so lacking in the elementary sense of justice and due discharge of his duties without fear or favour according to his pledge as to hesitate to make recommendations of the most suitable persons for appointments to the High Court for fear of recommendations not finding favour with the Chief Minister.' 'Such an attitude,' he continued, 'would be hardly in accord with even the ordinary standards of integrity and independence expected from judicial officers.'

Setalvad responded to Pant's letter in November[108] and said that paragraph 4 of the interim note needed modification in the light of the data that Pant had provided. However, the fact still remained, he wrote, that 'a vast body of opinion including that of extremely responsible persons [did] hold that some unsatisfactory personnel [had] been selected and that such selection [had] been due to extraneous considerations'. He was unsure about why unsatisfactory judicial appointments were being made despite the concurrence of the chief justice of India and high court chief justices, and wondered if this had something to do with the 'demoralisation of the State Chief Justices which the Chief Justice of India and other responsible persons have referred to'.

Pant's data perplexed Setalvad, who, satisfied that the data was accurate, asked himself, 'How could the Chief Justices of the High Courts have concurred in appointment of unsatisfactory personnel to the Court?'[109] Setalvad soon learnt that the chief justices had concurred 'under circumstances which had prevented them from exercising their choice freely and in favour of suitable and proper persons'.[110] High court chief justices realized that if they did not cooperate with the government, it would appoint candidates who would be 'incapable of rendering proper assistance or [who were] otherwise unsuitable'. They also did not want their newly appointed judges to feel that they had been appointed by the executive against the wishes of the chief justice. With this in mind, a high court chief justice decided to compromise with the executive government; he would not recommend 'someone whom he [had] reasons to know the executive [would] not favour' and would recommend 'someone who he believed would be acceptable to the executive'.[111]

Thus, a fiction was preserved that the appointment was eventually always made with the concurrence of the chief justice of India and high court chief justice, even though they may not have, strictly speaking, agreed with the appointment, or even if they had better judicial candidates in mind for the vacancy. The chief justice probably thought it better to compromise and get judges appointed to help deal with arrears rather than to put up a fight and get a worse candidate or no candidate at all.

In 1958, the Law Commission in its 14th report said that judicial appointments had been made on political and extraneous considerations. In its chapter on the Supreme Court, the Law Commission wrote that the 'general impression' was that 'now and again executive influence exerted from the highest quarters has been responsible for some appointments to the Bench'.[112] Even on appointments to the high court, the Law Commission noted that the 'almost universal chorus of comment' from 'Supreme Court Judges, High Court Judges, retired Judges, Public Prosecutors, numerous representative associations of the Bar, principals and professors of Law Colleges and very responsible members of the legal profession all over the country' was that 'selections are unsatisfactory and that they have been induced by executive influence'.[113] Appointments to high courts were made, noted the Law Commission, either 'out of considerations of political expediency or regional or communal sentiments', and that top-ranking members of the bar were not appointed to the high courts 'for reasons that can stem only from political, or communal or similar grounds'.[114] It was noted that some of the judges appointed to the high courts had not been recommended by the chief justices of those courts:[115] two judges were appointed to the Calcutta High Court against the wishes of the chief justice of that court;[116] a judge had been appointed to the Allahabad High Court against the wishes of the chief justice of that court;[117] and there were instances where the last person on a list of names submitted by the chief justice for appointment, in order of merit, was appointed to the court.[118]

The Law Commission summarized the procedure which was followed for appointing high court judges as follows: The chief justice of the high court forwarded his recommendation to the chief minister of the state. If the chief minister did not agree with the names suggested by the chief justice, he could suggest his own names, but the chief justice had to be given an opportunity to comment on the chief minister's names (a practice which was not always followed). The recommendations of the chief justice and chief minister were then forwarded to the Union home minister through the governor of the state (presumably with the governor's own recommendations). The home minister, in consultation with the chief justice of India, then advised the President about whom to appoint. The Law Commission noted that the chief minister's nominee was sometimes appointed in preference to the nominee of the high court chief justice.[119] However, in most cases, the chief justice of the high court would eventually concur with the appointment which was made,[120] thus preserving the fiction that no appointment was made without the concurrence of the chief justice. The Law Commission recommended that if the state government disagreed with a name proposed by the chief justice, it could voice its concerns and request the chief justice to suggest another name, but it must not suggest a name on its own.[121]

The Law Commission suggested that judicial appointments at the high courts must only be made on the recommendation of the high court chief justice, i.e. the executive government should not initiate names for appointing judges.[122] Further, akin to the recommendation made at the conference of Federal Court judges and high court chief justices, the Law Commission also opined that judicial appointments ought to be made only with the concurrence of the chief justice of India.[123]

Home Minister Pant strongly disagreed with Setalvad's hypothesis that chief justices were making compromise recommendations in the judicial appointments process. When the Law Commission's report was debated in the Rajya Sabha in 1959, Pant said that out of the 211 judicial appointments made since 1950, all but one (i.e. 210 in total) were made with the concurrence of the chief justice of India.[124] There were only fifteen cases in which there had been a difference of opinion between the chief justice and the chief minister or governor.[125] The government rejected the Law Commission's recommendations that appointments should only be made with the concurrence of the chief justice of India and that the state government should not be able to propose its own names.[126]

Limited Interference

However, the sense one gets is that the extent of executive interference was limited during this time. Two chief justices of India who served as such in the 1960s, B.P. Sinha and P.B. Gajendragadkar, later said that the executive always accepted their recommendations.

However, Sinha, who served as the chief justice between October 1959 and January 1964, repeatedly complained to Prime Minister Nehru about executive interference in judicial appointments, especially at the high courts. In November 1959, Sinha met Nehru and said that some chief ministers were interfering in the appointment of judges. He said that the appointment of two new judges in Bihar had been held up for two years because the chief minister of the state wanted one judge to be appointed, while the chief justice of India wanted another. Because of this, Sinha told Nehru, even the judge over whom there was no controversy was not being appointed. Concerned, Nehru informed Home Minister Pant about this.[127]

In March 1960, Sinha met Nehru again and repeated his complaint against the Bihar chief minister.[128] Sinha did not want to recommend the Bihar chief minister's judicial candidate because he did not consider him to be a man of integrity though he had a large practice. He also said that the chief minister of the new state of Gujarat, Dr Jivraj Mehta, was interfering in judicial appointments. Chief Minister Mehta wanted a man who was eighth or ninth in seniority at the Bombay High Court to be appointed as the chief justice of the Gujarat High Court. This judge, said Sinha, was related to Mehta, being 'some kind of a brother-in-law'. Mehta went to Sinha and suggested this judge's name. Sinha said no, but Mehta kept pressing the name on Sinha. Both Sinha and Mehta spoke with the governor of Bombay. Sinha wanted the chief Justice of the Bombay High Court, H.K. Chainani, to go to Gujarat as the chief justice of that high court. But Mehta's candidate had already gone to Ahmedabad and had started making preparations for moving there. Nehru agreed with Sinha. As he wrote to Home Minister Pant, Nehru thought that the reasons given by Sinha for rejecting Mehta's choice for the position of the high court chief justice were 'sound', and that 'this kind of narrow provincialism should not be encouraged by us'. 'The Chief Minister naturally should have a say in the appointment of the Chief Justice of a State,' wrote Nehru, 'but the Chief Justiceship should not be considered as a gift from the Chief Minister.'[129] It is not clear what happened next. However, we do know that Sinha's choice for the chief justiceship of the Gujarat High Court, Chainani, did not go to Gujarat for whatever reason. Justice S.T. Desai, a puisne judge of the Bombay High Court, became the Gujarat High Court's first chief justice in May 1960.[130]

Sinha complained to Nehru not merely about chief ministers but also about chief justices. He was unhappy with Chief Justice A.N. Bhandari of the Punjab High Court, and said that he had made unsatisfactory appointments. He also did not think very highly of Chief Justice Iqbal Ahmed of the Allahabad High Court, saying that he 'pushed his particular friends on to the Bench without much thought of other considerations' and 'brought down the level of the Allahabad High Court which used to be high previously'.[131] In fact, Sinha sometimes went with the chief minister's recommendation for a judicial appointment over that of the high court chief justice.[132]

That having been said, in his autobiography, Sinha referred to numerous instances where his decisions on judicial appointments were accepted by Prime Minister Nehru. In fact, Sinha wrote that though one of the recommendations made by his predecessor, S.R. Das, had not been accepted by the government,[133] it had agreed to all of his own recommendations which he had made while holding the office of chief justice of India.[134] He wrote that the Union government, unlike the state governments, appointed judges on the basis of merit, not extraneous matters.[135] For instance, Justice Harbans Singh, additional judge of the Punjab High Court, was not being made permanent by Chief Minister Partap Singh Kairon and Governor N.V. Gadgil, even though Sinha and the chief justice of the Punjab High Court were in favour of it. Sinha saw Nehru about this and, soon thereafter, Singh was made a permanent judge of the high court.[136] The chief minister of a northern state (possibly Punjab) also wanted a candidate to be appointed to the high court, while Sinha wanted another. Eventually, it was Sinha's candidate who was appointed.[137] Sinha rejected the appointment of S. Mohan Kumaramangalam to the Madras High Court, and his recommendation was accepted.[138]

Sinha's successor, Chief Justice Gajendragadkar, also said that the government accepted his recommendations for judicial appointments. He said that the Union government 'attached . . . decisive importance to the voice of the chief justice of India', adding that if he did not agree with a recommendation, that judge was not appointed.[139]

Asoke Sen, who served his first term as law minister between 1957 and 1966,[140] said that during that time, Prime Minister Nehru simply agreed with the recommendations of the chief justice of India and did not veto any of them. Nehru, said Sen, did not suggest any names to the chief justice of India.[141] Justice Vivian Bose, who served at the court in the 1950s, however, said that Prime Minister Nehru did occasionally try to influence an appointment, though the chief justice of India always got his way.[142] Justice S.K. Das agreed that Nehru always accepted the recommendations of the chief justice of India.[143] However, Das revealed that there was some political interference even in the 1950s, though not nearly as much as there was in the 1980s.[144] Justice A.K. Sarkar, who was the chief justice of India for a few months in 1966, recalled that he wanted to appoint Justice G.K. Mitter from the Calcutta High Court to the Supreme Court though Mitter was around the fourth in seniority there at the time. Mitter's senior colleagues went to the West Bengal chief minister and complained about this. The chief minister of Bengal wrote a letter to the home ministry in Delhi, which in turn sent a letter to Sarkar. However, Sarkar stood firm, and Mitter was appointed (though a few months after Sarkar retired as chief justice).[145] Something similar happened with Chief Justice Subba Rao. He had recommended Justice K.S. Hegde for appointment to the Supreme Court. However, Subba Rao resigned from the Supreme Court in April 1967 in order to contest elections as the United Opposition's candidate for President of India.[146] Though Subba Rao was essentially running against the government of the day, his judicial nominee, Hegde, was nonetheless appointed to the Supreme Court in July 1967.[147]

From 1971 to 1993

Committed Judges

However, there were signs of change after the Supreme Court decided the contentious case of *Golak Nath v. State of Punjab*[148] in February 1967. It was held in this case that the chapter in the Constitution on fundamental rights could not be amended or altered by Parliament. Parliament had been in the process of enacting laws to ensure that property would not be held in a few concentrated Indian hands. The Supreme Court's judgment in *Golak Nath* had thwarted Parliament's attempts to modify property laws. Chief Justice Subba Rao, who handed down the majority judgment in that case, resigned in April to run for office as President of India against the ruling Congress regime.

Though the election was hotly contested, Subba Rao lost to the Congress candidate, Zakir Husain.[149]

A few years later, sometime prior to August 1969, Chief Justice M. Hidayatullah, the last of the powerful chief justices of India, recommended three judges for elevation to the Supreme Court, including A.N. Ray, a Calcutta High Court judge.[150] Home Minister Y.B. Chavan then came to Hidayatullah and asked him if he knew what the 'political ideology' of the three judges was. This was perhaps the first time that judicial candidates' political ideologies were being inquired about. Hidayatullah responded to Chavan by saying that he did not know what their political ideology was, and added, 'I didn't know yours until four days ago when you said you were a socialist.' Nevertheless, the three judges recommended by Hidayatullah were appointed to the Supreme Court in August 1969.[151]

Soon thereafter, however, the Supreme Court handed down two contentious decisions in the *Bank Nationalization* case (February 1970[152]) and the *Privy Purses* case (December 1970[153]). In both, the Supreme Court foiled the policy measures of the Indira Gandhi government. It held that the government's decisions to nationalize banks and abolish the 'privy purses' paid to former Indian princes (who had agreed to join the Indian Union after the British left India) were illegal. Chief Justice Hidayatullah retired from the Supreme Court after these two cases had been decided, in December 1970. Before retiring, he had recommended the names of two judges, chief justice S.P. Kotval of the Bombay High Court and M.S. Menon of the Kerala High Court, for elevation to the Supreme Court. The government now ignored these recommendations.[154]

The government thereafter began to impose its will upon the chief justice of India on judicial appointments with greater frequency. The recommendations made by Chief Justice J.C.

Shah, who held office for only a few months, were ignored. When asked why this had happened, Shah said that 'ultimately, the Government has the appointing power'.[155]

It was around this time that the responsibility for appointing judges was transferred from the home minister to the law minister. The Indira Gandhi government (through Law Minister H.R. Gokhale, Minister of Steel and Mines S. Mohan Kumaramangalam, and Minister of Education, Youth Services and Culture Siddhartha Shankar Ray who thereafter became the West Bengal chief minister) started packing the court with judges with a view to overturn Golak Nath's case.[156] Judges started being appointed to the Supreme Court, for the first time, by openly considering their political ideologies, a topic which we will explore in greater detail in the next chapter.

Fictional Concurrence Continues

Chief Justice S.M. Sikri,[157] who followed Shah, was the first of the weak chief justices of India when it came to judicial appointments. Most of the judges who were appointed to the Supreme Court during his term were those whose names had been initiated and suggested by the government. Accordingly, Sikri had never known or even met judges like Justices S.C. Roy, D.G. Palekar, Y.V. Chandrachud or A.N. Alagiriswami. Among the nine judges who had been appointed during his tenure, seven sat on the bench to hear the *Basic Structure* case, which reconsidered the correctness of the *Golak Nath* case, and five of them held that the Constitution had no 'basic structure' which could not be amended. However, as before, Sikri fictionally concurred in the appointment of every judge—even those who had been suggested by the government. Sikri put his foot down and exercised a veto in only one case—Nagendra Singh. The government had tried to appoint Singh, but Sikri pointed out that he was an international law expert while the Supreme Court needed municipal law experts (Singh eventually served as a judge of the International Court of Justice from 1973–88, which included terms as the vice president and president of the court[158]). No judge was forced on Sikri.[159]

Sikri was also unable to control the flow of arguments during the hearing in the *Basic Structure* case, and he did not invite all his colleagues to the judicial conference to discuss the case, only including the ones whose views he did not know, which struck one of the judges on that case as improper.[160] Sikri, however, was said to have been responsible for bringing Khanna to the Supreme Court.[161] He also said that Chandrachud was 'completely my choice',[162] even though the name may have been initiated by Gokhale.

One of the judges who was appointed to the Supreme Court during Sikri's tenure as chief justice was S.C. Roy. His uncle was Dr Bidhan Chandra Roy,[163] who had been a prominent Congress chief minister of West Bengal. As Nehru and Bidhan Chandra were close friends, Roy and Prime Minister Gandhi must have met when they were children, surmised Roy's wife many years later. In 1970, Roy had been sent feelers by the government about coming to the Supreme Court, but he had refused. He was asked once again in 1971, before the general elections for the Lok Sabha. Prime Minister Gandhi had said to him, 'you must come to help me'.[164] Roy's appointment to the Supreme Court was initiated by Gokhale, S.S. Ray, Kumaramangalam and Attorney General Niren De. Roy, who practised law in Calcutta, was called to Delhi to meet Gokhale and asked to bring his biodata along.[165] In Delhi, Roy met Gokhale, Kumaramangalam and Ray, and they quizzed him about his views on various matters.[166] Following this meeting, Roy was appointed to the Supreme Court. Sikri, though a 'thorough gentleman',[167] was really a bystander in the whole process. After Roy was appointed to the Supreme Court, Prime Minister Gandhi asked him to take care of some legal work concerning her family property in Allahabad. However, he died of a heart attack in November 1971, a few months after his appointment. Many years later, Mrs Roy told Gadbois that after her husband's death, Prime Minister Indira Gandhi had all the files relating to the property dispute whisked away so that nobody would know.[168]

Hidayatullah thought that Sikri was a weak chief justice. He believed that Mrs Gandhi kept him in good humour, and accordingly got him to cooperate in making judicial appointments. Gadbois, however, thought that this criticism of Sikri was unfair.[169] On the other hand, Hidayatullah was not alone in his belief. Justice Mitter too maintained that Sikri, though 'a very good man', 'just couldn't withstand the pressure' put on him by the government.[170] Similarly, B.P. Sinha said that Sikri was a rich man's son who led an elegant lifestyle, that he was shy and withdrawn and did not visit the high courts.[171]

Similarly, Chief Justice Chandrachud[172] formally approved all the judges who were appointed to the Supreme Court during his tenure. He exercised a veto once, when it appeared that the judge in question had been credibly accused of sexual assault. Thus, he signed off on the appointment of Justice Baharul Islam in December 1980, an appointment which he considered the 'low point in the history of Supreme Court appointments'. Islam later resigned from the Supreme Court in order to contest elections as a Congress (I) candidate for a Lok Sabha seat,[173] after holding in favour of Bihar's Congress (I) chief minister, Jagannath Misra, in a controversial case where he had been accused of criminal wrongdoing and misuse of office.[174] Law Minister P. Shiv Shankar had pressed Chandrachud hard on

Islam's appointment and said that there would be 'no harm' in appointing him. Chandrachud had agreed.

Chandrachud also did not want M.P. Thakkar, a Gujarat High Court judge, to be appointed to the Supreme Court. Thakkar, said Chandrachud, had handed down some extreme judgments favouring labourers, including in a case involving a bank employee who had stolen money from the bank. However, after Prime Minister Gandhi mentioned Thakkar's name to Chandrachud two or three times, he agreed. Shiv Shankar was behind Thakkar's appointment as well. Chandrachud said that while he still had a veto, the Government tries 'artful persuasion, drops hints, [and] keeps egging you' until you agree to the appointment.[175] Consequently, many of his colleagues and members of the bar criticized Chandrachud for being a weak leader.[176]

A good example of what would happen to a chief justice of India if he was too rigid and did not accept the government's choice of candidates could be seen with Chief Justice P.N. Bhagwati.[177] He did not agree to the appointment of Prakash Narain, chief justice of the Delhi High Court, and threatened to resign if that appointment were made by the government. However, thereafter, many of Bhagwati's own recommendations for judicial appointments were completely ignored by the government. For instance, Bhagwati recommended Chief Justice P.D. Desai of the Himachal Pradesh High Court, Chief Justice Surjit Singh Sandhawalia of the Patna High Court and Chief Justice K.M. Lahiri of the Gauhati High Court for appointment to the Supreme Court, but nothing came of it.

Similarly, Chief Justice R.S. Pathak found that some of his recommendations for appointment to the Supreme Court, like Chief Justice T.P.S. Chawla of the Delhi High Court, were rejected by the government, often without reason.[178]

What had happened in the post-1971 period,[179] therefore, was that the essential process of appointing judges to the Supreme Court had not changed. The chief justice of India still signed off on all appointments made to the court. In Nehru's time, though Kania was not happy about the appointment of Basheer Ahmed Sayeed to the Madras High Court, he had gone along with the government's wishes. Now, though Chief Justice Chandrachud did not want judges like Baharul Islam and Thakkar at his court, he formally approved their appointments nonetheless. Where chief justices harboured strong feelings against a candidate, they exercised a veto—as Sikri did with Nagendra Singh and as Chandrachud did with the judge accused of sexual assault. Further, appointments were still being made on what the Law Commission had called 'extraneous' matters in 1958—considerations of region, religion and community. However, two things had changed after 1971. Firstly, the extent of interference in Supreme Court appointments by the executive was far more than it had been in the 1950s. In the early years, it was mostly confined to state government interference in high court appointments, but not Union government interference in Supreme Court appointments, at least not on the same scale as in the 1970s and thereafter. Secondly, during Chief Justice Sikri's tenure and later, appointments were being made, for the first time, on the basis of the ideology of the judge and not merely for reasons of political patronage or for doling out political favours. The government in the 1970s, as we shall see in the next chapter, was actively looking for 'committed' judges, which was not so earlier on.

Supersessions

After 1971, the government also followed a sustained policy of intimidating the judiciary and undermining judicial independence, using primarily three weapons in its armoury: supersessions, transfers and non-confirmations of additional judges and acting chief justices. The supersessions began when A.N. Ray was appointed chief justice of India. Since 1951, the convention was that the post of chief justice of India would go to the most senior Supreme Court judge, as we will see in the next chapter.[180] When Sikri retired from the Supreme Court in April 1973, he was supposed to be replaced with Justice J.M. Shelat, the most senior Supreme Court judge at the court at the time. Thereafter, the post was supposed to go to Hegde and A.N. Grover successively, the senior judges next in line. However, when Sikri retired, the chief justiceship went to Justice Ray, a judge who had consistently voted in favour of the government, though he was not in line to become the chief justice of India under the seniority norm. Ray was junior to Shelat, Hegde and Grover, having been appointed to the Supreme Court after them. The three judges were, in essence, penalized for having decided important cases like the *Basic Structure* case against the government. Of course, there had been an instance of supersession before this, as we have seen, when Imam was superseded by Gajendragadkar. However, in that case, Imam had been superseded not for political reasons but because he was medically unable to discharge the office of the chief justice of India. With Ray, it was the first time that a supersession had been carried out on politically vindictive grounds. After Ray retired, the chief justiceship was supposed to have gone to the next most senior judge at the court at the time, Justice Khanna. However, Khanna was superseded as well, because he had decided cases like the *Habeas Corpus* case and *Basic Structure* case against the government. A judge junior to Khanna, M. Hameedullah Beg, was appointed to the chief justiceship. When the Janata government came to power after the Emergency, though there was some talk about Chandrachud (the next most senior judge) being superseded, no supersession was carried out, and the chief justiceship of the Supreme Court has devolved according to seniority ever since.

Transfers

While the Constitution was being drafted, Orissa Governor K.N. Katju made a recommendation to the Constituent Assembly that 'a convention should be established whereby a proportion of judges in every high court could be recruited from outside the Province'.[181] In the 1950s, state boundaries in India were redrawn along linguistic lines. In 1953, the first linguistic state, Andhra, was created, followed by a large-scale reorganization of states in 1956. The States Reorganization Commission, in its report published in 1955, made recommendations for the re-division of state boundaries along linguistic lines. However, in order to arrest what it called 'parochial trends', the commission recommended that 'at least one-third of the number of Judges in a high court should consist of persons who are recruited from outside that State'.[182] The clear objective of this recommendation was to promote national and cultural integration in India.

The Law Commission in its 14th report did not devote much space to the transfer of judges.[183] However, it suggested that lawyers could be appointed to a high court from outside the state and that an all-India judicial service could be created so that some judges at the high courts were recruited from outside the states.[184] The Law Commission also recommended that when the most senior puisne judge of a high court was not qualified to become the court's chief justice, then the chief justice of the high court could come from outside the state.[185] However, the Law Commission did not endorse the view of the States Reorganization Commission that a third of the judges of a high court had to come from outside the state. It also did not favour a policy that all the chief justices of the high courts were to be appointed from outside the state. However, in a classified document, the Law Commission recommended that transfers of judges must take place only with the concurrence of the chief justice of India.[186]

Between 1950 and 1971, there were, broadly speaking, two kinds of transfers which took place: routine transfers and punitive transfers.

Routine transfers were those which were not necessitated by some problem with the transferred judge. For example, S.R. Das, a judge of the Calcutta High Court, was transferred as chief justice to the East Punjab High Court in January 1949 not because there was anything wrong with Das, but because East Punjab needed a stellar chief justice who would bring with him the traditions of an established court like the Calcutta High Court. Routine transfers typically took place when a puisne judge was transferred from one high court to the post of chief justice of another high court. This happened with numerous judges apart from Das: for instance, Wanchoo was transferred as a puisne judge from Allahabad to the chief justiceship of the Rajasthan High Court in January 1951, while B.P. Sinha was transferred as a puisne judge of the Patna High Court and made the chief justice of the Nagpur High Court in February 1951.

On the other hand, punitive transfers had to be made because of some fault or deficiency in the judge who was being transferred. For instance, as chief justice of India between 1964 and 1966, Gajendragadkar heard complaints that the chief justice of the Hyderabad High Court, P. Chandra Reddy, was not functioning in an independent manner. The allegations against him were that he was favouring members of the Reddy caste in judicial appointments and had close relations with the chief minister and executive government.[187] Gajendragadkar made inquiries and found that the complaints were valid. He then had Reddy transferred to the Madras High Court as its chief justice. Reddy put up a fight, but he was eventually transferred according to Gajendragadkar's wishes.[188] Similarly, Gajendragadkar learnt that the number-two judge in the Patna High Court was quite unpopular with his colleagues, and that groups and cliques were forming in that court. He had the man transferred as the chief justice of the Orissa High Court. Once again, there was some opposition to the move initially— Gajendragadkar had to convince Vice President Zakir Husain that the transfer was justified, which he succeeded in doing.[189]

Of course, punitive transfers of this sort were not meant to be used in every instance where a judge was found to be unsatisfactory, but only in cases where a transfer would help solve the problem.[190] For instance, in the colonial period, when a judge in Madras referred to Privy Councillor Lawrence Jenkins as a 'scoundrel' in open court, he was not transferred to another court, but forced to resign.[191] Similarly, when Prime Minister Nehru learnt that there were some serious allegations against Justice P.B. Mukharji of the Calcutta High Court, he told Home Minister Pant that 'the least [that] can be done in this matter is to call upon this judge to resign', and that '[i]t would be wholly inadequate to transfer him'.[192] Even when Gajendragadkar learnt that the Madras High Court chief justice may have been dishonest about his age and had already passed the age of retirement, he was persuaded to resign, instead of being transferred.[193]

However, it seems that the government did not, in the period between 1950 and 1971, extensively follow a policy of routine transfers of puisne judges. In the early 1960s, Home Minister Gulzari Lal Nanda wanted to transfer four puisne judges:

Harbans Singh (Punjab), S. Murtaza Fazal Ali (Kashmir), M. Hameedullah Beg (Allahabad), and G.C. Mathur (Allahabad). It is not clear why Nanda wanted to transfer these judges, though two of them, Beg and Fazal Ali, eventually became Supreme Court judges. However, Gajendragadkar believed that these transfers would interfere with the independence of the judiciary and opposed them,[194] and it appears that they did not go through.

Relying on a speech made by Law Minister Asoke Sen in 1963 in Parliament, Austin wrote that about twenty-five transfers took place prior to 1974, and all the judges who were transferred had consented to their transfers.[195] However, one wonders whether this is accurate. After all, Gajendragadkar's autobiography suggests that the Hyderabad High Court's chief justice, Chandra Reddy, had not consented to his transfer. On the other hand, it is possible that Reddy's consent was eventually obtained for the transfer on an understanding that he would serve as acting Governor of Madras.[196] Sen told Parliament in 1963 that the rule that a judge's consent was always taken prior to transferring him had evolved into a constitutional convention.[197]

However, in the post-1971 period, transfers of judges started being used by the government as an aggressive tool to intimidate the judiciary and undermine its independence. While the transfers of judges during this time were justified by citing the report of the States Reorganization Commission, the clear intent of the government was to harass and intimidate the judiciary into submission. After the Emergency was declared in June 1975, sixteen high court judges (some of whom were chief justices) were arbitrarily transferred by the government without their consent. A list of fifty-six judges who had either been transferred or whose names were being considered for a transfer was prepared and leaked to the press in order to intimidate the judiciary.[198] Unlike transfers which had taken place between 1950 and 1971, these were not routine transfers, nor were they punitive in the sense in which punitive transfers had taken place during those years (e.g., to penalize judges suspected of misconduct). Now, what the transferred judges were being penalized for was not any misconduct on their part, but their independence of judgment and courage to decide cases against the government. For instance, one of the sixteen transferred judges was Justice A.P. Sen, later a Supreme Court judge, who had delivered the judgment of the Madhya Pradesh High Court against the government, which came up in appeal before the Supreme Court and became the *Habeas Corpus* case.[199] The Supreme Court later held that the transferred judges' consent was not required.[200]

When the Janata Party government came to power after the Emergency, the Law Commission in its 80th report (prepared under Justice Khanna) suggested that the recommendations of the States Reorganization Commission ought to be implemented and a third of the judges of the high courts ought to be appointed from outside the state. This policy, thought the Law Commission, would have several benefits: it would promote national integration and ensure that judges were not excessively swayed by local influences. However, the Law Commission recommended that this policy should be implemented at the stage of making appointments, not through transfers.[201] The commission was generally against transferring judges, except in cases where it was absolutely necessary (i.e. punitive transfers), where impeachment was too harsh a remedy.[202] Further, it did not endorse the policy of appointing chief justices of high courts from outside the state. Instead, it opined that the chief justiceship of a high court must devolve according to seniority, and only in cases where the most senior judge of a high court was unfit for appointment as the court's chief justice was the chief justice to be brought from outside the state.[203]

During the Janata regime, many of the transferred judges opted to go back to their own states. However, when the Indira Gandhi government came back to power in 1980, it started transferring judges once again. In January 1981, Chief Justice M.M. Ismail of the Madras High Court (who, ironically, had turned down an offer of elevation to the Supreme Court in favour of the Madras High Court chief justiceship[204]) was transferred to the Kerala High Court (he resigned his office), while Chief Justice K.B.N. Singh of the Patna High Court was transferred to Madras. In March 1981, the law minister issued a circular addressed to state chief ministers and chief justices of high courts, asking them to take the consent of newly appointed judges to being transferred out of the state.[205] These controversies gave rise to the *First Judges* case,[206] where the Supreme Court once again held, among other things, that a judge could be transferred without his consent.[207]

In January 1983, the government announced its transfer of chief justices policy, according to which the chief justice of a high court was to be appointed from outside the state. It was only if a judge had less than a year to retire that he could be made the chief justice of his own high court.[208] Around the same time, the government instituted the transfer of judges policy, implementing the States Reorganization Commission report, whereby a third of the judges of a high court were to come from outside the state.[209] Today, the transfer of judges policy (i.e. the policy that a third of the judges of high courts must be appointed from outside the state) is no longer in force, but the transfer of chief justices policy (i.e. the policy that a judge cannot be appointed the chief justice of his own high court) is still in place.[210]

The transfer of judges policy was particularly unpopular in the judiciary and several judges spoke against it.[211] Justice P.K. Goswami told Gadbois that it had been put in place because Prime Minister Gandhi did not like independent judges.[212] Justice V.D. Tulzapurkar said that its intent was to keep high court chief justices and puisne judges on tenterhooks.[213] Even in 1995, noted advocate and constitutional law scholar, H.M. Seervai wrote a letter to the chief justice of India and said that the transfer of judges policy would have the effect of reducing 'great High Courts like the High Courts of Bombay, Calcutta and Madras . . . to the level of District Courts'. 'In my opinion,' he wrote, 'no self-respecting Advocate would accept a high court Judgeship for the simple reason that he can be transferred against his will to another high court.'[214]

There was generally less opposition to the policy of transferring chief justices. Some judges spoke in favour of it, saying it ensured that high courts were administered professionally without regard to local influences.[215] Justice K.J. Shetty, a puisne judge from the Karnataka High Court, was transferred to the Allahabad High Court as its chief justice in October 1986. When news came of his impending elevation to the Supreme Court around May 1987, a large delegation from Allahabad requested the chief justice of India, R.S. Pathak, to keep Shetty in Allahabad for at least another year, since he was doing good work there, uninfluenced by local dynamics.[216]

Confirming Temporary Judges

Apart from supersessions and transfers, in the post-1971 period, the government did not confirm the appointments of several additional judges who had decided cases against it,[217] and it did not regularize chief justices of high courts appointed on a temporary 'acting' basis for long periods of time in order to bully chief justices into cooperating with the government.[218]

The Three Changes of the Collegium System

'Primacy' of the Chief Justice Abandoned

In 1977, Gajendragadkar wrote a note to Prime Minister Morarji Desai which recommended that a new system (which resembled what we would now refer to as the collegium system) be put into place for appointing judges.[219] The collegium system came into force in the 1990s, as a result of a judgment of the Supreme Court, according to which judges are appointed on the basis of binding recommendations made by the chief justice of India and a certain number of his senior colleagues.[220] The collegium system had no real precedent in India, and made three broad changes to the system of appointing judges.

Firstly, it gave an institutionalized role to the senior colleagues of the chief justice of India, who had hitherto only been informally consulted, on occasion, over judicial appointments. Prior to the collegium system, it was not obligatory for the chief justice of India to consult his senior colleagues while recommending names for judicial appointments. We shall see below that chief justices like Hidayatullah, Ray and Chandrachud did not consult their senior colleagues while recommending names. This changed under the collegium system, after which the chief justice of India can no longer ignore the views of his senior colleagues while making appointments. In other words, the 'primacy' of the chief justice of India over his colleagues ended with the collegium system.

Prior to the collegium model of appointing judges, some chief justices of India would consult their senior colleagues (or colleagues who came from the same region as the judge who was being considered for elevation) before making judicial appointments, but this was an informal, not an institutionalized, practice. Its prevalence varied from one chief justice to the other.

Some of the early chief justices of India might have consulted their senior colleagues before recommending appointments. Justice S.K. Das, for example, who served at the Supreme Court as a puisne judge between 1956 and 1963, said that the chief justice of India, in his time, would consult senior judges prior to recommending names to the government for appointment.[221] Similarly, Justice Wanchoo,[222] who served between 1958 and 1968, said that in his time, the chief justice of India always consulted senior judges of the Supreme Court as well as judges of the Supreme Court from the region where the judge was being considered if the chief justice did not belong to that region. For example, if the chief justice of India hailed from a north Indian state, but a judge from a south Indian state was being considered for elevation to the Supreme Court, then the chief justice of India would consult his Supreme Court colleagues from the south. Wanchoo himself consulted Justice Hidayatullah (the most senior judge in the Supreme Court after Wanchoo) while appointing Justice Grover to the Supreme Court.[223] Chief Justice B.P. Sinha, who served as such between 1959 and 1964, said that while making his recommendations to the government for appointing judges, he collected the views of some of his colleagues and kept them informed. He would say to them, 'The Supreme Court is as much yours as [it is] mine.'[224] Sarkar, who served as chief justice for a few months in 1966, said that he consulted a few of his colleagues (including Subba Rao), but since the court was on vacation during his term as chief justice, there were not many people around.[225]

However, the one chief justice of India who definitely broke from this tradition was Hidayatullah. When Hidayatullah recommended the names of A.N. Ray, P. Jaganmohan Reddy[226] and I.D. Dua (these judges were appointed to the Supreme Court in August 1969), he did not consult his senior colleagues. Though Hidayatullah said that he had consulted most of his colleagues on these names (he even claimed to have been the first Supreme Court chief justice to have consulted his junior colleagues at the court on Supreme Court appointments),[227] his successor J.C. Shah said that he had not been consulted on these appointments or others made by Hidayatullah.[228] Shah said that not all chief justices consulted their colleagues—it all depended on the 'personal equation' of the chief justice with his colleagues. Justice Hegde (who was not, however, one of the most senior judges at the court in Hidayatullah's time) said that the Hidayatullah appointments of August 1969 took him and others by surprise.[229] Chief Justice Sikri said that it was his practice to consult his two most senior colleagues at the Supreme Court, and also colleagues who hailed from the same high court as the judge being considered for elevation.[230]

The practice of the chief justice of India consulting senior judges on Supreme Court appointments started disintegrating thereafter. Chief Justice A.N. Ray consulted his colleagues only infrequently.[231] Justice Chandrachud said that while he started off his tenure as chief justice by consulting his colleagues (he would initially consult four or five colleagues[232]), he stopped discussing judicial appointments with his colleagues once Bhagwati betrayed him on the M.N. Chandurkar nomination.[233] His rival, Justice Bhagwati, was quite miffed about this and said that Chandrachud had shown him a list of a few names[234] at the last minute before they were appointed in March 1983, and that he did not really seek Bhagwati's concurrence. Having served as second in line to Chief Justice Chandrachud for several years, Bhagwati was a strong advocate in favour of setting up a collegium system of judicial appointments.[235]

Chief Justice Pathak said that he consulted his colleagues, but did not seek their concurrence. '[T]he list,' he said, 'is ultimately mine,' adding, 'It is the responsibility of the [chief justice of India] to be the final determiner of the list.'[236]

Outsiders too were sometimes consulted by chief justices of India. For instance, Chief Justice Sinha consulted President Prasad, his benefactor and well-wisher.[237] Some chief justices of India would consult Attorney General Setalvad[238] (Hidayatullah said that Setalvad was upset that he was not consulted by Hidayatullah while making judicial appointments[239]). Chief Justice Sikri on occasion consulted the advocate general of a state.[240]

The Law Commission in its 80th report (which, we have seen, was prepared by Justice Khanna and submitted in 1979) recommended that a high court chief justice should consult his two most senior colleagues prior to recommending names to the government for judicial appointments to the high court. However, the chief justice's colleagues were not to have the ability to suggest their own names—they were only to comment on the suitability of the candidates proposed by the chief justice.[241] Likewise, for Supreme Court appointments, the Law Commission recommended that the chief justice of India must consult his three most senior colleagues before recommending names for appointment.[242] It was suggested that the names recommended by the chief justice and his senior colleagues in this manner should ordinarily be accepted.[243] However, the Law Commission did not mandate that the recommendations had to be made unanimously by the chief justice and his senior colleagues. It also did not say that the view of the chief justice and senior colleagues was necessarily binding on the government, though it was entitled to great weight.

In short, the collegium system essentially institutionalized the informal practice, which appeared to have been in vogue until Chief Justice Hidayatullah's time, of the chief justice of India consulting his most senior colleagues prior to making judicial appointments. However, never before, prior to the collegium system, were the opinions of senior colleagues binding on the chief justice of India. In other words, the collegium system did away with the 'preponderating voice'[244], the 'primacy', of the chief justice of India in judicial appointments.

From Fiction to Reality

Secondly, the collegium system made the recommendations of the chief justice of India and his senior colleagues binding on the executive government. No longer could a post-collegium minister prevail upon the chief justice, as Vallabhbhai Patel had over Kania in the matter of appointing Basheer Ahmed Sayeed to the Madras High Court or as Shiv Shankar had in forcing Chandrachud to appoint Baharul Islam to the Supreme Court. Earlier, a fiction was maintained that all appointments were made with the notional 'concurrence' of the chief justice of India, even when the chief justice had been essentially forced into a compromise. However, the collegium system converted that fiction into reality.

Other Forms of Intimidation

Thirdly, under the collegium system, the other methods which were used by the government to intimidate judges after 1971 are no longer in vogue. We have seen that there were many tools which the government used in order to tamper with the independence of high court judges: supersessions, transfers and the non-confirmation of additional judges and acting chief justices. We have also seen that the government used supersessions to curb the independence of Supreme Court judges. These tools ceased to be of any consequence after the collegium system came into place. However, there is one more weapon in the government's armoury which impacts the independence of the judiciary, and which has not been affected by the collegium system. It is post-retirement employment with the government. After retirement, some judges in India are offered positions by the government, and the collegium does not control the allocation of these positions.

Unlike federal judges in the US, judges in India do not have life tenure, i.e., they do not hold their offices for life. They continue in office until they reach the retirement age, which is sixty-five at the Supreme Court[245] and sixty-two at the high courts.[246] These judges do not hold their offices during the 'pleasure' of the President, but during good behaviour. In other words, they cannot be arbitrarily removed by the government once they are appointed, and can only be impeached by a supermajority[247] of both Houses of Parliament 'on the ground of proved misbehaviour or incapacity'.[248] The impeachment process is very difficult and never in the history of independent India has a judge been successfully impeached to date, though attempts have sometimes been made to do so.[249] Judges therefore enjoy security of tenure while holding office, which is essential for the maintenance of judicial independence.

However, the retirement of judges threatens to undermine judicial independence. This is because some judges, but not all, are offered post-retirement employment by the government, and it has often been feared that judges close to retirement

might decide cases so as to please the government in order to
get a favourable post-retirement position.

The Constitution provides that a retired Supreme
Court judge cannot 'plead or act in any court or before
any authority within the territory of India'.[250] Initially, the
Constitution imposed the same restriction on retired high
court judges as well. However, after 1956,[251] a retired high
court judge was allowed to practise in the Supreme Court
and in any high court in which that judge did not serve as
a permanent judge.[252] The rule for retired high court judges
was relaxed because it was considered to be '[a]n important
factor affecting the selection of high court judges from the
bar'.[253] Additional judges who are not made permanent
(including those who resign before being made permanent)
can practise in the same high court.

In the Constituent Assembly, K.T. Shah, an economist
and advocate,[254] suggested that high court and Supreme
Court judges should not take up an executive office with the
government, 'so that no temptation should be available to a
judge for greater emoluments, or greater prestige which would
in any way affect his independence as a judge'.[255] However, this
suggestion was rejected by Ambedkar because he felt that the
'judiciary decides cases in which the Government has, if at all,
the remotest interest, in fact no interest at all'. In Ambedkar's
time, the judiciary was engaged in deciding private disputes
and rarely did cases arise between citizens and the government.
'Consequently,' said Ambedkar, 'the chances of influencing
the conduct of a member of the judiciary by the Government
are very remote.'[256] This reasoning no longer holds true today
because the government is one of the largest litigants in courts.
Ambedkar also said that the services of retired judges would be
required in commissions of inquiry.

On retiring at the age of sixty-five from the Supreme Court in September 1951, Justice Fazl Ali's term was extended under the provision of the Constitution which allows the chief justice of India to get retired Supreme Court judges to serve at the court.[257] While he was serving this extended term of office, an announcement was made that Fazl Ali would be appointed as the Governor of Orissa.[258] This raised 'a question of constitutional propriety' relating to the independence of the judiciary.[259] After all, though the decision of the government in Fazl Ali's case might have been well intentioned, could the government not use such tactics in the future to reward judges who had decided cases in its favour?

In its 14th report in 1958, the Law Commission noted that retired Supreme Court judges used to engage in two kinds of work after retirement: firstly, 'chamber practice' (i.e. a term which would, today, mean giving opinions to clients and serving as arbitrators in private disputes) and secondly, 'employment in important positions under the Government'.[260] The Law Commission said that chamber practice was undesirable, but did not recommend that it be banned altogether. However, it did recommend banning post-retirement government employment for Supreme Court judges.[261] On chamber practice, the Law Commission opined that this was inconsistent with the dignity of a retired Supreme Court judge and inconsonant with the high traditions which retired judges observe in other countries.[262] Perhaps this was a little unfair because pensions paid to retired Supreme Court judges in India are not consistent with their dignity or consonant with what is paid in other countries, and retired Supreme Court judges cannot be expected to live on those pensions alone (though the Law Commission also recommended that pensions be raised[263]). The Law Commission called for banning post-retirement employment for Supreme

Court judges with the government since the government was a large litigant in the Supreme Court.[264]

The Law Commission made similar recommendations for high court judges. It said that chamber work was undesirable, but did not recommend banning it outright. However, it called for reintroducing the pre-1956 ban against high court judges practising in the Supreme Court or other high courts, and instituting a ban against retired high court judges getting employed by the government.[265] A 'leading counsel in Bombay' deposed before the commission and said that there were 'big clients' appearing before judges, who were, after the 1956 amendment, being seen as 'future clients' by judges, and large fees to the tune of Rs 10,000–Rs 20,000 were being charged by retired high court judges from these clients.[266] The Law Commission thought that allowing retired high court judges to engage in chamber practice would lead to a perception that sitting judges would not be impartial towards rich litigants, since they might be seen as potential future clients by those judges. It recommended reintroducing the bar against high court judges practising in the Supreme Court or other high courts, saying that this was beneath the dignity of courts (since retired judges often had to comment or rely on some of their own judgments).

The Law Commission's recommendations were never implemented, and Setalvad was unhappy with judges who took up government positions thereafter. He was highly critical of Chagla, chief justice of the Bombay High Court, for resigning his position in order to become India's ambassador to the US at Prime Minister Nehru's invitation.[267] Thereafter, Supreme Court judge Justice Kapur was due to retire in December 1962, and Setalvad wrote that 'like most of the retiring Judges', Kapur was 'trying to secure some suitable employment'. Kapur was appointed the chairman of the Law Commission while he was still serving as a Supreme Court judge.[268] 'The appointment was most unfortunate,' wrote Setalvad, 'and gravely affected the dignity and independence of the Supreme Court.'[269] Setalvad felt that as chairman of the Law Commission, Kapur would have had to advise the government on making law, and might have had meetings with government officials, which was inconsistent with his position as a Supreme Court judge, since those very laws could be under challenge in cases which came up before him.[270] Setalvad was also critical of Chief Justice Subba Rao who resigned his office in April 1967 to run as an opposition candidate for the position of President of India.[271]

While Chief Justice Hidayatullah was hearing the *Privy Purses* case, his last judgment as chief justice of India, a news story had appeared that he was being considered by the government for the World Court or for the position of Lokpal. Some lawyers and judges suggested to him that he should not hear the *Privy Purses* case since this was being contemplated. However, Hidayatullah made it clear that even if he were offered these positions, he would not accept them.[272]

After he retired as the chief justice of India in March 1966, Gajendragadkar became the chairman of the Law Commission, a position he held for a long time. As chief justice of India, Gajendragadkar had blocked the appointment of Shanti Bhushan as a judge at the high court of Allahabad on the grounds that Bhushan was under forty years of age. Decades later, Bhushan became the law minister of India in the Janata government. Bhushan's autobiography[273] conveys the impression that Gajendragadkar was thereafter extremely worried that he was going to be removed as chairman of the Law Commission by Bhushan. Gajendragadkar sought meetings with Bhushan several times and requested him not to terminate his services (Bhushan assured Gajendragadkar that he would be retained). If this story is true, Gajendragadkar's plight was certainly beneath the dignity of a retired Supreme Court chief justice.

Several judges told Gadbois that post-retirement employment with the government was undermining the independence of the judiciary.[274] Chandrachud said that some judges were looking for post-retirement positions and writing judgments with that in mind.[275] Bhagwati added that most judges hanker after a good retirement job because it enables them to have a rent-free house, car and driver, and allowances, and also gives them some status.[276] Pathak believed that judges with short tenures at the Supreme Court tended to be more pro-government in their approach since they were looking for a suitable position after retirement.[277]

We have seen that in January 1983, Justice Baharul Islam resigned as a Supreme Court judge in order to contest a Lok Sabha seat as a Congress (I) candidate. This was shortly after he had decided a controversial case in favour of the Congress (I) chief minister of Bihar, against whom allegations had been levelled of misuse of office.[278]

The collegium system has not been able to entirely free judges from their dependence on the executive government for post-retirement employment.

6

Criteria for Selecting Judges

So far, we know why lawyers and judges turned down offers to become high court and Supreme Court judges. But at a more fundamental level, what were the criteria employed to decide whom to select for a judgeship in the first place?[1] This chapter examines the qualities which were considered to be crucial for the quintessential judge in the 1980s. We will see that, above everything else, an effort was made to ensure that the Supreme Court was reflective of the diversity of India in terms of region, religion, caste and, to a far lesser extent, gender. Apart from diversity, the ideological leanings of the judge were important. In the 1970s and 1980s, chief justices and governments considered the social and economic philosophy of judges, and even their political leanings, in order to decide whether they were fit for appointment. A person who even remotely identified himself with an opposition party was blackballed—this is what happened to Chief Justice M.N. Chandurkar of the Madras High Court, whose only offence was attending the funeral of and eulogizing an RSS leader. We will also see that chief justices looked at the family background of judicial candidates—a person who came from a well-known family was considered an especially suitable candidate. In this matter, selecting a judge for the high court or Supreme Court, thought Gadbois, was very much like selecting a match for one's son or daughter in an arranged marriage. The personal life of potential judicial candidates was also investigated, often by the government's intelligence agencies. For example, a person was considered unsuitable if he was a 'womanizer' or taken to 'drunkenness'. One wonders whether a candidate's personal life ought to be taken into account in this manner for determining whether he or she is fit for appointment to the Supreme Court if these matters have no impact on the judge's professional performance. Of course, these were not the only criteria for judicial selection. The merit of candidates was looked into. Some chief justices went through judgments of the potential candidate in order to determine his ability. Subject-matter expertise was, at times, an important consideration. Integrity was essential. Interestingly, in the early years, a judge's knowledge of English and American cases was considered an advantage while determining whether he was fit for elevation to the Supreme Court. Many of the criteria for judicial selection discussed in this chapter continue to remain relevant in the present day. Apart from the ideological orientation of judges, which has been abandoned in today's collegium system of judicial appointments, it would be safe to assume that many of these criteria continue to be employed today while determining whether or not to appoint a person as a judge.

'A Zoo with All Species'

Among other criteria, appointments to the Supreme Court are made on the basis of region, religion, caste and gender.[2] An effort is made to ensure that judges from different regions and states in India, and from religious minority communities and backward castes are appointed to the Supreme Court. In countries like the US, diversity in courts is officially considered to be important, but in India it is spoken of in a negative manner.[3] The feeling which is often harboured in India is that diversity comes to the court at the cost of the merit of judicial candidates. Quoting someone else, Justice S.K. Das lamented that the Supreme Court was 'a zoo with all species'.[4] In 1958, the Law Commission (which included among its members Chief Justice M.C. Chagla of the Bombay High Court, who was a Muslim) in its 14th report strongly deprecated this practice of 'communal and regional considerations' which had 'prevailed in making the selection of the Judges', calling them 'extraneous considerations' and attributing them to 'executive influence' in the judicial appointments process.[5]

There has been a steady attempt to ensure that the different regions of India are represented in the Supreme Court.[6] Larger, politically significant states now have 2–3 seats reserved in the Supreme Court, while smaller states get no more than 1–2 seats. Justice A.M. Ahmadi agreed that part of the reason he was appointed to the Supreme Court in December 1988 was that the state of Gujarat, where he had served as a high court judge, required representation at the Supreme Court.[7] Three Gujarat judges, D.A. Desai, P.N. Bhagwati and M.P. Thakkar, had retired from the Supreme Court in May 1985, December 1986 and November 1988 respectively, leaving Gujarat completely unrepresented at the Supreme Court. Likewise, Justice K.N. Saikia agreed that the fact that he was from the North-east 'must have been' a factor in his appointment to the Supreme Court in December 1988.[8]

In the 1950s, Justice Vivian Bose, who came from the Nagpur High Court, found it difficult to build lasting bonds with the Supreme Court's south Indian judges (probably judges like M. Patanjali Sastri, N.C. Aiyar, or T.L.V. Ayyar). He said that they were hard to get to know, and culturally very different from the north and central Indian judges.[9] Bose was not alone. Another judge, Justice Mehr Chand Mahajan, who was from the north, once asked a newly appointed judge from south India (probably either Aiyar or Ayyar) to wear trousers on the bench, not a dhoti as was customary in the south.[10] Likewise, some southern judges felt discriminated against. Justice Chinnappa Reddy said that his transfer from Andhra Pradesh to Chandigarh as a high court judge helped him, because no matter how good a southern judge was, he hardly got noticed in Delhi. Being a Chandigarh judge gave him visibility where it mattered.[11] Justice A.P. Sen felt that Supreme Court judges 'are a bunch of strangers, disparate elements drawn from distant parts of this vast subcontinent'. 'We have nothing in common,' he said, adding, '[we] can't make friends, there is no sense of brotherhood, we come from different states, and we don't have mutual respect for each other.'[12] Perhaps this was why the transfer of judges policy instituted later on was not an entirely misconceived experiment, as it sought to promote national integration. Under the policy in place at present, most Supreme Court judges serve as chief justices of a high court apart from the one in which they served as puisne judges. The Supreme Court judge of today is therefore more culturally integrated with his brethren from the different regions of India than his counterpart was in earlier times.

Some judges also found that there were regional variations in the cases which came to the Supreme Court. A.P. Sen believed that very few SLPs came to the court from places like Calcutta or Kerala, but that almost every case from Bombay ended up as an SLP, and that a large volume of cases came from northern areas like Punjab and Haryana, and Delhi.[13] Likewise, Justice D.P. Madon found that most SLPs came from northern states like Punjab and Haryana, and Rajasthan.[14] These anecdotal vignettes have been confirmed in a relatively recent empirical study conducted by Nick Robinson and others.[15]

Judges from smaller, politically less important states complained that they did not have an equal opportunity to get appointed to the Supreme Court as judges from larger states did. Justice Ranga Nath Misra, who was appointed to the Supreme Court in March 1983 from the Orissa High Court, was the first judge to have been appointed to the court since March 1953 (when Justice B. Jagannadhadas was appointed to the court) from Orissa. When he was asked why it took thirty years for another Orissa judge to come to the Supreme Court, Misra said that the link between Orissa and the Centre was weak, that big states got more recognition while little attention was paid to small states like Orissa. He implied that Orissa was not a politically important state, and that it consequently paid the price when it came to appointments in high places. Misra noted that there were, in April 1983, three judges at the Supreme Court from Bombay (Y.V. Chandrachud, V.D. Tulzapurkar, Madon), three from Gujarat (Bhagwati, Desai and Thakkar), and two from Calcutta (A.N. Sen and Sabyasachi Mukharji), which he saw as evidence of a bias towards big states in the Supreme Court.[16] However, Justice L.M. Sharma believed that even a large and politically significant state like Bihar was not sufficiently represented at the Supreme Court after the early 1960s because other states are politically stronger and have more clout in Delhi, aside from the fact that the standard of the Patna bar and bench had fallen since then.[17]

A Muslim Judge Appointed Out of Turn

There has, of course, been a 'Muslim seat' at the Supreme Court since its inception, i.e., one seat at the court has been reserved for a Muslim judge.[18] As the number of judges at the Supreme Court has risen over the years, the number of seats reserved for Muslims has also gone up.[19] Justice S. Fazl Ali, a Muslim judge, was appointed to the Federal Court in June 1947 and was at the court when the Constitution came into force and the Supreme Court came into being. After his retirement, he was replaced successively by Ghulam Hasan, who was followed by S.J. Imam, both Muslim judges. In the 1950s, Nehru even tried to get Chagla, the Muslim chief justice of the Bombay High Court, appointed chief justice of the Supreme Court, because he wanted a Muslim chief justice of India.[20] In the 1960s, when the time came for P.B. Gajendragadkar to supersede Imam, a Muslim, because Imam was suffering from a mental infirmity, Nehru allegedly expressed concern about what Pakistan would think if a Muslim judge were superseded.[21]

Justice M. Hidayatullah was the one exception to the 'Muslim seat' phenomenon—he insisted that he wanted to be appointed to the Supreme Court on his own merit, not on the Muslim seat,[22] and he was accordingly appointed to the Supreme Court in December 1958, when Imam was still at the court. Initially, the chief justice of India, S.R. Das, asked Hidayatullah whether he would be interested in taking Justice K.C. Das Gupta's place as chief justice of the Calcutta High Court. Das planned to elevate Das Gupta to the Supreme Court first, and said that Hidayatullah would get his chance to move to the Supreme Court once Justice Imam retired. 'This meant that I was to get,' wrote Hidayatullah in his autobiography many years later, 'what had till then become a Muslim seat in the Supreme Court.'[23] Hidayatullah rejected Das's offer. Yet, he was appointed before Das Gupta to the Supreme Court, when Imam was still at the court. In Hidayatullah's own words, he was, thus, 'a Muslim Judge appointed out of turn'.[24]

There was a feeling that some Muslim judges were being appointed because of their religion and not on their own merit. Gadbois noted that one judge told him that Hasan was appointed to the Supreme Court because he was a Muslim, and that he was not of the calibre of the other Supreme Court judges of his day.[25] Likewise, he noted that another judge, appointed to the court in August 1966, told him that Muslim judges were being appointed to the Supreme Court regardless of their merit, and that Hidayatullah was the only good one.[26]

In December 1971, Justice M. Hameedullah Beg was appointed to the court because he was the most senior Muslim judge in the country,[27] and the court had to have a Muslim judge after Hidayatullah retired in December 1970.[28] This was despite the fact that Beg was junior to R.S. Pathak[29] as a puisne judge of the Allahabad High Court. Pathak and Beg had been appointed to the Allahabad High Court in October 1962 and June 1963 respectively, though Beg was made chief justice of Himachal Pradesh before Pathak. Justice Beg himself was very frank about the fact that the court had a Muslim seat, and that the government wanted a Muslim judge at the Supreme Court, which is why he had been appointed.[30] Justice S. Murtaza Fazal Ali was also appointed to the court in April 1975 because he was a Muslim, even though he was not a 'prominent' judge, according to a former member of the court.[31] In December 1988, Justice Ahmadi was appointed to the Supreme Court because he was a Muslim, and the court needed a Muslim judge after the retirement of Justice V. Khalid in 1987.[32] His rival, Justice Kuldip Singh, informed

Gadbois that Ahmadi belonged to a sect of Islam which did not qualify him as a Muslim.[33]

A few Supreme Court judges told Gadbois that there was some religious discrimination among their colleagues at the court. However, this was not the predominant view. Justice Khalid, a Muslim Supreme Court judge who came from the Kerala High Court, and who was appointed to the Supreme Court in June 1984, told Gadbois that he believed that B.P. Sinha was appointed before Imam because Sinha was a Hindu and Imam a Muslim.[34] Justice Khalid also felt that chief justice Pathak was not interested in appointing Ahmadi to the Supreme Court because he was a Muslim,[35] though Justice Sharma, on the other hand, said that Pathak was actively looking for a competent Muslim judge to appoint to the Supreme Court.[36] Sharma believed that there was no competent senior Muslim judge in the high courts at the time, and felt that Pathak would be constrained to appoint a junior Muslim high court judge to the Supreme Court. Ahmadi, whom Pathak eventually appointed, was not the most senior Muslim high court judge in the country—Justice Syed Ali Ahmad of the Patna High Court was.[37] Similarly, Justice Madon felt that Justice Tulzapurkar was critical of Justice Fazal Ali because he was a Muslim.[38] Madon, on the other hand, was impressed by the fact that his non-drinking Muslim colleagues like Khalid and Fazal Ali served alcohol to him and their other imbibing guests.[39]

Justice R.S. Sarkaria's appointment to the Supreme Court in September 1973 had a lot to do with the fact that he was a Sikh. In 1973, both Giani Zail Singh (who was, at the time, the chief minister of Punjab) and G.S. Dhillon (the Speaker of the Lok Sabha[40]) went to Union Law Minister H.R. Gokhale and Prime Minister Indira Gandhi and requested that Sikhs be given a chance at the Supreme Court. Both Gokhale and Indira Gandhi agreed, and Gokhale then made a trip to Chandigarh in search of what Sarkaria called 'a suitable Sikh'. Gokhale had lunch with all the judges of the court, and the first rumour was that a very junior and radical Sikh judge by the name of Dhillon[41] was going to be selected. Thereafter, a dinner was hosted by the chief ministers of Punjab and Haryana in honour of Gokhale, which high court judges attended. Rumours began to abound about who would be appointed to the court. Everyone knew that Gokhale was looking for a Sikh judge. A few days thereafter, Zail Singh (whom Sarkaria called a 'kingmaker') called Sarkaria and arranged a meeting at a neutral venue, possibly a guest house. Zail Singh requested Sarkaria to accept a Supreme Court judgeship. Sarkaria initially declined for personal reasons: he was not ambitious and he liked to go to Patiala on weekends to work on his farm. One of Sarkaria's colleagues at the high court, Justice P.C. Pandit,[42] who was then the number two judge at the court, urged Sarkaria to accept the judgeship. Sarkaria then talked it over with his wife, and she agreed that he ought to accept the offer. He tried to get in touch with Zail Singh who, by then, had gone to Delhi. He had some difficulty locating him, but when he did, Sarkaria told Zail Singh that he had changed his mind. It turned out that Zail Singh was about to meet Prime Minister Gandhi to let her know that Sarkaria had turned down the offer. Gokhale then put Sarkaria in touch with Chief Justice A.N. Ray over the telephone, and the appointment soon went through.[43]

Justice Kuldip Singh believed that he had been appointed to the Supreme Court because he was an excellent advocate and had impressed all of the court's judges during his sixteen-month tenure as additional solicitor general of India. He said that he never hesitated to tell the judges if he had a bad case, and practised at the Supreme Court almost daily. Though he agreed that the court needed a judge from Punjab after the retirement of Justice A.D. Koshal in March 1982, and that his being from Punjab might have been a factor in his appointment to the court, he did not himself bring up the fact that he was a Sikh.[44] However, Chief Justice Pathak, during whose term Singh was appointed to the court, confirmed that his being a Sikh was a major consideration in the appointment.[45]

Religious considerations apply in judicial appointments to the high courts as well. Justice Fazal Ali, who was from Bihar, was appointed a puisne judge of the Jammu and Kashmir High Court in April 1958 because Prime Minister Nehru and the home ministry felt that it was necessary to have an outsider, who had to be a Muslim.[46] In January 1972, Justice Baharul Islam was appointed to the Gauhati High Court by Chief Justice P.K. Goswami because the court needed a Muslim judge, and the only other option was a relatively junior Muslim lawyer.[47] Islam may have been the first Muslim judge at the Gauhati High Court.[48] Justice Balakrishna Eradi, chief justice of the Kerala High Court between 1980 and 1981, said that while there were no anti-Brahmin sentiments which affected judicial appointments at that court, there was a great deal of clamour for community representation along religious lines.[49]

A Human Being and an Indian

Likewise, caste considerations have had a role to play in judicial appointments. In June 1983, Justice Rajagopala Ayyangar told Gadbois that the backward community got all the advantages, that there were only a handful of Brahmins at the Madras High Court at that time.[50] Likewise, T.V. Balakrishnan, son of the 1950s' supreme court judge T.L.V. Ayyar, said that since 1960, appointments to the Madras High Court were made on the basis of community and caste, that members of the forward community were discriminated against at that court and appointed late, and that there were just two Brahmins at the high court by June 1983.[51] Balakrishnan said that the Madras High Court had not been appropriately represented at the Supreme Court because appointments to that court were made on communal considerations, not merit, and that consequently there were few competent judges at the Madras High Court.

Appointed in September 1956, Justice P. Govinda Menon was the first non-Brahmin judge from south India to be appointed to the Supreme Court.[52] He was previously a judge of the Madras High Court. Menon's son said that there was an exclusiveness to south Indian Brahmins because they were Brahmins. He said that south Indian Brahmins were very traditional, not cosmopolitan.[53] Justice E.S. Venkataramiah said that south Indian Brahmins were generally exiting to the US on account of a lack of opportunity in India.[54] Chief Justice Sinha was accused of appointing judges who belonged to his Rajput caste, but he was able to convince Prime Minister Nehru that those charges were bogus.[55]

Justice A.P. Sen told Gadbois that Brahmins used to dominate the judiciary at Calcutta, Bombay and Madras, but that caste was not a factor in the decision-making of courts.[56] Justice P. Jaganmohan Reddy believed that Brahmin judges were more conservative than others, because the whole Brahmin ethos was conservative.[57] In 1980, Justice Krishna Iyer said that the Supreme Court was mainly Brahmin and upper class (no Scheduled Caste judge had been appointed to the court at that time). He concluded that judges' backgrounds affect their decisions.[58] Justice Madon added that since the time of Chief Justice P.B. Gajendragadkar, Brahmin judges from Bombay were preferred at the Supreme Court. He seemed to be especially

angry with Chief Justice Chandrachud for seeking to appoint
Brahmin judges from Bombay to the Supreme Court. He said
that many high court chief justices made recommendations
for judicial appointments on caste considerations and that
it was not only the government which was doing so.[59] He
suggested that for this reason, the transfer of judges policy of
the government, under which the chief justice of a high court
was appointed from outside the state,[60] was a good one, as it
prevented chief justices from enforcing their own deep-seated
caste prejudices in their own high courts. Another judge felt
that his appointment to the Supreme Court was held up in 1979
because Chandrachud wanted to appoint a Bombay Brahmin,
V.S. Deshpande, to the Supreme Court (though Deshpande was
a Delhi High Court judge and chief justice).[61]

Justice D.A. Desai, himself a Brahmin, found it humorous
that the Karnataka reservations case, *K.C. Vasanth Kumar v.
State of Karnataka*,[62] was decided by a bench of five judges,
none of whom belonged to the backward castes. He joked about
five Brahmins making decisions about Scheduled Castes and
backward castes.[63] Chief Justice Pathak pointed out to Gadbois
that all the five judges who decided the historic case of *Kehar
Singh v. Union of India*,[64] involving the scope of the presidential
power of pardon, arising out of the Indira Gandhi assassination
case, were Brahmins.[65] In fact, Gadbois made a note that 'Some
Brahmin judges [are] very much aware of other Brahmins in
high posts.'[66] In 1988, Justice Khalid criticized the Brahmin-
dominated Supreme Court and suggested that both chief
justices Chandrachud and Pathak preferred Brahmin judges.[67]
Justice Hidayatullah said that his name was proposed for
appointment to the Supreme Court ahead of Justices K. Subba
Rao and K.N. Wanchoo, but that Nehru pushed him down in
favour of Wanchoo, a Kashmiri Brahmin.[68]

Justice A.N. Sen was disillusioned with the involvement of caste criteria in judicial appointments. He believed that if a Scheduled Caste judge was 40 per cent competent, and a Forward Caste judge was 60 per cent competent, then it would be fine to appoint the Scheduled Caste judge. However, if the Scheduled Caste judge was 0 per cent competent, and the Forward Caste judge was 90 per cent competent, then the Scheduled Caste judge ought not to be appointed. Sen was referring to the appointment of Justice B.C. Ray to the Supreme Court in October 1985 during the tenure of Chief Justice Bhagwati. Sen had recommended A.K. Sen (a senior Calcutta High Court judge) for the appointment, but Ray was appointed instead.[69] Interestingly, Gadbois noted that Ray's father was a zamindar, and his family was relatively well off.[70] In fact, Chief Justice Pathak referred to B.C. Ray as being 'very rich'.[71]

Others disagreed. Justice Sabyasachi Mukharji, for instance, said that caste was never taken into account at the Calcutta High Court while making judicial appointments.[72] Justice M.H. Kania said that while caste was not a factor at the Bombay High Court, it may have been taken into account in places like Andhra Pradesh, Uttar Pradesh and elsewhere.[73] In a long, handwritten letter to Gadbois in 1984, Justice Chinnappa Reddy, who belonged to the Reddy caste, whose father was a fifth-generation Roman Catholic and mother a non-Brahmin Hindu, eloquently wrote, 'I refuse to be classified to any religion or any community. I prefer to be a human being and an Indian. I will certainly feel offended if you call me a Hindu or a Christian or a member of any caste.' He also added, 'I must say that I profess and practice no religion, my wife does not and my children do not.' Reddy was quick to point out that whatever the 'origins' of Supreme Court judges were, 'almost all' belonged 'to the socially elite classes', that 'human beings change their attitudes' with the 'acquisition of knowledge, wealth, status and other symbols', and that judges were no exception to this. Reddy also said that inquiring about the religion at birth of a judge was meaningless, because judges could change their religious views over time. He wrote about his friend, Justice Gangadhara Rao of the Andhra Pradesh High Court, who came from 'a devout Brahmin Landlord family', but was 'an atheist and an ardent believer in Socialism and Marxism', and about his friend Justice K.A. Muktadar,[74] 'at one time an agnostic and a believer in the humanism of Bertrand Russell', who had 'now suddenly found faith in Islam, the religion of his forefathers'.

Ironically, Chinnappa Reddy was appointed to the Supreme Court in July 1978 as a replacement for Justice K.K. Mathew, who had retired in January 1976. Mathew was a devout Christian,[75] and Chief Justice Chandrachud, who appointed Reddy, thought that Reddy was a Christian too. It was only later that he realized that Reddy was not really a Christian.[76] Reddy found it particularly amusing that after he retired, he was replaced by Justice T.K. Thommen,[77] a Christian, who was appointed at least in part because he was a Christian,[78] and was meant to represent Reddy's identity on the court.

Justice N.L. Untwalia said that though he was recommended for a judgeship of the Patna High Court in August 1957, his appointment was delayed because a judge who was a Bhumihar Brahmin was preferred in his place.[79] Untwalia was eventually appointed to the Patna High Court in January 1958. On the other hand, Justice Eradi said that his father, a district and sessions judge in Madras, was not appointed to the high court because he was a Brahmin and a wave of anti-Brahmin sentiment stood in his way, that non-Brahmins junior to him were appointed to the high court.[80]

Several law ministers and politicians brought caste considerations into judicial appointments. For instance, Chief Justice Sinha accused Home Minister G.B. Pant of favouring a Brahmin candidate for appointment to the Supreme Court in the 1960s.[81] When Shanti Bhushan became law minister after the Janata government came to power in 1977, several judges complained that he made a large number of high court appointments on the basis of caste, preferring judges from the bania caste.[82] Prime Minister Morarji Desai did not like Bhushan at all and he told Chief Justice Chandrachud this several times.[83] It was Bhushan who, as law minister, essentially set a precedent for making judicial appointments along caste lines.[84] In August 1980, Law Minister Shiv Shankar wrote a letter to high court chief justices requesting that more Scheduled Caste and Scheduled Tribe judges be appointed.[85]

When asked why Justice N.P. Singh was not appointed to the Supreme Court earlier, Chief Justice Pathak informed Gadbois that the law minister, B. Shankaranand,[86] being a Scheduled Caste man himself, wanted judges from the Scheduled Castes to be appointed to the Supreme Court,[87] and Singh was a Bhumihar Brahmin. He was also opposed by Law Minister B. Dubey, who was a Brahmin, but who did not accept Bhumihar Brahmins as real Brahmins.[88] The irony was not lost on Gadbois, who noted that Singh had been 'shot down by Bihar Brahmins who don't like Bhumihars, and by [Shankaranand], who doesn't want any Brahmins'. Pathak was also unable to appoint Justice Chittatosh Mookerjee to the Supreme Court because there were already three Calcutta judges at the Supreme Court and because Mookerjee was a Brahmin.[89] Shankaranand, who held up several appointments on account of his insistence on appointing Scheduled Caste judges,[90] was partly the reason that Justice S.R. Pandian, a backward caste judge, was appointed to the Supreme Court.[91]

However, while Supreme Court judges are proud of their seniority, they are less willing to acknowledge that their appointment might have had something to do with their caste, religion or gender. Justice B.C. Ray, for instance, did not acknowledge that his caste might have had something to do with his appointment,[92] and Justice Kuldip Singh did not mention that his being a Sikh was related to his appointment,[93] though those responsible for these appointments (chief justices Bhagwati and Pathak) said that caste and religion were factors in these appointments.[94]

Women

The first woman to be appointed a high court judge in India was Justice Anna Chandy,[95] who was appointed to the Kerala High Court in February 1959 and served until April 1967.[96] Chief Justice of India S.R. Das had recommended her appointment, and he mentioned this as an 'achievement' at his farewell dinner while retiring from the court in September 1959.[97] However, the first woman to be appointed to the Supreme Court was Justice M. Fathima Beevi, also a former judge of the Kerala High Court, in October 1989. Since then, only a handful of women have served in the Supreme Court (Justices Sujata Manohar, Ruma Pal, Gyan Sudha Misra, Ranjana Desai and R. Banumathi).[98] Chief Justice Leila Seth of the Himachal Pradesh High Court was the first chief justice of any high court in India.[99]

Chief Justice Chandrachud said that Prime Minister Gandhi urged him to appoint a woman to the Supreme Court, but at that time there were no candidates who were senior enough. He met one woman judge from a southern state in India who was very senior, but he did not think that she was competent enough, and had even heard that she used to sleep in court.[100]

Thereafter, Chief Justice Pathak wanted to appoint a woman to the Supreme Court. During his chief justiceship, Justice Beevi had retired as a puisne judge of the Kerala High Court. Pathak thought that the best woman judge in the country was Justice Manohar (he said she came from a good family—her father, K.T. Desai, had been chief justice of the Gujarat High Court), but thought that she was too junior at the time.[101] Manohar was fifty-four years old then, and a puisne judge of the Bombay High Court. After serving as the chief justice of the Bombay and later Kerala High Courts, she was brought to the Supreme Court in November 1994 at the age of sixty. Pathak tried to recommend the name of Leila Seth for elevation to the Supreme Court, but nothing happened.[102] Pathak resigned as chief justice in June 1989 (in order to serve on the International Court of Justice). His successor, Chief Justice Venkataramiah, also told Seth that he wanted her to be appointed to the Supreme Court[103] but, during his tenure, Justice Beevi, a retired judge of the Kerala High Court, was appointed in Seth's place. Seth said that she had been told by '[a] couple of Supreme Court judges' that Beevi had lobbied for the position on the grounds that 'she would be the first Muslim woman in the world to be a judge of a Supreme Court', and that she would also be the only Muslim judge in the court at that time. Beevi, like Kuldip Singh, did not believe that Justice Ahmadi was a Muslim—she said that he was an Ahmadi, whom even Pakistanis did not consider Muslims.[104] Seth was very disappointed when Beevi was appointed to the Supreme Court. As she later wrote in her autobiography:

It showed that lobbying worked. It showed that politics worked. It showed that the misuse of religion worked. Above all, it showed that every decent convention could be broken and that merit was no consideration.[105]

Interestingly, when Seth accepted a judgeship of the Delhi High
Court, Chief Justice T.V.R. Tatachari told her that she should
not be influenced by her husband while deciding matters.[106]
Tatachari later felt awkward sitting with Seth on the bench
when she had been newly appointed as a judge (the practice
was that the new judge sat with the chief justice), because he
was apprehensive about being with a woman in open court and
in closed chambers for discussion.[107]

Ideological Leanings

Prior to the 1970s, a judicial candidate's political ideology was
not much of a concern in the judicial appointments process. In
1958, the Law Commission wrote in its iconic 14th report that
there may sometimes have been political reasons for appointing
a judge to a court,[108] but this had more to do, as we have seen,
with political patronage than ideology. However, things began
to change when, in February 1967, a bench of eleven judges of
the Supreme Court held, by a slender majority of six judges to
five,[109] in *Golak Nath v. State of Punjab*,[110] that Parliament had
no power to amend the Constitution to take away or abridge
the fundamental rights, including the right to property.[111] The
Supreme Court also handed down 'two catalytic defeats' to the
Indira Gandhi government in the *Bank Nationalization* case
and *Privy Purses* case.[112]

Judicial appointments started being overseen by the law
ministry in the government instead of the home ministry, and
ministers in the Indira Gandhi government thereafter started
attempting to pack the court in order to overrule the judgment
of the Supreme Court in Golak Nath.[113] One of those ministers
was S. Mohan Kumaramangalam, cabinet minister for steel
and mines. Kumaramangalam had been the advocate general

of Madras who had appeared in Golak Nath, on the losing side, at the Supreme Court. Kumaramangalam openly advocated the doctrine that the ideology of judges must be considered while determining whether they were fit for appointment to the Supreme Court.[114] He became bold about saying this while justifying the supersession of the three judges, J.M. Shelat, K.S. Hegde and A.N. Grover, after they had decided against the government in the *Basic Structure* case,[115] where the court held that Parliament did not have the power to amend certain 'basic features' of the Constitution. Though Kumaramangalam died in a plane crash in May 1973,[116] Kumaramangalam's legacy, said Justice Pathak in 1983, was that the social philosophy of judges had begun to be considered while appointing them.[117]

Thereafter, while ascertaining whether or not to appoint someone as a judge, the government started looking at whether that person had identified himself, even in the most inconsequential manner, with an opposition party. According to Asoke Sen, who served his second term as law minister between 1984 and 1987, the government during that time would not appoint anyone with known anti-Congress views, though it was not looking for minions who would agree with it on everything.[118] Gadbois himself thought that this was reasonable. Chief Justice Chandrachud said that the government was looking for judicial candidates who would support it in general. The government would look at a judge's judgments and antecedents, and especially at whether he had been close to opposition groups or had attended functions organized by such groups, for example, the RSS.[119] The government then rejected candidates who they thought did not fit their ideology.

This is what happened with Chandurkar,[120] a Bombay judge who was chief justice of the Bombay High Court in early 1984 and thereafter the Madras High Court between 1984 and

1988.[121] Chief Justice Chandrachud recommended him for appointment to the Supreme Court in 1982[122] and 1985, a few months before his own retirement. Justice Bhagwati refused to support this appointment and 'torpedoed' it by going to the prime minister and saying bad things about Chandurkar. This was despite the fact that Bhagwati had told Chandrachud that he would support Chandurkar's appointment.[123] The government informed Chandrachud that Chandurkar had attended the funeral of RSS leader M.S. Golwalkar and had said nice things about Golwalkar in a eulogy. Golwalkar had been a friend of Chandurkar's father. Chandrachud thought it was preposterous that Chandurkar should have been labelled an RSS man for merely attending a funeral. However, Prime Minister Gandhi told Chandrachud, 'my party people think he's not good', and for the first and only time, frankly told him, 'Chandurkar is not likely to be helpful to us' (i.e. to her Congress government).

The government also rejected judges who were too independent-minded. For example, G.P. Singh, chief justice of the Madhya Pradesh High Court, was recommended by Chief Justice Chandrachud for appointment to the Supreme Court. Chandrachud wanted Singh in the Supreme Court 'very badly'.[124] However, the government rejected this appointment. This was because, as chief justice, Singh had refused to recommend names for appointment to the high court which were suggested by a Congress (I) chief minister.[125] Apart from this, his reputation as an independent judge hurt him. Every time Chandrachud tried to suggest Singh's name, the government would say 'please suggest another name', without giving him any reasons for rejecting it. 'The Government could always oppose,' said Chandrachud, 'but never impose.'[126] When Singh retired as chief justice in 1984, G.L. Oza took over as acting chief justice and appointed all the names recommended by the government to the high court. Thereafter, he was made permanent chief justice and then promoted to the Supreme Court.[127]

Justice A.P. Sen believed[128] that Indira Gandhi did not want G.P. Singh in the Supreme Court because he had refused to yield to her wishes in an election petition involving V.C. Shukla, one of Sanjay Gandhi's 'enforcers' during the Emergency[129] and an important political figure in Congress (I). However, this version may not be entirely accurate. Shukla and his electoral rival, P.L. Kaushik, were contesting for a Lok Sabha seat from the Mahasamund parliamentary constituency in Madhya Pradesh. Kaushik objected to Shukla's candidature on the grounds that Shukla had been convicted of an offence by a court in Delhi and sentenced to imprisonment for more than two years, rendering him ineligible to contest elections under the relevant electoral law. Shukla was subsequently acquitted by the Supreme Court. However, Kaushik filed an election petition against Shukla at the Madhya Pradesh High Court, and the petition was allowed. But the judgment of the Madhya Pradesh High Court was rendered by Justice J.S. Verma, not Justice G.P. Singh.[130] The judgment was eventually reversed by the Supreme Court.[131] Justice Sen told Gadbois that Prime Minister Gandhi kept trying to influence Singh's judgment at the Madhya Pradesh High Court, but the case was in fact decided by J.S. Verma, not Singh himself. It is possible, therefore, that Sen's memory was failing him while recounting this story. It is also possible, on the other hand, that what the government was unhappy about was not Singh's judgment in the case, but his assignment of this case to an independent judge like Verma.

Chief Justice Pathak wanted to appoint the chief justice of the Delhi High Court, T.P.S. Chawla, to the Supreme Court.[132] He considered Chawla to be a man of integrity and a scholar.

As chief justice, Chawla had exposed a scandal in the registry at the Delhi High Court. Law Minister Shankar shot down Chawla's candidature. Pathak referred to Shankar as a savvy, clever man, who wanted to do some horse-trading with Pathak on judicial appointments. Of the four law ministers Pathak had to deal with as chief justice of India (Asoke Sen, Shiv Shankar, B. Dubey, and B. Shankaranand), Shankar gave him the most trouble. Shankar asked senior lawyer K. Parasaran and Supreme Court judge A.P. Sen to speak to Chief Justice Pathak about not appointing Chawla. Sen did not want Chawla to be appointed to the Supreme Court because Chawla was his neighbour and had threatened to shoot one of his dogs.[133]

On several occasions, the government simply did not offer any substantive reasons why a candidate had been rejected.[134] This happened to at least three successive chief justices—Chandrachud, Bhagwati and Pathak. During Charan Singh's caretaker government, in late 1979, Chief Justice Chandrachud suggested the name of Justice Yasoda Nandan of the Allahabad High Court for elevation to the Supreme Court. However, the President refused to appoint Nandan since a caretaker government was in power, and elections were soon going to take place. No further development took place on this appointment once the Indira Gandhi government came to power.[135] Thereafter, Chief Justice Bhagwati found it 'absurd' and 'humiliating' that the government said absolutely nothing about his list of three judges (Chief Justice P.D. Desai of the Himachal Pradesh High Court, Chief Justice Surjit Singh Sandhawalia of the Patna High Court and Chief Justice K.M. Lahiri of the Gauhati High Court) whom he wanted to appoint to the Supreme Court.[136] It was as though the government simply ignored Bhagwati's recommendations. Next, Chief Justice Pathak tried to appoint Chief Justice H.N. Seth of the

Punjab and Haryana High Court to the Supreme Court, but his name simply vanished as the government did nothing.[137]

In 1988, Chandrachud believed that the government was desperate to find judges who were going to help it. He told Gadbois that the government was worried about the upcoming elections of 1989 and election petitions, and was trying to pack the court.[138] Similarly, around the same time, when Justice Bhagwati was asked what selection criteria the government used for appointing judges, he said that the government wanted judges who were favourable towards it, especially at the high courts where election petitions were being heard.[139]

Justice Chinnappa Reddy agreed that the government carefully examined a nominee's past in order to see if he was pro- or anti-government. If the Justice Department, Prime Minister's Secretariat or Crime Branch[140] of the police said that the judge belonged, say, to the RSS or to left-wing parties, then his name was dropped. He believed that this was wrong, that since parties like the RSS were not illegal or banned organizations, a person who identified himself with these parties could not be dropped as a judicial candidate for that reason alone. Reddy was disillusioned with the Supreme Court. He said that in one case, he was sitting with a senior Supreme Court judge, who told him that the government would be angry with them if they did not decide the case in its favour. Reddy told the judge that they must not worry about the government's reaction. He said that judges trying to please the government was the 'new ethos' of the Supreme Court, that this was happening especially in big political cases.[141] However, Justice Goswami subscribed to the optimistic view that even if judicial appointments were made on political criteria, most judges became independent once appointed to the court.[142]

It was not only the government which was looking at the ideological leanings of judges. Chief Justice P.N. Bhagwati looked at the social and economic philosophies of judges before deciding whether to appoint them.[143] For example, Bhagwati did not appoint the Bombay High Court Chief Justice Chittatosh Mookerjee (who held that post between 1987 and 1991[144]), grandson of Sir Asutosh Mookerjee (an important colonial-era educationist),[145] because he thought Mookerjee was too conservative, i.e., he did not satisfy Bhagwati's preference for activist judges.[146] Mookerjee was later recommended by Bhagwati's successor, Chief Justice Pathak, but Law Minister Asoke Sen rejected his candidature.[147] Between late July 1979 and January 1980, Charan Singh's caretaker government held power at the Centre,[148] in between the Morarji Desai and Indira Gandhi governments. During this time, Chief Justice Chandrachud went directly to the President of India, N. Sanjiva Reddy, for judicial appointments. When Chandrachud tried to suggest the name of Chief Justice Deshpande of the Delhi High Court for appointment to the Supreme Court, Bhagwati went to President Reddy and killed the nomination.[149] Bhagwati also vetoed the appointment of Prakash Narain, chief justice of the Delhi High Court.[150] Ten days after he became the chief justice of India, the government tried to get Bhagwati to accept Narain's appointment to the Supreme Court, but Bhagwati threatened to resign if the appointment went through,[151] though it is not clear from the interview notes why this was so. Bhagwati had a hand in the appointment of Justice M.M. Dutt to the Supreme Court in March 1986, because he thought Dutt would have progressive views, having been involved in legal aid in West Bengal.[152]

Similarly, Chief Justice Beg[153] wanted the chief justice of the Gujarat High Court, B.J. Diwan, to be appointed to the Supreme Court. However, Justice Bhagwati wanted to appoint Justice D.A. Desai, who was an activist judge, but who was fourth[154] in seniority at the Gujarat High Court. Bhagwati persuaded the government to choose Desai over Diwan.[155] Diwan was popular with the bar, whereas Desai was not (especially because he was not courteous to lawyers).[156] In fact, when Desai was appointed to the Supreme Court in September 1977, superseding Diwan, the bar boycotted the swearing-in ceremony. Members of the bar apologized to Justice Tulzapurkar, who was sworn in on the same day as Desai, and informed him that the boycott of the swearing-in ceremony was targeted at Desai, not Tulzapurkar.[157] The Gujarat Bar protested Desai's elevation, and drew support from the Supreme Court Bar Association.[158] Justice Oza believed that he was selected for the Supreme Court by Chief Justice Bhagwati because their points of view on many issues were similar.[159]

Selecting judges on the basis of their presumed ideological leanings, however, is not always without its risks. As Chief Justice Bhagwati found out, though a judge might seem to have a particular voting preference at the high court, it is not always easy to predict how a judge will vote once he actually gets to the Supreme Court. Bhagwati said he made a 'big mistake'[160] appointing Justice S. Natarajan to the Supreme Court in March 1986. He thought that Natarajan was 'progressive in outlook', but once at the court, Bhagwati said that Natarajan 'didn't fall in line with my philosophy'.[161] Bhagwati was miffed about how Natarajan voted in the case involving Bihar Chief Minister Jagannath Mishra.[162] Mishra fell out of power between 1977 and 1980. During that time, a criminal case was filed against him, alleging that he had misused his office in order to prevent the promoters of the Patna Urban Cooperative Bank from being criminally prosecuted for engaging in some financial misdealing. It was said that the bank had given out large sums of money as loans without proper documentation (e.g., loan application forms) and that Mishra had sought to protect the bank's officers from being prosecuted. Once

Mishra became the chief minister of the state again in 1980, his government withdrew the case filed against him. A bench of three judges of the Supreme Court, by a majority of 2–1[163] held in favour of Mishra. A review petition was admitted against that judgment,[164] and the case came up before a bench of five judges of the Supreme Court, which included Bhagwati and Natarajan. The court once again voted in favour of Mishra. Chief Justice Bhagwati dissented in this case, and Natarajan voted the other way.[165]

Merit, Integrity and Good Health

The Law Commission in its 14th report had hoped judicial appointments would be made on the basis of '[m]erit and character alone', and that the 'fittest person' would be selected for judicial office.[166] However, while merit is not the sole criterion for judicial appointments, it is certainly not irrelevant. Chief Justice Pathak said that the integrity and ability of a judge were more important than regional and communal representation.[167] At least four chief justices of India—Gajendragadkar, Sikri,[168] Chandrachud[169] and Pathak—would read judgments of the judicial candidate who was being considered for appointment to the Supreme Court, in order to determine whether he was fit for that office. Gajendragadkar, for instance, read several judgments of Justice R.S. Bachawat,[170] and they 'struck [him] as very cogent, lucid and brief in the presentation of his viewpoints'.[171] Similarly, Chief Justice Pathak said that Justice Thommen was scholarly and wrote very good judgments—a factor taken into account while appointing him to the Supreme Court.[172]

Judges were sometimes appointed to the Supreme Court on the basis of subject-matter expertise. If the Supreme Court needed, say, a tax specialist or a labour specialist, then the specialization of a high court judge would be a relevant factor to be considered.[173] For instance, Chief Justice Gajendragadkar appointed Justice Bachawat to the Supreme Court because he 'wanted a judge who had both Original and Appellate experience and who was familiar with company law and other mercantile laws with which the Original Side judges had always to deal'.[174] Chief Justice Sikri threatened to resign if the government forced the appointment of Nagendra Singh through to the Supreme Court.[175] Sikri said that he knew Singh, and they were friends, but Singh was an expert strictly in international law, while the Supreme Court needed judges who were knowledgeable in Indian law.[176] Singh was appointed to the World Court in 1973.[177] Sikri, on the other hand, said that D.G. Palekar was appointed because he was a specialist in civil matters, and that the Supreme Court needed someone with that background.[178] Chief Justice Pathak briefly said that a judge's area of expertise was also relevant, that he had a hard time composing a bench to hear the case involving Indira Gandhi's assassination because there were very few judges at the Supreme Court who had much criminal experience.[179] He appointed Justice S. Ranganathan because the Supreme Court needed an income-tax specialist.[180]

The integrity and honesty of a candidate were also essential. Chief Justice Pathak said that these were among his main criteria for selecting judges.[181] Chief Justice Chandrachud vetoed the appointment of the chief justice of the high court of a northern state against whom there was a credible (and apparently, very public and scandalous) allegation of sexual assault.[182] Rumour had it that the judge was having an affair with the wife of an advocate, and that he had also tried to sexually assault her daughter. The daughter fought the man, went the rumour, and the judge came to court the next day with a bandaged face, alleging that he had merely fallen on his face.[183] Chief Justice

Chandrachud also rejected the appointment of one chief justice
of the high court of a western state because there were credible
intelligence bureau reports against him—the judge might have
been involved in corruption.[184]

As chief justice of the Andhra Pradesh High Court in
the late 1960s, Jaganmohan Reddy told the chief minister
of the state that it was the role of the chief justice to initiate
names for judicial appointment to the high court, but that
the chief minister could reject a name on some grounds like
if the candidate was a womanizer, or taken to drunkenness,
corruption, and so on.[185] At some level, one wonders whether
the instrumentalities of the state like intelligence-gathering
bodies ought to be deployed in determining whether a judicial
candidate is having an extramarital affair, or consumes alcohol
excessively. It certainly does seem like an intrusion of that
judge's privacy, and it is questionable whether something which
a judge does in his personal life ought to be anybody's business
if it does not impact his official work. On the other hand, one
might say that a judge who is having an extramarital affair
might be amenable to being blackmailed on that account, and
so it is better to keep him off the Supreme Court. Headed by
Prime Minister Morarji Desai, the Janata government insisted
on making judges sign an undertaking that they would refrain
from consuming alcohol.[186]

Chief Justice Hidayatullah did not appoint a Calcutta
High Court chief justice to the Supreme Court, not merely
because the man was 'canvassing' for the job, but also because
he had cancer.[187] He appointed three judges to the Supreme
Court in 1969 because they were highly educated, two of them
in England.[188] One of these judges, Justice I.D. Dua, who was
a Delhi High Court judge, was appointed by Hidayatullah
because they were virtually neighbours in Delhi; Hidayatullah

knew Dua personally and their sons played together.[189] Chief
Justice Bhagwati did not consider appointing Justice B. Lentin
of the Bombay High Court to the Supreme Court because,
he said, Lentin played to the gallery, liked press coverage,
or spoke to the press too much.[190] When Gadbois spoke to
Pathak in October 1988, Pathak had not yet recommended
Lentin, though he hadn't ruled him out. Pathak said that
the government did not like the fact that Lentin talked to
the press.[191] Justice Leila Seth, in her autobiography, wrote
that Chief Justice Pathak repeatedly recommended Lentin,
whom she called 'a distinguished and independent judge', for
elevation to the Supreme Court.[192]

Many of these criteria probably varied with the individual
preferences of the chief justice of India. Justice Palekar said that
the chief justice of India or appointing authority likes to pick
'someone whom he knows'.[193]

Family Background

The family background of a judicial candidate was important.
If he came from a well-known legal family, then that was a
factor taken into account in his favour.[194] Justice S.K. Das, who
was appointed to the Supreme Court in April 1956 during the
tenure of Chief Justice of India S.R. Das, said that he knew S.R.
Das very well prior to his appointment, that their families had
been very close for a long time (in fact, after they both retired
from the Supreme Court, their families became related through
marriage).[195] President Rajendra Prasad initially hesitated
about appointing Justice J.R. Mudholkar to the Supreme Court
in 1960, but he was convinced when Chief Justice Sinha told
him that Mudholkar's father had been president of the Indian
National Congress one year.[196]

Perhaps Chief Justice Pathak was someone who emphasized family background the most.[197] For instance, Pathak recommended the name of Chittatosh Mookerjee, chief justice of the Bombay High Court, for appointment to the Supreme Court, at least partly because his 'lineage [was] excellent'. Mookerjee was the grandson of educationist Sir Asutosh Mookerjee.[198] However, Pathak looked not merely at the candidate's ancestors but also at his children. For instance, Pathak was impressed with how Justice Pandian had raised his children. Two of his children were in the US which, thought Pathak, indicated that they had received 'good training in the family'. One of those children, thought Pathak, was doing very well.[199]

Justice A. Varadarajan said that if a person's parents were well placed (as they were in the cases of Justice P.N. Bhagwati, whose father had been a Supreme Court judge, and R.S. Pathak, whose father had been the vice president of India), then it was much easier to succeed in India. Varadarajan himself had no such family background.[200] Justice Sarkaria also made the point that several persons had become judges because of their fathers, and that the son of a judge has a big advantage in these matters.[201]

On the other hand, a person's family background could also work to the detriment of a candidate. As chief justice of India between 1959 and 1964, B.P. Sinha blocked the appointment of Kumaramangalam to the Madras High Court because, according to Sinha, he came from a family of communists.[202] Shanti Bhushan's family background worked against him when it came to his appointment to a judgeship at the Allahabad High Court. Both Bhushan and his brother-in-law, Satish Chandra, were recommended for appointment to the high court at the same time. However, Chief Justice Sinha said that it would not look good for two relatives to be appointed simultaneously, and therefore suggested that Bhushan's appointment ought

to be delayed. However, then Gajendragadkar became the
chief justice of India, and Bhushan's appointment never went
through (because Gajendragadkar suggested that Bhushan be
made to wait until he turned forty, and Bhushan withdrew his
consent for being appointed a judge).[203]

Age and Seniority

Prior to the advent of the collegium system, factors like age and
seniority had not taken a firm hold on the judicial appointments
system.[204] However, age and seniority were not irrelevant in the
judicial appointments process prior to the collegium. The Law
Commission in its 14th report noted that unnecessary emphasis
was being placed on matters like age, seniority and judicial
experience.[205] The high court appointments of both Law Minister
Bhushan and Justice A.P. Sen were held up on account of their
age. We have seen that Bhushan had given his consent for being
appointed a judge of the Allahabad High Court. He was not yet
forty at the time, but Chief Justice Gajendragadkar said that
judges could only be appointed to the high court after the age
of forty-five, and that an exception could be made in Bhushan's
case once he turned forty. Bhushan withdrew his consent, and
never became a judge.[206] Justice A.P. Sen's name was first sent up
for a judgeship of the Madhya Pradesh High Court in 1958, when
he was only thirty-five years old. Though his candidature was
supported by the chief justice of India, S.R. Das, it was rejected
by the home ministry on account of his age. It was sent up again
a year later, in 1959, but this time around, Chief Justice Sinha
refused to appoint him because he was under forty. However,
during the chief justiceship of B.P. Sinha, both Justices Bhagwati
and Pathak were appointed to their respective high courts under
the age of forty. Thereafter, Chief Justice Gajendragadkar put in

place a policy that no person could be appointed to a high court under the age of forty-five.[207] Sen was finally appointed to the court in November 1967, at the age of forty-four.[208]

Justice Ahmadi was very critical of elderly, short-term Supreme Court appointments. He said that it takes about a year to settle in at the Supreme Court, and that older judges leave less of a mark on the court. He felt that younger men ought to be appointed to the court.[209] Justice Natarajan believed that the government preferred having older judges at the Supreme Court so that there would be a quicker turnover of judges (the retirement age is sixty-five), giving more judges a chance to serve at the Supreme Court.[210] Even Justice J.C. Shah was unhappy about the fact that 'old men' were being appointed to the Supreme Court, 'who serve just two or three years' at the court, and 'leave no clear impress of their personality'. Shah, who we have seen tried to get Bhagwati appointed to the Supreme Court at a very young age, wanted younger men to be appointed to the Supreme Court.[211]

Seniority is one of the most important criteria for appointing judges to the Supreme Court today, but it was not so prior to the establishment of the 'collegium' system of appointing judges. It was only after certain decisions of the Supreme Court in the 1990s and thereafter,[212] that senior judges of the court set up the collegium system. According to this system, Supreme Court judges are appointed by a collegium of the chief justice of India and the four most senior judges of the court. High court judges, on the other hand, are appointed by a collegium consisting of the chief justice of India and the two most senior judges of the Supreme Court. The collegium system has placed a premium on the seniority of judges much more than it had been before. Under this system, it is now almost always high court chief justices who get appointed as Supreme Court judges.[213]

The collegium system was not in place when Gadbois interviewed the judges in the 1980s. At that time, the procedure for appointing judges was different, as we have seen in the previous chapter. Seniority was not entirely irrelevant in the pre-collegium period. Senior judges were still miffed when they were superseded by junior ones. Seniority, however, played a very important role in the Supreme Court in the pre-collegium period, when it came to the succession to the post of chief justice of India.

When the chief justice of the Supreme Court of India retires from office, his post is offered to the most senior judge in the court at the time of the retirement of the outgoing chief justice. The seniority of a Supreme Court judge is determined by the date of the judge's appointment to the court, and not by age. Thus, for example, let us say that when the chief justice of India retires, the two most senior judges on the court are Justices *A* and *B*. *A* is fifty-nine years old but was appointed to the Supreme Court in April 2017, while *B* is fifty-eight years old but was appointed in January 2017. Though *B* is younger than *A*, he will be appointed as the next chief justice of the Supreme Court because he is senior to *A*, having been appointed to the Supreme Court earlier.

This rule, sometimes referred to as the seniority convention, evolved in 1951.[214] The first chief justice of the Supreme Court of India, Harilal J. Kania, died while holding office in November 1951. A question then arose as to who would replace him as the chief justice. There are three different stories about what happened next.[215]

The most credible story is that when Chief Justice Kania passed away, the post of chief justice of the Supreme Court was first offered to the attorney general of India, Motilal C. Setalvad, by Home Minister K.N. Katju.[216] Setalvad had already surpassed

the retirement age for Supreme Court judges of sixty-five years.
Setalvad apparently suggested to Nehru that Chief Justice Chagla
of the Bombay High Court, who was 'always a great favorite
of the Government',[217] could be appointed.[218] Nehru wanted a
Muslim to hold the post of chief justice of India.[219] However, all
the judges threatened to resign[220] if the chief justiceship were
not given to the most senior judge on the Supreme Court at
the time, Justice Patanjali Sastri. Prime Minister Nehru was not
fond of Sastri, and was not averse to superseding him.[221] Justice
Ranga Nath Misra told Gadbois that Nehru thought Sastri was
a weak judge, and he preferred strong people in high office,
unlike his daughter.[222] Since all the judges had threatened to
resign, the move to bring Chagla to the Supreme Court never
materialized, and Justice Sastri was eventually sworn in as chief
justice of India.[223] In 1958, as chairman of the Law Commission,
Setalvad strongly criticized the seniority convention in the
matter of appointing the chief justice of India, saying that the
chief justice had to be a 'competent administrator' in addition
to having the 'ability and experience' necessary for being a
Supreme Court judge.[224]

After recommending Chagla's name to Nehru, Setalvad left
for England. Apparently, he was so confident that Chagla would
be appointed chief justice that when he returned, he asked his
junior, G.N. Joshi, at the airport, whether Chagla was now well-
settled in Delhi.[225] When Chagla was offered a puisne judgeship
of the Federal Court (the precursor to the Supreme Court) by
Chief Justice Kania, Setalvad had recommended to Chagla that
he should turn it down, and only accept the chief justiceship of
the court.[226]

This incident was mentioned by Chagla in his autobiography,
but not by Setalvad in his. Setalvad had some harsh things to say
about Chagla in his autobiography. He was critical of Chagla for

having resigned the chief justiceship of the Bombay High Court in order to be appointed India's ambassador to the US. Setalvad claimed that Chagla had 'always yearned to be in politics', and that his 'action was characteristic of the self-seeking attitude of many of our leading men'.[227] Perhaps Setalvad had changed his opinion of Chagla by the time he wrote his autobiography (the first edition was published in 1970, nearly two decades after the 1951 incident), and he therefore omitted to mention the fact that he had suggested that Chagla be appointed to the post of chief justice. Incidentally, on reading his autobiography, one gets the sense that Setalvad had strong and somewhat harsh views on many judges.[228] In fact, Gadbois himself advised me not to quote from Setalvad's autobiography in my master's thesis at Stanford Law School because he felt that Setalvad's opinions were far too caustic.

The second story is that when Chief Justice Kania died, the post of chief justice was offered to a judge who was the third most senior judge in the court at the time, Justice B.K. Mukherjea.[229] This rumour had gained a lot of currency and strength over the years. For instance, Chief Justice Hidayatullah believed this to be the correct version. Hidayatullah believed that Mukherjea too had offered to resign, and that he did not want to supersede his colleague.[230] Gadbois had a hard time believing Hidayatullah because Hidayatullah 'didn't get on with Chagla'.[231] Some thought that Mukherjea was Nehru's first choice, while Chagla was second.[232] The nephew and son of Justices Sastri and Mukherjea respectively told Gadbois that this version of events was only a rumour.[233]

The third version was propounded only by Chief Justice B.P. Sinha.[234] Sinha said that Nehru did not want Sastri to be the chief justice of India because Sastri would have had less than four years in office, and Nehru wanted a chief justice

with at least a four-year term. Sinha said that Nehru therefore
wanted to make S.R. Das, first cousin of 'Deshbandhu' C.R.
Das (a leading member of the Congress),[235] who was the fourth
most senior judge in the court at the time, the chief justice
of India, not Chagla or Mukherjea. Sinha said that when this
was proposed, all the judges, except Das, threatened to resign.
Sinha was certain that his version was correct.[236] He appeared
to have been in 'excellent mental health', and his memory
was 'very sharp', at the time that he recounted this story to
Gadbois.[237] However, he was not at the court in 1951 when the
incident occurred. He was appointed to the Supreme Court in
December 1954.

Knowledge of Foreign Law

Interestingly, in the early years, if a judge was familiar with
and knowledgeable about English and American cases, this
was seen as an advantage, something to be taken note of
while deciding whether to appoint him to the Supreme Court
or not. Justice S.K. Das, for instance, who was appointed to
the Supreme Court in April 1956, said that while he was a
Patna High Court judge, judges of the Supreme Court were
impressed with his judgment in the *Bihar Zamindari* case,[238]
in which he had cited English and American authorities. This
was part of the reason, thought S.K. Das, why Chief Justice
S.R. Das appointed him to the Supreme Court.[239] Similarly,
while looking for a lawyer to be directly appointed from the
bar to the Supreme Court in February 1964, Chief Justice
Gajendragadkar thought of Sikri and found him suitable
because he was 'quite familiar with the doctrines and decisions
of American courts as well as the decisions of the House of
Lords and the English courts'.[240]

Canvassing and Lobbies

Even though there is no formal application process for becoming a high court or Supreme Court judge, for decades, there has been some amount of canvassing for appointment to the Supreme Court. The Law Commission considered 'the prevalence of canvassing for judgeships' at the high court to be a 'distressing development', one which had come into being '[w]ithin a few years of Independence'.[241] Chief Justice Gajendragadkar wrote in his autobiography that a high court chief justice once called on him on a Saturday and, over a cup of tea, asked Gajendragadkar to appoint him to the Supreme Court. Gajendragadkar refused to appoint him.[242] When Hidayatullah was serving as the chief justice of the Madhya Pradesh High Court, a conference of high court chief justices was held in Delhi in 1957. While attending the conference, Hidayatullah was staying with Justice Vivian Bose, a retired[243] Supreme Court judge. Hidayatullah asked Bose if he was expected to visit the chief justice of India or whether this would be seen as 'an attempt to canvass for a seat on the Supreme Court'. Bose advised Hidayatullah against meeting the chief justice, since 'every Chief Justice except one or two would call on the Chief Justice of India' to canvass for an appointment.[244] Justice Bhagwati believed that high court judges in the post-1971 period would walk the halls of Shastri Bhavan, the building in New Delhi where the ministry of law is located, seeking to meet the law minister.[245] Others agreed that there was a lot of canvassing for judgeships.[246] Canvassing continues under the collegium system as well.[247]

Over the years, Supreme Court judges were conflicted over whether to accept invitations for dinners and parties from lawyers or outsiders. In February 1949, Governor General C. Rajagopalachari was invited to a private party which was being thrown for Justice M.C. Mahajan of the Federal Court, at the Roshanara Club in Delhi. Rajaji was quite unhappy about this, and he wrote to Home Minister Vallabhbhai Patel, saying 'I don't much like this growing practice of public parties organised by private gentlemen to honour officials, judges etc.'[248] Patel spoke with Chief Justice Kania about this, and conveyed his views to Mahajan as well. He then wrote back to Rajaji and said, '[i]t is possible that the engagement may be cancelled'.[249] However, when Mahajan retired from the Supreme Court in 1954, he said that he was thrown 'the usual garden party by the Bar and the Staff'.[250]

Setalvad, who had harsh things to say for just about anyone, was critical of Chief Justice Gajendragadkar for 'accept[ing] at about the time of his retirement entertainments from private lawyers' when he retired in March 1966, which Setalvad thought was 'contrary to the usual decorum observed by retiring Judges'.[251] However, many judges, especially from Bombay, found this practice of attending parties thrown by lawyers to be quite odd. Gajendragadkar himself said that he did no such thing. As a Supreme Court judge, he had found it amazing that retiring judges were given dinners by lawyers. He said that this practice contrasted against his 'Bombay background' (though the editor of Gajendragadkar's autobiography, his son-in-law and judge of the Bombay High Court, R.A. Jahagirdar,[252] said that the 'Bombay background' had 'considerably changed' by the time Gajendragadkar's autobiography was published in 1983).[253] Similarly, when Justice Palekar (later a Supreme Court judge) was appointed to the Bombay High Court in October 1961, he cloistered himself—he did not visit his friends and they did not visit him.[254] However, this was not a practice restricted to Bombay alone. When Leila Seth retired as chief justice of the Himachal Pradesh High Court in 1992, the chief minister of the state wanted to host a farewell dinner in her honour. Seth herself felt that there was nothing wrong in attending the dinner, but her colleagues told her not to accept, so it was cancelled at the last minute.[255]

Some judges believed that a few such bar entertainments given to judges were a part of the canvassing process for getting judgeships. During his tenure on the court, Gajendragadkar had refused a lawyer's invitation for a dinner party. However, he later found that that lawyer had been appointed a high court judge, and hinted that his canvassing had worked.[256] When Hidayatullah was in Delhi for the conference of chief justices in 1957, he was advised by Justice Bose, to 'refuse private invitations to dinner from lawyers'.[257] Bose told him that those lawyers were 'hopefuls' for a judicial appointment. He was told by another judge, Justice Imam, that this 'vicious practice' was encouraged because some Supreme Court judges did accept such invitations, though Imam refused them as well.[258]

Hidayatullah said that at the Nagpur High Court, no such invitations were accepted unless there was an occasion like a marriage. Questions of propriety, however, were raised even in marriages. When his son was getting married, Justice Grover wanted to invite President V.V. Giri and Vice President G.S. Pathak, who were his friends, for the wedding. However, Chief Justice Hidayatullah advised him against this, saying that it would not look proper. They were accordingly not invited.[259] Justice Khalid, who served at the court in the 1980s, was unhappy about the fact that some judges mingled with ministers. He also felt that some advocates got what they wanted in court on account of their close relations with judges.[260] Today, there is an informal norm (followed at least at the Bombay High Court) that when a person is appointed a judge of the high court, he or she has to delete all social media accounts, including Facebook.[261]

On the other hand, when it becomes known that a person is likely to be appointed a judge of the Supreme Court, lobbies sometimes form in order to block that appointment. Chief Justice Chandrachud said that as soon as a name is rumoured to be under consideration, lobbies form, mainly against the candidate.[262] Similarly, Justice Eradi said that 'lobbies for and against a nominee are part of our culture'.[263]

Perhaps the most famous example of a lobby against a judge was the case of Justice P.B. Sawant. When it became known that Sawant, a relatively junior judge of the Bombay High Court, was being considered seriously for appointment to the Supreme Court by Chief Justice Bhagwati in 1986, a lobby formed to block Sawant's appointment. At the time, Sawant was about eighth in seniority at the Bombay High Court.[264] Sawant had somewhat of a rivalry going with another judge of the Bombay High Court, Justice Lentin. Both Sawant and Lentin were appointed to the high court one day apart, in March 1973.[265] Lentin had been promoted from the City Civil Court, whereas Sawant had been appointed from the bar. When a bar judge (like Sawant) and a service judge (like Lentin) are appointed on the same day, the convention in such cases was that the bar judge got seniority over the career judge. However, Lentin was sworn in a day prior to Sawant,[266] and he was one of the judges whom Sawant was going to supersede.

In March 1986, Sawant was told by Chief Justice Bhagwati to be in Delhi as his name would be cleared for appointment to the Supreme Court on the night of 6 March 1986 (a Thursday), and that on 10 March 1986 (the following Monday) he would be sworn in as a Supreme Court judge. Sawant had a prior speaking engagement at Madurai, which Justice Bhagwati requested him to cancel. Accordingly, Justice Sawant arrived in Delhi and was present on the specified date, but his name was not declared.

Only three judges were appointed to the Supreme Court on 10 March 1986 (M.M. Dutt, K.N. Singh and S. Natarajan), but Sawant was not on the list. Chief Justice Bhagwati later told Justice Sawant that his name had been on Prime Minister Rajiv Gandhi's table for some time, but that he had telephoned Bhagwati and told him that for some reason his name was being kept back only for a month, and that after a month Sawant would be named a Supreme Court judge. However, Bhagwati failed in getting Sawant to the Supreme Court during his tenure.[267] This is because judges who were senior to Sawant at the Bombay High Court went to the government and threatened to resign, and senior advocates made representations as well.[268] H.R. Bhardwaj, minister of state in the law ministry, handled this delicate matter. One of the personal secretaries to the prime minister was a friend of a senior judge whom Sawant would supersede. The government did not want the Bombay High Court harmed by Sawant's appointment, so it refused to appoint Sawant.[269] He was eventually appointed to the Supreme Court in October 1989 (though he was around fourth in seniority at the time).[270]

Something similar also happened to Justice N.P. Singh of the Patna High Court, who could have been appointed to the Supreme Court in the 1980s, had it not been for lobbies which formed against him.[271] He was eventually appointed to the court in June 1992 after having served as chief justice of the Calcutta High Court.

Acknowledgements

This book could not have been written without Professor Gadbois and the painstaking and meticulous research he conducted in the 1980s, which he preserved and refined in the decades thereafter. His legacy lives on in his precious interview notes, which were the culmination of his life's work, which I was both blessed and honoured to receive. I am also grateful to many who helped me in the process of writing this book. Thank you, Pranay Chitale, for visiting the National Archives and Nehru Library in Delhi to pull out archival materials for me yet again. Many thanks to Mrs Uma Narayan for helping me locate rare judicial autobiographies and materials. Thank you, Vikram Raghavan, for helping me access some of the Granville Austin papers at Princeton, and for providing photographs of Professor Gadbois. Thank you, Arun Natessan, for helping me find rare books. Thank you, Vasujith Ram and Professors Upendra Baxi and Mitra Sharafi, for corresponding with me in connection with this book. Many thanks to Fali Nariman, Arshad Hidayatullah, Satish Shah, Anjali Chandurkar and Judy Gadbois for providing photographs that have been used in this book. Many thanks to Dr Nozer Sheriar and Dr Phiroze

Soonawala. Thank you, Meru Gokhale, Premanka Goswami, Arpita Basu, Saloni Mital, Ahlawat Gunjan, and the entire team at Penguin, for making this book possible. Many thanks are owed to my research assistants, Shreyas Narla and Shivani Chimnani, for checking citations and helping spot errors. Thank you, Professor K.L. Daswani. I owe everything to my family, to Dad and Kalpana, Aai and Baba, without whom this book could not have been written. A thousand apologies to Radha who put up with me in the month of May 2017 while I researched and wrote this book instead of spending the court vacation with her.

Notes

The Gadbois Interviews

1. The reason I cannot be precise is because the records of some interviews appear to be missing. For instance, though Gadbois interviewed Justice H.R. Khanna in 1983, the notes of that interview are missing. There may be other such examples.
2. He also corresponded with many of the judges and their relatives, and this book relies on letters exchanged between Gadbois and the judges (or their relatives).
3. Gadbois in his interview notes wrote 'Ms G's people' (i.e. Mrs Indira Gandhi's people).
4. Interview with Mrs Archana Subimal Roy (29 June 1983).
5. See, Sumit Mitra, 'Supreme Court: Tug of War', *India Today*, 15 January 1986, available at: http://indiatoday.intoday.in/story/bad-vibes-between-cji-sen-and-law-minister-bhagwati-cast-shadow-on-judicial-appointments/1/348083.html (last visited 19 May 2017).
6. Gadbois in his notes wrote that the judge said that the lawyer was a 'well known liar' and that he also called him 'crooked'.
7. Interview with Justice P.N. Bhagwati (3 October 1988). Bhagwati also informed Gadbois that he had introduced the American doctrine of 'procedural due process' into Indian constitutional law, though he had not called it this in his judgment (he was obviously referring to his judgment in the famous case of *Maneka Gandhi v. Union of India,* [1978] 1 SCC 248, where the Supreme

Court rejected the intent of the framers of India's Constitution to delete the American 'due process clause' from the Constitution). Procedural due process, said Bhagwati, means that procedures set up by the government for depriving rights must be fair, reasonable and acceptable to the Supreme Court. Interview with Justice P.N. Bhagwati (24 January 1980).

8.   Interview with Justice Y.V. Chandrachud (8 December 1988).

9.   Interview with Chief Justice R.S. Pathak (22 December 1988).

10. Interview with Justice Y.V. Chandrachud (8 December 1988). Gadbois wrote in his interview notes that Indira Gandhi told Chandrachud, 'my party people think he's no good' and 'Chandurkar is not likely to be helpful to us'. Perhaps one should not judge a judge by his attendance at a person's funeral. Even P. Jaganmohan Reddy, as chief justice of the Andhra Pradesh High Court, felt awkward attending the Nizam's funeral because of the 'sensitivities' of his office. P. Jaganmohan Reddy, *The Judiciary I Served* (Hyderabad: Orient Longman Ltd, 1999), p. 143.

11. Interview with Chief Justice R.S. Pathak (22 December 1988).

12. Interview with Justice S. Natarajan (24 April 1988). However, Justice R.S. Bachawat had fed Gadbois 'fresh pineapple juice [not tinned], Mango, three different fried items, Bengal sweets, ice cream, etc'. Gadbois noted: 'He asked what other judges had fed me, just to make sure no one did better than him.' Bachawat, noted Gadbois, was a 'Jolly fellow', with 'a great sense of humor'. They 'laughed a lot' during that interview, and Gadbois felt 'exhausted and not very sharp' by the time this interview took place, the last interview in Calcutta, at least in 1983.

13. *Kesavananda Bharati v. State of Kerala*, AIR 1973 SC 1461.

14. Interview with A.N. Ray (29 June 1983).

15. The interview with this judge took place on 7 November 1988. It is said that this particular judge missed his train from Delhi to Bombay, after his retirement, because of his penchant for alcohol.

16. Interview with Justice R.S. Sarkaria (15 July 1983).

17. Interview with Justice M.N.R. Venkatachaliah (1 September 1988).

18. Gadbois wrote to me in his email dated 22 June 2016: 'What you do with the interview material is entirely up to you.'

19. Abhinav Chandrachud, *The Informal Constitution: Unwritten Criteria in Selecting Judges for the Supreme Court of India* (New Delhi: Oxford University Press, 2014); Abhinav Chandrachud, *An Independent, Colonial Judiciary: A History of the Bombay High*

Court During the British Raj, 1862–1947 (New Delhi: Oxford University Press, 2015).

20. George H. Gadbois, Jr., *Judges of the Supreme Court of India, 1950-1989* (New Delhi: Oxford University Press, 2011). Where he wrote about something the judges told him, e.g., about G.P. Singh not being elevated to the Supreme Court; he barely scratched the surface of what they told him.

21. Though his book was eventually published in 2011, he had started working on it much earlier. Ill health prevented him from completing the manuscript sooner. In 1989, he became ill, spent quite a bit of time on leave, and opted for early retirement in 1991. During that time, he put aside all his writing projects. When his health improved, he moved on to other matters. It was only around 2007, possibly earlier, that he resumed his book on the judges. See, email from Gadbois to Justice Natarajan, dated 6 August 2009.

22. Gadbois wrote to me in his email dated 22 June 2016: 'I think enough time has passed to feel OK about the interviews now being accessible to anyone. I didn't promise any particular amount of time. Very little was off the record anyway. I labelled quite a bit of what your grandfather told me as off the record, though I don't think he ever attached that restriction. But feel free to edit out portions of what he told me.'

23. Much of Gadbois's biographical information is from his Curriculum Vitae, which is on file with the author.

24. Vikram Raghavan and Vasujith Ram (eds.), George H. Gadbois, Jr., *Supreme Court of India: The Beginnings* (New Delhi: Oxford University Press, 2017), p. xi.

25. Ibid.

26. 'Evolution of the Federal Court of India: An Historical Footnote', *Journal of the Indian Law Institute*, vol. 5 (January–March 1963), pp. 19–46; 'The Federal Court of India: 1937-1950', *Journal of the Indian Law Institute*, vol. 6 (April–September 1964), pp. 253–315.

27. The Indian Law Institute (ILI) was inaugurated by President Rajendra Prasad, with Prime Minister Nehru in attendance, on 12 December 1957. See, S. Gopal (ed.), *Selected Works of Jawaharlal Nehru*, 2nd Series, (New Delhi: Jawaharlal Nehru Memorial Fund, 1989), available at: http://nehruportal.nic.in/writings (last visited 25 May 2017), vol. 40, p. 303. See further, Nehru to Morarji Desai, letter dated 13 March 1960. Gopal, ibid., vol. 58, p. 184. For more on the founding of the ILI, see, B.P. Sinha, *Reminiscences and*

Reflections of a Chief Justice (Delhi: B.R. Publishing Corporation, 1985), pp. 123–44.

28.   Gadbois may have met some judges of the Supreme Court during this visit. For instance, in Gadbois's papers, there is a letter from K. Subba Rao, who had by then retired as the chief justice of India, to Gadbois, dated 14 March 1970, agreeing to meet with Gadbois on 24 March.

29.   'Indian Supreme Court Judges: A Portrait', *Law & Society Review*, vol. 3 (November 1968–February 1969), pp. 317–36.

30.   'Indian Judicial Behaviour', *Economic & Political Weekly*, vol. 5 (Annual Number, 1970), pp. 149–166.

31.   Gadbois sent several judges a copy of his 'Indian Judicial Behaviour' paper. Hidayatullah wrote a letter to Gadbois on 6 December 1988, saying: 'Of course your cabalistic signs are difficult to comprehend to me who have "little arithmetic and no Algebra", but the text was clear.' Similarly, in a letter dated 3 March 1970, Justice J.M. Shelat thanked Gadbois for sending him a copy of this paper, and said, 'I am glad to assure you of my appreciation of its excellent objectivity and the very large industry which obviously you have put into it. It was a very unique experience to find the judgments of the Supreme Court critically analysed and the attitudenal behaviour of each of us carefully dissected.' Chief Justice Chandrachud wrote a letter to Gadbois on 12 September 1985 thanking him for sending a copy of another paper.

32.   Interview with Justice G.K. Mitter (28 June 1983). 'Hell of a nice fellow,' wrote Gadbois about Mitter.

33.   P.B. Gajendragadkar, *To the Best of My Memory* (Bombay: Bharatiya Vidya Bhavan, 1983), p. 214. Gajendragadkar wrote that a friend of his informed him, after his retirement, that 'an American student had contributed an article to the *Journal of the Indian Law Institute*, in which he had dealt with what he called the behavioural pattern of the judges of the Supreme Court'. In Gadbois's copy of Gajendragadkar's autobiography, Gadbois wrote, in green ink along the margin, 'EPW'. Gajendragadkar was clearly referring to Gadbois's article published in the EPW. Gajendragadkar wrote that an American student contacted Gajendragadkar and asked to meet him, though Gajendragadkar wrote a 'polite letter' to him saying that he would 'be happy to meet him', but that he 'would not be able to assist him in his study of what he called [Gajendragadkar's] behavioural pattern'. On the margins of Gadbois's copy of

Gajendragadkar's autobiography, once again in green ink, Gadbois wrote, 'not me!' Perhaps Gadbois never received Gajendragadkar's letter, or perhaps Gajendragadkar had some facts mixed up; the letter he wrote could have possibly been written to someone else, though the research paper on the behavioural voting patterns of judges was clearly that of Gadbois.

34. M. Hidayatullah, *My Own Boswell: Memoirs* (Bombay: N.M. Tripathi Pvt. Ltd, 1992), pp. 208–09.
35. R.M. Sahai, *A Lawyer's Journey* (New Delhi: Universal Law Publishing Pvt. Ltd, 2005), p. 95.
36. Visiting Scientist, United States–India Exchange of Scientists Program, December 1979–February 1980.
37. He held the following positions: Senior Faculty Research Fellowship, American Institute of Indian Studies, New Delhi, 1982–83; Senior Faculty Research Fellowship, American Institute of Indian Studies, New Delhi, 1988–89.
38. *Waman Rao v. Union of India*, (1981) 2 SCC 362. In this case, the Supreme Court upheld the constitutional validity of Articles 31-A, 31-B and (the unamended Article) 31-C of the Constitution. These provisions were inserted in order to give immunity to some laws from being challenged for violating fundamental rights.
39. Gadbois's notes in Interview with Justice A.P. Sen (11 May 1983).
40. *Supreme Court Advocates on Record Association v. Union of India*, (2016) 5 SCC 1 (paragraph 189). Justice Khehar recorded that Gadbois's work had been cited in support of the incident which occurred in 1951 after the death of Chief Justice Kania, which will be explored in this book.
41. Constitution (Ninety-Ninth) Amendment Act, 2014.
42. See, Coomi Kapoor, 'Supreme Court: The Conflicts Within', *India Today*, 15 November 1984, available at: http://indiatoday.intoday. in/story/has-chief-justice-y.v.-chandrachud-succeeded-in-his-mission-to-win-prestige-back-for-sc/1/361161.html (last visited 19 May 2017).
43. Letter from Gadbois to Tulzapurkar, 28 April 1983.
44. Letter from Tulzapurkar to Gadbois, 3 May 1983.
45. Interview with Justice V.D. Tulzapurkar (14 July 1983).
46. Interview with Justice D.P. Madon (7 November 1988). See, Upendra Baxi, 'The Horse and the Rider: Court, Constitution and Civil Servants', vol. 23, Mainstream, p. 59 (1985).
47. (1983) 1 SCC 305.

48. Interview with Justice D.A. Desai (29 September 1988).
49. Upendra Baxi, 'Socialism for the Superannuated: A Critique of *Nakara*', AIR 1983 Journal 105.
50. Interview with Justice Krishna Iyer (22 January 1980).
51. Interview with Justice A.N. Grover (24 May 1983). Apparently, Grover did not trust what Baxi wrote because he did not identify Justice Mathew as a communist in one of his books.
52. Interview with Justice Baharul Islam (4 October 1988).
53. Interview with Fali S. Nariman (16 July 1983).
54. For example, Justice K.S. Hegde's two daughters were in the US. See, Hegde to Gadbois, letter dated 29 April 1976. Chief Justice Chandrachud's daughter was at Indianapolis in the US. Interview with Chief Justice Y.V. Chandrachud (3 May 1983). Justice A. Varadarajan had two daughters who were, at the time of the interview, applying for post-graduate study in the US. Interview with Justice A. Varadarajan (13 May 1983). Justice M.H. Kania's wife had relatives in the US. Interview with Justice M.H. Kania (23 April 1988).
55. Gadbois wrote a letter to Chandrachud on 27 August 1985, inviting him to the University of Kentucky for a lecture if he was visiting his daughter in Indianapolis. Chandrachud replied to Gadbois on 12 September 1985, informing him that his daughter and family were still at Indianapolis in the US, and 'It is always a pleasure to visit them but now we have an added reason for going there since we can also come to Lexington and, if possible, I can deliver a lecture at your University.' Though Chandrachud eventually never went to Kentucky to visit Gadbois or to deliver a lecture there, Gadbois and Chandrachud played a round of golf and had lunch (with their respective wives) at the Delhi Golf Club during Gadbois's next trip to Delhi in 1988, after Chandrachud's retirement. See, letter from Chandrachud to Gadbois, dated 13 December 1988.
56. Interview with Justice M.M. Dutt (24 April 1988).
57. Interview with M. Hidayatullah (17 June 1983).
58. Madon to Gadbois, letter dated 23 February 1990. Gadbois then interviewed Madon when Madon visited Kentucky on 28 May 1990.
59. Letter from Vivian Bose to Gadbois dated 12 May 1983.
60. Interview with Justice R.B. Misra (27 October 1988).
61. Reference will repeatedly be made in this book to the iconic 14th Report of the Law Commission of India. Nehru had approved the formation of the first Law Commission in his letter to Home

Minister K.N. Katju in July 1954. See, Nehru to Katju, letter dated 19 July 1954, Gopal, *Selected Works of Jawaharlal Nehru*, vol. 26, p. 265. Nehru, however, initially wanted the former chief justice of the Calcutta High Court, Sir Arthur Trevor Harries, to be its chairman. The appointment of the Law Commission was eventually announced on 5 August 1955, and it was chaired by Motilal C. Setalvad.

62. See, Chandrachud, *An Independent, Colonial Judiciary*.
63. 'Didn't Want to Shift to Allahabad HC for Just 10 Months ...', *The Hindu*, 27 September 2017, available at: http://www.thehindu.com/news/national/karnataka/didnt-want-to-shift-for-just-10-months-jayant-patel/article19758953.ece (last visited 16 October 2017).
64. Even so, readers should read the footnotes, recognize what the source for each story is, and perhaps take each story with a pinch of salt if it is derived from a one-sided source. This book will also indicate to readers whenever this is so.
65. Interview with Vivian Bose (21 June 1983). Bose 'couldn't communicate well' and was '[a]ssisted in [the] interview by [his] daughter and son in law ...'
66. In fact, one of the judges whom Gadbois interviewed in the 1980s, P. Jaganmohan Reddy, wrote an autobiography which was published in 1999, and much of what Gadbois recorded of their meeting was also said by Reddy in the autobiography.

1. Judicial Rivalries

1. Justices Jasti Chelameswar, Ranjan Gogoi, Madan Lokur and Kurian Joseph.
2. Interview with M. Hidayatullah (17 June 1983).
3. Interview with B.P. Sinha (17 July 1983). Interestingly, Sinha's name was really 'Singh', but his university listed his name as 'Sinha' so he just went with it.
4. (1959) SCR vii, pp. xv–xvi.
5. Sinha did not name Imam's family member in his autobiography, though he narrated this story. He said that he had powerful enemies like 'the Chief Minister of Bihar, the Revenue Minister and others'. B.P. Sinha, *Reminiscences and Reflections of a Chief Justice* (Delhi: B.R. Publishing Corporation, 1985), pp. 155–56.
6. Interview with B.P. Sinha (17 July 1983).
7. Interview with Justice Rajagopala Ayyangar (25 June 1983).

8.   This is confirmed in Motilal C. Setalvad, *My Life, Law and Other Things* (Gurgaon: LexisNexis, 2017 reprint), p. 507.

9.   P.B. Gajendragadkar, *To the Best of My Memory* (Bombay: Bharatiya Vidya Bhavan, 1983), p. 158.

10. Interview with Justice L.M. Sharma (24 April 1988).

11. Ibid. Sharma bore no animosity towards Imam. In fact, he was keen to emphasize that Imam was a very good man, a good judge and an excellent criminal lawyer. He was very close to Imam and his family.

12. According to Gadbois's notes, Sinha had some unflattering things to say about Imam's wife, which have not been repeated here.

13. Interview with Justice L.M. Sharma (24 April 1988).

14. Setalvad, *My Life, Law and Other Things*, p. 508.

15. Ibid.

16. Gajendragadkar said that Nehru met Imam 'half a dozen times' and that he himself came to the conclusion that Imam could not be appointed as the chief justice. Gajendragadkar, *To the Best of My Memory*, pp. 158–59.

17. Sinha, *Reminiscences*, pp. 89–90, 171–72.

18. Gajendragadkar to Gulzari Lal Nanda, letter dated 12 February 1964, available at: Gajendragadkar Papers, NMML.

19. Website of the Delhi High Court, available at: http://delhihighcourt.nic.in/history.asp (last visited 27 May 2017).

20. Gajendragadkar to Gulzari Lal Nanda, letter dated 12 February 1964, available at: Gajendragadkar Papers, NMML.

21. Ibid.

22. Sinha, *Reminiscences*, p. 142.

23. Sinha did not mention Gajendragadkar in the version of this story in his autobiography. Ibid, pp. 142–43.

24. Ibid, p. 143.

25. Ibid, p. 92.

26. Interview with S.K. Das (14 May 1983).

27. Gajendragadkar, *To the Best of My Memory*, p. 200.

28. Interview with B.P. Sinha (17 July 1983).

29. In this book, the old names of Indian cities have been used since that is how they were known at the time that the incidents narrated in this book took place.

30. Interview with Justice A.K. Sarkar (28 June 1983).

31. Interview with Justice R.S. Bachawat (30 June 1983); Interview with Justice V. Ramaswami (22 June 1983). Justice P. Jaganmohan

Reddy also confirmed the story of Gajendragadkar trying to get Sarkar superseded, though Reddy was appointed to the Supreme Court in 1969, and both Gajendragadkar and Sarkar had retired in 1966. Interview with P. Jaganmohan Reddy (20 June 1983). Gajendragadkar and Hidayatullah did not get along too well either, and according to Hidayatullah, Gajendragadkar hoped for him to be superseded. Interview with M. Hidayatullah (17 June 1983).

32. Confidential 'prefatory note' from Gajendragadkar to Prime Minister Morarji Desai, dated 8 July 1977, available at: Gajendragadkar Papers, NMML.

33. Gajendragadkar to Desai, ibid.

34. Gajendragadkar to Home Minister Gulzari Lal Nanda, letter dated 28 January 1966, available at: Gajendragadkar Papers, NMML.

35. See, Gajendragadkar to Prime Minister Indira Gandhi, letter dated 24 August 1977, available at: Gajendragadkar Papers, NMML.

36. M. Hidayatullah, *My Own Boswell: Memoirs* (Bombay: N.M. Tripathi Pvt. Ltd, 1992), p. 209.

37. Interview with M. Hidayatullah (17 June 1983).

38. (1970) 3 SCC 400.

39. Interview with M. Hidayatullah (17 June 1983).

40. *Ranjit D. Udeshi v. State of Maharashtra*, AIR 1965 SC 881 (decided by five judges).

41. Interview with M. Hidayatullah (4 November 1988).

42. *R.C. Cooper v. Union of India*, (1970) 1 SCC 248.

43. K.S. Hegde, 'A Dangerous Doctrine', in *Supersession of Judges* (Kuldip Nayar ed., New Delhi: Indian Book Company, 1973), p. 47.

44. After interviewing S.C. Roy's wife, Gadbois wondered whether the government had contemplated replacing Shah with Roy. Interview with Mrs Archana Subimal Roy (29 June 1983). Roy had been sent 'feelers' by the government about his being appointed to the Supreme Court in 1970, but he had refused.

45. Interview with M. Hidayatullah (17 June 1983). Justice G.K. Mitter was among those who were willing to resign. Interview with Justice G.K. Mitter (28 June 1983). See further, P. Jaganmohan Reddy, *The Judiciary I Served* (Hyderabad: Orient Longman Ltd, 1999), p. 226.

46. Interview with Justice A.N. Grover (24 May 1983).

47. Ibid.

48. Interview with Justice K.S. Hegde (14–15 November 1988). Hegde referred to the case as the 'Gupta case'. Hegde was sitting with Shah

on the bench, and though Hegde wrote the judgment in the case, Shah had made some critical remarks about Gupta during oral arguments. Gupta had powerful political friends. This was the case of: *State of U.P. v. Om Prakash Gupta*, (1969) 3 SCC 775. *Cf*, Sunil Sethi, 'High Priest of Justice', *India Today*, 30 November 1977, available at: http://indiatoday.intoday.in/story/justice-j.c.-shah-a-patrician-and-a-strict-disciplinarian/1/436092.html (last visited 2 June 2017).

49.   Interview with M. Hidayatullah (17 June 1983). In fact, Hidayatullah also succeeded in convincing Dhillon to disallow any discussion regarding the conduct of the judges in the *Bank Nationalization* case. There had been allegations that the judges who were hearing the case had shares in the nationalized banks. However, the only judge who had shares, Sikri, had openly disclosed his holdings to Attorney General Niren De, and De had said that the Government had no objection to Sikri hearing the case. Reddy, *The Judiciary I Served*, p. 188.

50.   Interview with Justice K.S. Hegde (14–15 November 1988).

51.   Hidayatullah, *My Own Boswell*, p. 278.

52.   Rajasthan, Madhya Pradesh, Punjab, Bihar, Himachal Pradesh and Orissa.

53.   (1977) 3 SCC 592 (Para 178).

54.   This incident also finds mention in Fali S. Nariman, *Before Memory Fades* (New Delhi: Hay House India, 2016 reprint), pp. 181–82, 199.

55.   Under Article 143 of the Constitution, the President of India has the power to ask the Supreme Court for an advisory opinion on any question of law or fact.

56.   Interview with Justice M. Hameedullah Beg (2 May 1983).

57.   Ibid.

58.   Interview with Justice P.K. Goswami (8 July 1983).

59.   Interview with Chief Justice A.N. Ray (29 June 1983).

60.   That is, the convention that when the chief justice of the Supreme Court of India retires, the next most senior judge on the court (where seniority is determined on the basis of the date of appointment and not according to age) assumes the office.

61.   AIR 1973 SC 1461.

62.   Cambridge dictionary, available at: http://dictionary.cambridge.org/dictionary/english/snow-job (last visited 13 May 2017).

63.   Kuldip Nayar, 'The 13th Chief Justice', Kuldip Nayar (ed.), *Supersession of Judges* (New Delhi: Indian Book Company, 1973), p. 9.

64. Reddy said that Shelat and Hegde resigned immediately, while Grover delayed his resignation up to 1 June; Reddy, *The Judiciary I Served*, p. 245. However, Shelat and Hegde resigned with effect from 30 April; George H. Gadbois, Jr., *Judges of the Supreme Court of India, 1950-1989* (New Delhi: Oxford University Press, 2011), pp. 116, 130. Grover resigned with effect from 31 May; Gadbois, ibid, p. 134.

65. See, Section 13 read with the Schedule to the Supreme Court Judges (Conditions of Service) Act, 1958, as it stood at the time. The seven-year requirement was done away with in 2005. The High Court and Supreme Court Judges (Salaries and Conditions of Service) Amendment Act, 2005.

66. Interview with P. Jaganmohan Reddy (20 June 1983). See further, Reddy, *The Judiciary I Served*, p. 245.

67. Interview with Justice K.S. Hegde (14–15 November 1988).

68. Interview with P. Jaganmohan Reddy (9 November 1988); Reddy, *The Judiciary I Served*, p. 243. Reddy even asked Ray why Kumaramangalam had congratulated Ray, but Ray said that he did not know; Reddy, *The Judiciary I Served*, p. 243.

69. Interview with Justice K.K. Mathew (17 November 1988); Interview with Justice K.S. Hegde (14–15 November 1988). Grover disagreed, and said that Mathew was much too junior to have been offered the chief justiceship. Interview with Justice A.N. Grover (24 May 1983). Jaganmohan Reddy also did not believe that Mathew was offered the chief justiceship. Interview with P. Jaganmohan Reddy (20 June 1983). Likewise, Justice Goswami believed that it was Beg, not Mathew, who would have been offered the job if Ray did not accept. Interview with Justice P.K. Goswami (4 June 1983). Justice C.A. Vaidialingam believed that Attorney General Niren De had been offered the chief justiceship, but that he had declined because he would not have had a very long tenure on the bench. It was only thereafter that Mathew was offered, he thought. Interview with Justice C.A. Vaidialingam (25 May 1983).

70. Kuldip Nayar, 'The 13th Chief Justice', p. 11.

71. Interview with Justice K.S. Hegde (14–15 November 1988).

72. *A.D.M., Jabalpur v. Shivakant Shukla*, (1976) 2 SCC 521.

73. See further, interview with Justice P.K. Goswami (8 July 1983).

74. Interview with Justice R.S. Pathak (1 October 1988).

75. Ibid. A.N. Sen, who was then a puisne judge of the Calcutta High Court (and who would go on to become the chief justice of the Calcutta High Court, and a Supreme Court judge), did not write

Ray a congratulatory letter either, though his and Ray's families
had been very close. This caused a falling out between the two.
Interview with Justice A.N. Sen (24 October 1988).
76. Interview with L.M. Singhvi (7/12 July 1983); Interview with Justice
H.R. Khanna (3 October 1988).
77. Sikri also said that he could not understand Krishna Iyer's
judgments. Interview with Justice S.M. Sikri (6 May 1983).
78. (1974) 2 SCC 831.
79. Interview with L.M. Singhvi (7/12 July 1983).
80. Interview with Justice A.N. Sen (24 October 1988).
81. Interview with Justice R.S. Bachawat (30 June 1983).
82. Interview with Justice K.S. Hegde (14–15 November 1988). Grover
also could not understand why Ray was sworn in ahead of the two, and
thought that Hidayatullah had something to do with that. Interview
with Justice A.N. Grover (23 October 1988). Jaganmohan Reddy also
thought that Ray had some influence over Hidayatullah. Interview
with P. Jaganmohan Reddy (9 November 1988). Likewise, A.C. Gupta
believed that Hidayatullah was responsible for Ray's appointment to
the Supreme Court. Interview with A.C. Gupta (22 October 1988).
83. Interview with P. Jaganmohan Reddy (9 November 1988).
84. Interview with Justice R.S. Bachawat (30 June 1983).
85. Interview with K.S. Hegde (13 January 1980).
86. See, Supreme Court Judges (Conditions of Service) Amendment
Act, 1976, available at: http://lawmin.nic.in/legislative/
textofcentralacts/1976.pdf (last visited 17 October 2017), p. 261.
87. Interview with K.S. Hegde (13 January 1980).
88. Interview with Justice A.N. Grover (24 May 1983); Interview with
Justice K.S. Hegde (14–15 November 1988).
89. Interview with Justice A.N. Grover (23 January 1980).
90. Interview with P. Jaganmohan Reddy (9 November 1988).
91. Interview with Justice Y.V. Chandrachud (8 December 1988).
92. Interview with Justice Ranga Nath Misra (20 April 1983). See
further, K.N. Bhat, 'Obituary: Former Chief Justice of India, A.N.
Ray', *Law and Other Things*, 16 January 2011, available at: http://
lawandotherthings.com/2011/01/obituary-former-chief-justice-
of-india/ (last visited 2017).
93. Conversation with Justice P.N. Bhagwati (20 August 1988).
94. See, Abhinav Chandrachud, *An Independent, Colonial Judiciary: A
History of the Bombay High Court During the British Raj, 1862–
1947* (New Delhi: Oxford University Press, 2015).

95. Interview with Justice Y.V. Chandrachud (8 December 1988).
96. On how S.T. Desai, not K.T. Desai, became the first chief justice of the Gujarat High Court; see, Gajendragadkar, *To the Best of My Memory*, pp. 149–50.
97. See, Gadbois's notes on interview with Justice Y.V. Chandrachud (8 December 1988).
98. Interview with Justice P.N. Bhagwati (20 April 1983).
99. Gajendragadkar, *To the Best of My Memory*, pp. 154–55. However, Justice Palekar said that Chandrachud was recommended by Justice Chainani, chief justice of the Bombay High Court, before Bhagwati was appointed to the Gujarat High Court, but that the chief justice of India, B.P. Sinha, had objected to the appointment since Chandrachud was not yet forty-five years old, and because he preferred high court judges to be at least forty-five years of age prior to their appointment. Interview with Justice D.G. Palekar (4 November 1988).
100. The case came before the Bombay High Court on 8 February 1960. It was finally decided by the court in March 1960. See, Gyan Prakash, *Mumbai Fables* (Noida: HarperCollins Publishers, 2011), pp. 186–88.
101. Interview with B.P. Sinha (17 July 1983); Interview with M. Hidayatullah (4 November 1988); Interview with Justice R.S. Pathak (17 April 1983) (recounting the words of Justice Gajendragadkar).
102. Later, Justice S.K. Kapur of the Delhi High Court was similarly identified as a future judge of the Supreme Court. However, he died in office as a high court judge on 13 October 1969. Interview with Justice P.N. Bhagwati (20 April 1983). See further, Justice Hardy, *Struggles and Sorrows: The Personal Testimony of a Chief Justice* (New Delhi: Vikas Publishing House Pvt. Ltd, 1984), p. 97. See, 'Former Judges', Website of the Delhi High Court, available at: http://delhihighcourt.nic.in/formerjudges.asp?currentPage=18 (last visited 21 May 2017).
103. Interview with P. Jaganmohan Reddy (9 November 1988).
104. Interview with S.M. Sikri (17 October 1988).
105. Interview with Justice D.A. Desai (29 September 1988). Desai told Gadbois that Shah told him that Sikri had rejected Bhagwati's nomination, and Shah consequently withdrew it a day or two before he retired.
106. Interview with Justice Y.V. Chandrachud (8 December 1988).
107. Interview with Justice J.C. Shah (3 November 1988).

108. Author's interview with P.N. Bhagwati (12 October 2011).

109. Interview with Justice P.N. Bhagwati (3 October 1988).

110. Interview with S.M. Sikri (17 October 1988); Interview with P. Jaganmohan Reddy (9 November 1988); Interview with Justice P.S. Kailasam (24 June 1983).

111. Chief Justice Sikri said that Gajendragadkar pushed only Krishna Iyer. Interview with S.M. Sikri (17 October 1988).

112. Interview with Justice Y.V. Chandrachud (8 December 1988).

113. Interview with S.M. Sikri (17 October 1988).

114. Ibid.

115. Reddy, *The Judiciary I Served*, p. 223.

116. Interview with Justice K.S. Hegde (14–15 November 1988); Interview with Justice P.N. Bhagwati (20 April 1983).

117. Interview with Justice K.S. Hegde (14–15 November 1988).

118. Ibid.

119. Interview with Justice A.N. Grover (23 October 1988); Interview with Justice D.P. Madon (7 November 1988).

120. Interview with Justice P.N. Bhagwati (on 31 March 1988).

121. Interview with Justice K.S. Hegde (14–15 November 1988).

122. *State of Rajasthan v. Union of India*, (1977) 3 SCC 592.

123. Gadbois's notes in interview with Justice A.C. Gupta (13 May 1983). See further, Abhinav Chandrachud, 'Voice of a Bygone Era', *Frontline*, 8 February 2013, available at: http://www.frontline.in/books/voice-of-a-bygone-era/article4328398.ece (last visited 31 May 2017).

124. *A.D.M., Jabalpur v. Shivakant Shukla*, (1976) 2 SCC 521.

125. Interview with Chief Justice Y.V. Chandrachud (3 May 1983). See further, Shanti Bhushan, *Courting Destiny: A Memoir* (Kindle: Penguin Books, 2008), at chapter 41 and appendix 10. Jayaprakash Narayan wrote a letter to Bhushan suggesting that both Chandrachud and Bhagwati ought to be superseded. Narayan to Bhushan, letter dated 14 July 1977, id. Bhushan replied on 31 July 1977, saying that he wanted to discuss the matter in detail with Narayan. Bhushan then met Narayan and convinced him that they should stick with the principle of seniority. However, he addressed letters to all Supreme Court judges and high court chief justices in order to make the consultation process prescribed under the Constitution for appointment of the chief justice as broad as possible.

126. Interview with Justice P.S. Kailasam (24 June 1983).

127. Bhushan, *Courting Destiny*, chapter 41.

128. Interview with Chief Justice R.S. Pathak (1 October 1988); Interview with Justice H.R. Khanna (3 October 1988).

129. Interview with Justice Y.V. Chandrachud (8 December 1988).
130. Ibid.
131. Interview with Justice Y.V. Chandrachud (8 December 1988); Interview with Chief Justice R.S. Pathak (1 October 1988); Interview with Justice P.N. Bhagwati (3 October 1988).
132. Interview with L.M. Singhvi (7/12 July 1983).
133. *S.P. Gupta v. Union of India*, (1981) Supp SCC 87.
134. D.Y. Chandrachud, 'Evolving Trends in Locus Standi: Models for Social Justice Dispensation', *Journal of the Bar Council of India*, vol. VIII (4), 1981, p. 672.
135. Y.V. Chandrachud, 'We Are Not Spineless', *India Today*, 31 July 1985.
136. Interview with Justice D.P. Madon (7 November 1988).
137. Granville Austin, *Working a Democratic Constitution: A History of the Indian Experience* (New Delhi: Oxford University Press, 2003 reprint), p. 529.
138. Interview with B.P. Sinha (17 July 1983).
139. Austin, *Working a Democratic Constitution*, pp. 528–29.
140. (1981) Supp SCC 87, at paragraph 114. Bhagwati was referring to a statement made in Chandrachud's counter-affidavit that full and effective consultations had taken place between the chief justice of India and central government over the question of transferring Singh. See further, Coomi Kapoor, 'Supreme Court: The Conflicts Within', *India Today*, 15 November 1984, available at: http://indiatoday.intoday.in/story/has-chief-justice-y.v.-chandrachud-succeeded-in-his-mission-to-win-prestige-back-for-sc/1/361161.html (last visited 17 May 2017).
141. Interview with Justice D.G. Palekar (4 November 1988).
142. The four judges were Gupta, Tulzapurkar, Pathak and Venkataramiah. The ones who voted against Chandrachud were Bhagwati, Fazal Ali and Desai.
143. Austin, *Working a Democratic Constitution*, p. 529.
144. Interview with Justice P.N. Bhagwati (31 March 1988).
145. Ibid.
146. (1980) 2 SCC 591 and (1980) 3 SCC 625.
147. Interview with A.C. Gupta (22 October 1988).
148. Ibid.
149. Kapoor, 'Supreme Court: The Conflicts within'.
150. Chandrachud, 'We Are Not Spineless'.
151. *S.P. Gupta v. Union of India*, (1981) Supp SCC 87.
152. Austin, *Working a Democratic Constitution*, p. 527.

153. Interview with B.P. Sinha (17 July 1983); Interview with Justice R.S. Bachawat (30 June 1983). Justice Chandrachud referred, several times, to the factions in the court. Interview with Chief Justice Y.V. Chandrachud (3 May 1983). See further, interview with Justice V. Ramaswami (22 June 1983); Interview with Justice A.N. Grover (24 May 1983). See, Hardy, *Struggles and Sorrows*, p. 141.
154. Interview with Justice R.S. Pathak (17 April 1983).
155. See, Anuj Bhuwania, *Courting the People: Public Interest Litigation in Post-Emergency India* (Delhi: Cambridge University Press, 2017), pp. 7–8.
156. *A.D.M., Jabalpur v. Shivakant Shukla*, (1976) 2 SCC 521.
157. See, paragraphs 530–31 of the judgment.
158. See further, Abhinav Chandrachud, 'Dialogic Judicial Activism in India', *The Hindu*, 18 July 2009, available at: http://www.thehindu.com/todays-paper/tp-opinion/Dialogic-judicial-activism-in-India/article16557560.ece (last visited 25 May 2017).
159. Interview with Justice P.N. Bhagwati (24 January 1980).
160. Abhinav Chandrachud, *Due Process of Law* (Lucknow: Eastern Book Company, 2011); Abhinav Chandrachud, 'Due Process', *in* Madhav Khosla et al (eds.), *The Oxford Handbook of the Indian Constitution* (New Delhi: Oxford University Press, 2016).
161. (1978) 1 SCC 248.
162. Chandrachud, *Due Process of Law*; Chandrachud, 'Due Process'.
163. Interview with Justice P.N. Bhagwati (24 January 1980).
164. Ibid.
165. Interview with Justice Krishna Iyer (22 January 1980).
166. Ibid.
167. (1983) 1 SCC 305.
168. Those governed by the 1972 rules and army pension regulations.
169. Interview with Justice D.A. Desai (29 September 1988). Desai had another similar experience. Interview with Justice D.A. Desai (30 April 1983).
170. Interview with Justice D.A. Desai (29 September 1988). Justice Balakrishna Eradi agreed with this. Interview with Justice Balakrishna Eradi (28 October 1988).
171. However, even Justice A.K. Sarkar, who served in the court between 1957 and 1966 (including a brief term as chief justice), supported the 1973 supersession. He said that the superseded three were 'cussedly against the Government' and that they had 'made it impossible for the Government to carry on'. Interview with Justice A.K. Sarkar (28 June 1983).

172. Interview with Justice D.A. Desai (30 April 1983).
173. Bhagwati was in no way responsible for Thakkar's appointment to the Supreme Court, though he was responsible for Desai's appointment. See, Interview with Justice P.N. Bhagwati (20 April 1983). See further, Interview with Justice M.P. Thakkar (29 April 1983).
174. Interview with Justice M.P. Thakkar (29 April 1983).
175. Ibid.
176. Interview with Justice G.L. Oza (22 April 1988).
177. Ibid.
178. Interview with Justice D.P. Madon (7 November 1988).
179. (1986) 3 SCC 156.
180. Paragraph 26.
181. Interview with Justice P.K. Goswami (30 September 1988).
182. H.R. Khanna, *Neither Roses Nor Thorns* (Lucknow: Eastern Book Company, 1982), p. 63.
183. Ibid, pp. 63–64.
184. It is not clear which judgment Justice Tulzapurkar was referring to, and whether the judgment was reported or not. The case of *D.C. Roy v. Presiding Officer*, (1976) 3 SCC 693, decided by Justices Chandrachud and Krishna Iyer, on a similar set of facts, went against the employee. However, at paragraph 13 of this judgment, the Supreme Court held that where the employer dismisses an employee from service without observing even a semblance of the principles of natural justice, then even if it is subsequently found by the labour court that the dismissal was justified, the employee must still get back wages up to the date of the order of the labour court. Justice Tulzapurkar was possibly referring to this judgment.
185. Interview with Justice V.D. Tulzapurkar (14 July 1983).
186. Interview with Justice A.P. Sen (11 May 1983).
187. (1979) 3 SCC 646.
188. Interview with Justice A.P. Sen (11 May 1983). Desai's statement was reported in Kapoor, 'Supreme Court: The Conflicts Within'.
189. Interview with Justice A.P. Sen (11 May 1983).
190. Interview with Justice P.S. Kailasam (24 June 1983).
191. Interview with Justice A. Varadarajan (13 May 1983).
192. Ibid.
193. Interview with Justice R.S. Pathak (17 April 1983).
194. See further, Interview with Justice Rajagopala Ayyangar (25 June 1983).
195. Interview with S.K. Das (14 May 1983).

196. Ibid.
197. Interview with S.K. Das (18 October 1988).
198. Interview with Justice A.K. Sarkar (28 June 1983). See further, Interview with Justice I.D. Dua (6 July 1983).
199. Interview with M. Hidayatullah (17 June 1983).
200. Ibid.
201. M. Hidayatullah, 'Highways and Bylanes of Justice', (1984) 2 SCC J 1. See further, Justice B.N. Srikrishna, 'Skinning a Cat', (2005) 8 SCC J 3.
202. Interview with Justice A.N. Grover (24 May 1983).
203. Interview with Justice I.D. Dua (6 July 1983). See further, Interview with Justice R.B. Misra (1 June 1983). Misra, however, did not say this about Krishna Iyer in particular.
204. Interview with Justice G.K. Mitter (28 June 1983). See further, Interview with Justice Raghubar Dayal (2 June 1983).
205. Interview with P. Jaganmohan Reddy (20 June 1983).
206. Interview with S.K. Das (14 May 1983).
207. Interview with Justice A.N. Grover (24 May 1983). See further, Abhinav Sekhri, 'Vignettes—Man Mohan Das and the Indian Supreme Court', *Lawandotherthings Blog*, 6 February 2018, available at: http://lawandotherthings.com/2018/02/vignettes-man-mohan-das-and-the-indian-supreme-court/ (last visited 16 March 2018).
208. Interview with Justice A.N. Grover (24 May 1983). He was referring to the majority judgment of Justice J.C. Shah.
209. Interview with Justice D.A. Desai (30 April 1983). Desai seemed to be unhappy about Hidayatullah's foreword in a then recent edition of O.P. Malhotra's book on labour law, in which Hidayatullah had criticized recent trends in that branch of law. Desai was also very critical of Setalvad, who, he said, had a big ego and was pro-British.
210. Interview with Justice Chinnappa Reddy (10 May 1983).
211. Justice Chinnappa Reddy to Gadbois, letter dated 15 May 1983.
212. Ibid.
213. Gadbois, 'Indian Supreme Court Judges', p. 325.
214. See, Gadbois, *Judges of the Supreme Court of India*, pp. 356–58.
215. Ibid, p. 358.
216. Interview with Justice A.C. Gupta (13 May 1983); Interview with Justice Sabyasachi Mukharji (1 October 1988); Interview with Justice B.C. Ray (22 April 1988).
217. See, Chandrachud, *An Independent, Colonial Judiciary*. Justice Dayal, who was a member of the ICS, thought that his time in

Cambridge was really a holiday. Interview with Justice Raghubar Dayal (2 June 1983).

218. Interview with M. Hidayatullah (4 November 1988).
219. Hidayatullah, 'Highways and Bylanes of Justices'.
220. Interview with Justice D.A. Desai (30 April 1983).
221. Ibid.
222. Interview with Justice A. Varadarajan (13 May 1983).
223. Interview with P. Jaganmohan Reddy (20 June 1983).
224. Interview with Justice M.N.R. Venkatachaliah (1 September 1988).
225. Interview with Justice L.M. Sharma (24 April 1988).
226. Article 124(2), first proviso, Constitution of India.
227. See, Hidayatullah, *My Own Boswell*, p. 227. The practice varied according to the chief justice.
228. Chief Justice Chandrachud was consulted on the appointment of his successor. He said that his 'unquestioned choice was Justice Bhagwati'. Chandrachud, 'We Are Not Spineless', p. 43.
229. Interview with Justice Y.V. Chandrachud (8 December 1988).
230. 'Supreme Choice', *India Today*, 31 May 1986, available at: http://indiatoday.intoday.in/story/dilemma-over-choosing-successor-to-supreme-court-chief-justice-p.n.-bhagwati/1/348495.html (last visited 15 May 2017).
231. Interview with Justice P.N. Bhagwati (3 October 1988).
232. Interview with Chief Justice R.S. Pathak (1 October 1988).
233. Ibid.
234. Prabhu Chawla, 'Judiciary: Presidential Tact', *India Today*, 15 December 1986, available at: http://indiatoday.intoday.in/story/govt-names-r.s.-pathak-as-next-chief-justice-of-sc-president-zail-singh-intervenes/1/349110.html (last visited 15 May 2017).
235. Interview with Chief Justice R.S. Pathak (1 October 1988).
236. Interview with Justice P.N. Bhagwati (3 October 1988).
237. Interview with Justice P.N. Bhagwati (31 March 1988).
238. Gadbois's notes on the P.N. Bhagwati interview (31 March 1988).
239. Interview with Justice R.S. Pathak (17 April 1983).
240. P.N. Bhagwati, *My Tryst with Justice* (New Delhi: Universal Law Publishing, 2013), p. 94.
241. Interview with Justice Kuldip Singh (1 January 1989).
242. Singh was born in January 1932, and Ahmadi in March 1932.
243. Interview with Chief Justice R.S. Pathak (22 December 1988); Interview with Justice Kuldip Singh (1 January 1989).

244. *Supreme Court Advocates on Record Association v. Union of India,* (1993) 4 SCC 441.
245. Paragraph 399.
246. Interview with Kuldip Singh (1 January 1989).
247. This was not all that uncommon. Both Justices A.C. Gupta and K.J. Shetty were also actually two years younger than their official age. Interview with Justice A.C. Gupta (13 May 1983); Interview with Justice K.J. Shetty (25 April 1988). During Gajendragadkar's term as the chief justice, there was an allegation that the chief justice of the Madras High Court had already reached the retirement age of sixty-two, which Gajendragadkar had to investigate, and which was found to be true. Gajendragadkar, *To the Best of My Memory,* pp. 166–69; Setalvad, *My Life, Law and Other Things,* p. 564. During Chief Justice B.P. Sinha's term in office, there was an allegation that Justice J.P. Mitter of the Calcutta High Court had not been truthful about his age. Sinha, *Reminiscences,* pp. 82–83.
248. Interview with Chief Justice R.S. Pathak (22 December 1988).
249. See, notes of Gadbois on interview with Justice A.M. Ahmadi (1 January 1989).

2. Disagreement without Dissent

1. Section 23(2), Constitutional Reform Act, 2005, available at: http://www.legislation.gov.uk/ukpga/2005/4/pdfs/ukpga_20050004_en.pdf (last visited 17 May 2017).
2. Hugh Tomlinson, 'Selecting the Panel and the Size of the Court', *UKSC Blog,* 4 October 2009, available at: http://ukscblog.com/selecting-the-panel-and-the-size-of-the-court-updated/ (last visited 17 May 2017).
3. Tomlinson, id.
4. AIR 1973 SC 1461.
5. If there are two judges on the bench, then both judges must agree with the outcome.
6. (1978) 2 SCC 213.
7. Interview with Justice Krishna Iyer (22 January 1980).
8. AIR 1950 SC 27.
9. Motilal C. Setalvad, *The Indian Constitution: 1950–1965* (Bombay: University of Bombay, 1967), p. 51.
10. George H. Gadbois, Jr., 'Indian Judicial Behaviour', *Economic and Political Weekly,* vol. 5, No. 3/5, January 1970,

pp. 149–66, p. 151. Gadbois wrote that out of 3272 reported judgments during that time, dissents were recorded in only 274 cases.

11. Ibid., p. 153.
12. Article 145(3), Constitution.
13. In 11 per cent cases there was at least one dissent, and in 4 per cent cases there was at least one dissent and one concurrence. Nick Robinson et al, 'Interpreting the Constitution: Supreme Court Constitution Benches since Independence', *Economic and Political Weekly*, 26 February 2011, pp. 27–31, 28.
14. Ibid.
15. Abhinav Chandrachud, 'Speech, Structure, and Behavior on the Supreme Court of India', *Columbia Journal of Asian Law*, vol. 25, issue 2, Summer 2012, pp. 222–74, 252.
16. Ibid.
17. Nick Robinson et al., 'Interpreting the Constitution', p. 28. This includes decisions with only a concurring judgment (8 per cent) and decisions with both concurring and dissenting judgments (4 per cent).
18. Chandrachud, 'Speech, Structure, and Behavior . . .', p. 252.
19. Abhinav Chandrachud, *An Independent, Colonial Judiciary: A History of the Bombay High Court During the British Raj, 1862-1947* (New Delhi: Oxford University Press, 2015).
20. Clause 36 of the Letters Patent of the Bombay High Court. After 1927, if two judges were equally divided over a question, that question would then be referred to a third judge.
21. Acting judges are now usually no longer appointed to courts in India, as a matter of practice.
22. Chandrachud, *An Independent, Colonial Judiciary*.
23. Ibid.
24. Lee Epstein, William M. Landes and Richard A. Posner, 'Are Even Unanimous Decisions in the United States Supreme Court Ideological?', *Northwestern University Law Review*, vol. 106, 2012, pp. 699–714, p. 701. The data relates only to orally argued cases.
25. Chris Hanretty, 'Dissenting Opinions in the UKSC', *UK Supreme Court Blog*, 19 August 2010, available at: http://ukscblog.com/dissenting-opinons-in-the-uksc/ (last visited 17 May 2017).
26. Katalin Kelemen, 'Dissenting Opinions in Constitutional Courts', *German Law Journal*, 2013, vol. 14, No. 8, pp. 1345–71, 1365 (n. 88).
27. Gajendragadkar described the process of the judicial conference at the end of a case, at which the judges discussed their views on

the case. He said that if differences persist after discussion, then a dissent is written. P.B. Gajendragadkar, *To the Best of My Memory* (Bombay: Bharatiya Vidya Bhavan, 1983), pp. 146–47. See further, M. Hidayatullah, *My Own Boswell: Memoirs* (Bombay: N.M. Tripathi Pvt. Ltd, 1992), p. 208.

28. One of those judges was P. Jaganmohan Reddy. P. Jaganmohan Reddy, *The Judiciary I Served* (Hyderabad: Orient Longman Ltd, 1999), pp. 166–67.
29. Hidayatullah, *My Own Boswell*, p. 209.
30. Gajendragadkar, *To the Best of My Memory*, pp. 135–36, 197–98.
31. *T.V. Vatheeswaran v. State of Tamil Nadu*, (1983) 2 SCC 68.
32. It was delivered on 16 February 1983. Sher Singh's case was decided on 24 March 1983.
33. *Sher Singh v. State of Punjab*, (1983) 2 SCC 344.
34. Interview with Justice A. Varadarajan (13 May 1983).
35. *A.D.M., Jabalpur v. Shivakant Shukla*, (1976) 2 SCC 521.
36. As the chief justice of the Andhra Pradesh High Court, P. Jaganmohan Reddy (later a Supreme Court judge) noticed that his 'newly appointed' colleagues hesitated to dissent. He put them at ease by telling them that they were free to dissent, but that they should not dissent merely to demonstrate that they were independent. Reddy, *The Judiciary I Served*, p. 167.
37. *Premier Automobiles Ltd v. Union of India*, (1972) 4 SCC (N) 1.
38. Likewise, Justice Benjamin Cardozo, in his first year at the US Supreme Court, suppressed his own dissent, so that the view taken by the court would be unanimous. Ruth Bader Ginsburg, 'Remarks on Writing Separately', *Washington Law Review*, vol. 65, Issue 133, 1990, pp. 133–50, at p. 142.
39. H.R. Khanna, *Neither Roses Nor Thorns* (Lucknow: Eastern Book Company, 1982), p. 62.
40. P.N. Shinghal to Gadbois, letter dated 27 April 1983. Similarly, as the chief justice of the Hyderabad High Court, P. Jaganmohan Reddy told his colleagues not to dissent 'for the sake of dissent' only to demonstrate their independence. Reddy, *The Judiciary I Served*, p. 140.
41. Interview with Justice A.C. Gupta (13 May 1983). The *Judges* case was *S.P. Gupta v. Union of India*, (1981) Supp SCC 87.
42. Interview with Justice Krishna Iyer (22 January 1980).
43. Ibid.
44. *Rustom Cavasjee Cooper v. Union of India*, (1970) 1 SCC 248.

45. Interview with P. Jaganmohan Reddy (20 June 1983). See further, Reddy, *The Judiciary I Served*, p. 177.
46. Reddy, *The Judiciary I Served*, p. 177.
47. Ibid.
48. Gajendragadkar, *To the Best of My Memory*, p. 133. See further, Hidayatullah, *My Own Boswell*, p. 204. Interview with B.P. Sinha (17 July 1983); Interview with P. Jaganmohan Reddy (20 June 1983); Interview with Justice M. Hameedullah Beg (2 May 1983).
49. Interview with Chief Justice R.S. Pathak (1 October 1988).
50. Interview with Justice Chinnappa Reddy (10 May 1983).
51. Ibid.
52. Interview with Justice M.P. Thakkar (29 April 1983).
53. See further, Bhadra Sinha, 'Home-cooked Food, Gossip and Bonhomie: How SC Judges Bond over Weekly Lunches', *Hindustan Times*, 16 April 2017, available at: http://www. hindustantimes.com/india-news/food-gossip-and-bonhomie-how-supreme-court-judges-bond-over-weekly-lunches/story-cp2pyvmMNhiGXLTJpCSZPI.html (last visited 18 May 2017).
54. Mehr Chand Mahajan, *Looking Back* (London: Asia Publishing House, 1963), p. 211.
55. Ibid., p. 196.
56. Interview with Justice Rajagopala Ayyangar (25 June 1983).
57. Interview with M. Hidayatullah (17 June 1983).
58. *Lt. Col. Khajoor Singh v. Union of India*, AIR 1961 SC 532; *State of West Bengal v. Union of India*, AIR 1963 SC 1241.
59. Donald P. Kommers, *The Constitutional Jurisprudence of the Federal Republic of Germany* (1997). As cited in Kelemen, 'Dissenting Opinions in Constitutional Courts'.
60. See, Lord Kerr of Tonaghmore, 'Dissenting Judgments—Self Indulgence or Self-Sacrifice?', *The Birkenhead Lecture*, 8 October 2012, available at: https://www.supremecourt.uk/docs/speech-121008.pdf (last visited 18 May 2017).
61. See, Brooke Donald, 'At Stanford, Justice Ginsburg Says Collegiality Is Not Swayed by Bitter Battles', *Stanford News*, 18 September 2013, available at: http://news.stanford.edu/news/2013/september/ginsburg-law-talk-091813.html (last visited 18 May 2017); Adam Liptak, 'For a Collegial Court, Justices Lunch Together, and Forbid Talk of Cases', *New York Times*, 1 June 2016, available at: https://www.nytimes.com/2016/06/02/us/politics/for-a-collegial-court-

justices-lunch-together-and-forbid-talk-of-cases.html?_r=0 (last visited 18 May 2017).

62. Garance Franke-Ruta, 'Justice Kagan and Justice Scalia are Hunting Buddies—Really', *Atlantic*, 30 June 2013, available at: https://www.theatlantic.com/politics/archive/2013/06/justice-kagan-and-justice-scalia-are-hunting-buddies-really/277401/ (last visited 18 May 2017).

63. Interview with Justice A.C. Gupta (13 May 1983); Interview with Justice A.P. Sen (11 May 1983); Interview with Chief Justice Y.V. Chandrachud (3 May 1983).

64. Interview with Chief Justice Y.V. Chandrachud (3 May 1983).

65. Lee Epstein, William M. Landes and Richard A. Posner, 'Why [And When] Judges Dissent: A Theoretical and Empirical Analysis', *Journal of Legal Analysis*, Spring 2011, vol. 3, Issue 1, pp. 101–37.

66. He said that the atmosphere at the Supreme Court was different from that at the high court. At the high court, the majority of appointments were made from the bar, so everybody knew everybody else. At the Supreme Court, judges came from different regions, and the same level of collegiality that was found at the Bombay High Court was missing there. Gajendragadkar, *To the Best of My Memory*, pp. 131–32.

67. Law Commission of India, 14th Report, 1958, vol. 1, pp. 52–53.

68. Interview with Justice S. Murtaza Fazal Ali (24 April 1983).

69. Interview with Justice A. Varadarajan (13 May 1983). However, he also said that the judges in the 1950s had less work, which is why they developed the habit of writing multiple judgments.

70. Interview with Justice Krishna Iyer (22 January 1980).

71. See, Thomas Roe, 'Dissenting Judgments', *3 Hare Court*, 5 June 2015, available at: http://www.3harecourt.com/assets/asset-store/file/Thomas%20Roe%20dissenting%20judgments.pdf (last visited 18 May 2017). This was by virtue of the Judicial Committee (Dissenting Opinions) Order, 1966.

72. B.P. Sinha, *Reminiscences and Reflections of a Chief Justice* (Delhi: B.R. Publishing Corporation, 1985), p. 75.

73. Nick Robinson, 'Structure Matters: The Impact of Court Structure on the Indian and U.S. Supreme Courts', *American Journal of Comparative Law*, vol. 61, no. 1 (2013).

74. This is also what Justice Gajendragadkar said in his autobiography. Gajendragadkar, *To the Best of My Memory*, p. 132.

75. Interview with Justice R.S. Sarkaria (15 July 1983).
76. Interview with Justice S. Murtaza Fazal Ali (24 April 1983).
77. Interview with Justice V.D. Tulzapurkar (14 July 1983).
78. Interview with K.S. Hegde (13 January 1980).
79. Interview with Justice P.N. Bhagwati (24 January 1980). Of course, one may have to take into account the fact that Bhagwati thought that Gajendragadkar (along with H.R. Gokhale) cost him a long term as chief justice of India.
80. Interview with Justice Y.V. Chandrachud (23 January 1980).
81. *S.P. Gupta v. Union of India*, (1981) Supp SCC 87.
82. Granville Austin, *Working a Democratic Constitution: A History of the Indian Experience* (New Delhi: Oxford University Press, 2003 reprint), p. 524 (n. 27). The three judges were: Chinnappa Reddy, A.D. Koshal and A.P. Sen.
83. Interview with Chief Justice R.S. Pathak (1 October 1988). He was referring to the case of *Kehar Singh v. State (Delhi Administration)*, (1988) 3 SCC 609, which was decided by a bench of three judges, viz., G.L. Oza, B.C. Ray and K.J. Shetty.
84. Interview with Justice Krishna Iyer (22 January 1980).
85. Interview with B.P. Sinha (17 July 1983).
86. Gadbois, 'Indian Judicial Behaviour', p. 153.
87. Ibid., p. 151.
88. Ibid., p. 166.
89. There is no record of this interview between Gadbois and Subba Rao. There is only a letter from Subba Rao to Gadbois dated 14 March 1970, in which Subba Rao gave Gadbois an appointment to meet him on 24 March 1970. The meeting between Gadbois and Subba Rao probably took place then. Gadbois told me that this is what Subba Rao had said to him.
90. Hidayatullah, *My Own Boswell*, p. 209.
91. Ibid.
92. Robinson et al., 'Interpreting the Constitution', p. 31.
93. Hidayatullah, *My Own Boswell*, p. 220.
94. Interview with Justice A.P. Sen (10 September 1988). Gadbois found this to be curious, because he thought that A.P. Sen and Chandrachud would have had similar ideas, so there would be no reason for Chandrachud to keep Sen off a constitution bench.
95. Interview with Justice C.A. Vaidialingam (25 May 1983).
96. See, speech of Justice B.P. Sinha at the retirement of Chief Justice S.R. Das, (1959) SCR vii, pp. x–xi.

97. Interview with Justice R.S. Pathak (17 April 1983).

98. Interview with Justice V.D. Tulzapurkar (14 July 1983).

99. Interview with Justice A.P. Sen (10 September 1988).

100. Hidayatullah, *My Own Boswell*, p. 222.

101. Exceptions include Estonia, Greece and Spain. Kelemen, 'Dissenting Opinions in Constitutional Courts'.

102. See, James Markham, 'Against Individually Signed Judicial Opinions', *Duke Law Journal*, vol. 56, issue 3, December 2006, pp. 923–52.

103. See, Ginsburg, 'Remarks on Writing Separately'.

104. For example, some judgments of the Supreme Court of Canada were delivered for the court as per curiam opinions. Peter McCormick, '"By the Court": The Untold Story of a Canadian Judicial Innovation', *Osgoode Hall Law Journal*, vol. 53, 2016, pp. 1048–82.

105. Ginsburg, 'Remarks on Writing Separately'.

106. Kelemen, 'Dissenting Opinions in Constitutional Courts'; Rosa Raffaelli, 'Dissenting Opinions in the Supreme Courts of Member States: Study', Policy Department C: Citizens' Rights and Constitutional Affairs, European Parliament, November 2012, available at: http://www.europarl.europa.eu/document/activities/cont/201304/20130423ATT64963/20130423ATT64963EN.pdf (last visited 18 May 2017).

107. Kelemen, ibid., pp. 1362–63.

108. Karl M. ZoBell, 'Division of Opinion in the Supreme Court: A History of Judicial Disintegration', *Cornell Law Quarterly*, vol. 44, 1959, pp. 186–214; Markham, 'Against Individually Signed Judicial Opinions'. There is now some debate about whether plurality opinions should start making their way into the decisions of the UK Supreme Court. See, Brenda Hale, 'Judgment Writing in the Supreme Court', *UK Supreme Court Blog*, 25 October 2010, available at: http://ukscblog.com/judgment-writing-in-the-supreme-court-brenda-hale/ (last visited 18 May 2017).

109. An order the Privy Council published in 1627 said: 'When the business is to be carried according to the most voices, no publication is afterwards to be made by any man, how the particular voices and opinions went.' ZoBell, 'Division of Opinion in the Supreme Court', p. 188. However, the name of the author of the single judgment would be revealed by the Privy Council.

110. Section 59, Senior Courts Act, 1981, available at: http://www.legislation.gov.uk/ukpga/1981/54/contents (last visited 18 May 2017). See further, Roe, 'Dissenting Judgments'.

111. See, Ginsburg, 'Remarks on Writing Separately', p. 135; Kelemen, 'Dissenting Opinions in Constitutional Courts', p. 1363. Both cite the work of Louis Blom-Cooper and Gavin Drewry.

112. Gajendragadkar, *To the Best of My Memory*, pp. 132–33.

113. ZoBell, 'Division of Opinion in the Supreme Court'.

114. Ginsburg, 'Remarks on Writing Separately', p. 135.

115. Ibid. See further, James Markham, 'Against Individually Signed Judicial Opinions'.

116. Ginsburg, ibid.; James Markham, ibid.

117. ZoBell, 'Division of Opinion in the Supreme Court', p. 192.

118. James Markham, 'Against Individually Signed Judicial Opinions'.

119. ZoBell, 'Division of Opinion in the Supreme Court', p. 193.

120. Ibid., p. 194.

121. Ibid., p. 195.

122. *Boos v. Barry*, 108 S. Ct. 1157 (1988). Ginsburg, 'Remarks on Writing Separately', p. 148.

123. See, ZoBell, 'Division of Opinion in the Supreme Court'.

124. Ginsburg, 'Remarks on Writing Separately'.

125. Ibid, p. 140; James Markham, 'Against Individually Signed Judicial Opinions', p. 946.

126. 410 U.S. 113 (1973).

127. Ginsburg, 'Remarks on Writing Separately', p. 140.

128. ZoBell, 'Division of Opinion in the Supreme Court', p. 211; Claire L'Heureux-Dubé, 'The Dissenting Opinion: Voice of the Future?', *Osgoode Hall Law Journal*, vol. 38, no. 3, pp. 495–517.

129. Ginsburg, 'Remarks on Writing Separately', p. 144.

130. Ibid.

131. Ibid.; William J. Brennan, Jr., 'In Defense of Dissents', *Hastings Law Journal*, 1986, vol. 37, pp. 427–38.

132. Ginsburg, ibid., p. 139.

3. Special Leave, a Special Burden

1. I have dabbled in this kind of criticism myself. See, Abhinav Chandrachud, 'My Dear Chagla', *Frontline*, 7 February 2014, available at: http://www.frontline.in/the-nation/my-dear-chagla/article5589838.ece (last visited 15 May 2017).

2.   Sections 109(a)-(b), 110, Code of Civil Procedure, 1908
      (CPC). In such cases, the litigant had to obtain a certificate
      from the high court that the value of the subject matter was
      indeed Rs 10,000 or more. See, Sir D.F. Mulla, *Code of Civil
      Procedure* (Bombay: N.M. Tripathi & Co., 8th edition, 1926),
      pp. 287–93, available at: https://archive.org/stream/in.ernet.
      dli.2015.548582/2015.548582.The-Code#page/n467/mode/2up
      (last visited 16 May 2017). The corresponding provisions
      in the Code of Civil Procedure, 1882, were sections 595–96.
      See, Mulla, ibid., available at: https://archive.org/details/
      codecivilproced00mullgoog (last visited 16 May 2017).
3.   Section 110, CPC.
4.   Order XLV Rule 3, CPC.
5.   Section 109(c), CPC. This provision allowed an appeal not merely
      against a decree but also against an 'order', and not merely 'final
      order' which are the words used in Section 109(a)-(b). In other
      words, even interim orders could theoretically be appealed before
      the Privy Council.
6.   Order XLV, Rules 7-8, CPC.
7.   For a discussion of the colonial-era law on appeals by special
      leave, see, William Macpherson, *The Practice of the Judicial
      Committee of Her Majesty's Most Honorable Privy Council*
      (London: H. Sweet, 1873), p. 22, available at: https://catalog.
      hathitrust.org/Record/011724372 (last visited 16 May 2017); Frank
      Safford, *The Practice of the Privy Council . . .* (London: Sweet and
      Maxwell, 1901), available at: https://babel.hathitrust.org/cgi/
      pt?id=uiug.30112021632499;view=1up;seq=803 (last visited 16 May
      2017).
8.   There was, thus, no provision in the Code of Criminal Procedure,
      1898 (CrPC), akin to the provisions in the CPC, dealing with
      appeals to the Privy Council. See further, speech of Bakshi
      Tek Chand, Constituent Assembly Debates of India (New
      Delhi: Lok Sabha Secretariat) (CAD), vol. 8, p. 611. However,
      Section 411-A(4), inserted into the CrPC by Act XXVI of 1943,
      provided a right to appeal where a division bench of the high
      court (which heard an intra-court appeal) certified that the case
      was fit for appeal. Available at: http://lawmin.nic.in/legislative/
      textofcentralacts/1943.pdf (last visited 16 May 2017).
9.   Bakshi Tek Chand was a member of the Constituent Assembly
      representing   East   Punjab.   See,   'Constituent   Assembly

Membership', website of the Rajya Sabha, available at: http://rajyasabha.nic.in/rsnew/constituent_assembly/constituent_assembly_mem.asp (last visited 17 March 2018). He had been a legislator and a former judge of the Lahore high court. G.S. Aujla, 'Founding Fathers', *Tribune*, 22 January 2000, available at: http://www.tribuneindia.com/2000/20000122/windows/main1.htm (last visited 17 March 2018).

10. CAD, vol. 8, p. 611.
11. Ibid.
12. Ibid, p. 851.
13. The Federal Court was established in 1937. Abhinav Chandrachud, *The Informal Constitution: Unwritten Criteria in Selecting Judges for the Supreme Court of India* (New Delhi: Oxford University Press, 2014).
14. Section 205, Government of India Act, 1935, available at: http://lawmin.nic.in/legislative/textofcentralacts/GOI%20act%201935.pdf (last visited 16 May 2017).
15. Article 132, Constitution. The original text of the Constitution is available at: https://dl.wdl.org/2672/service/2672.pdf (last visited 18 February 2018). See further: https://archive.org/stream/constitutionofin029189mbp#page/n181/mode/2up (last visited 18 February 2018).
16. Bakshi Tek Chand believed that increasing the value would reduce the number of appeals. CAD, vol. 8, p. 610. He said that three quarters of the cases that went to the Privy Council were of the value of between Rs 10,000 and Rs 20,000. Therefore, he conjectured, by introducing the cap of Rs 20,000, the framers of the draft Constitution had reduced appeals in civil cases by 75 per cent.
17. Article 133, Constitution of India.
18. Constitution (Thirtieth Amendment) Act, 1972 (with effect from 27 February 1973). Available at: http://indiacode.nic.in/coiweb/amend/amend30.htm (last visited 16 May 2017).
19. Constitution (Forty-fourth Amendment) Act, 1978 (with effect from 1 August 1979). Available at: http://indiacode.nic.in/coiweb/amend/amend44.htm (last visited 16 May 2017).
20. Article 134, Constitution.
21. See, Granville Austin, *The Indian Constitution: Cornerstone of a Nation* (New Delhi: Oxford University Press, 2015 reprint), pp. 214–16; B. Shiva Rao, *The Framing of India's Constitution: Select Documents* (New Delhi: Universal Law Publishing Co. Pvt. Ltd,

2012 reprint) ('BSR'), vol. 5, p. 493. In the draft Constitution dated 21 February 1948, there was no general right of appeal in criminal cases. See, BSR, vol. 3, pp. 509, 557. Article 110 dealt with the right of appeal in constitutional cases (whether civil or criminal), Article 111 gave a right of appeal in civil cases, and Article 112 dealt with special leave to appeal. However, many members of the Constituent Assembly objected to the absence of a general right to appeal in criminal cases, with the effect that B.R. Ambedkar eventually moved an amendment introducing a right of appeal to the Supreme Court in criminal cases. Articles 110-112 of the draft Constitution of February 1948 were extensively debated in the Assembly from 3 June 1949 onwards; CAD, vol. 8, p. 591 onwards. The appellate powers of the Supreme Court were debated again on 13 June 1949; CAD, vol. 8, p. 820 onwards.

22.   Article 136, Constitution.

23.   Article 112, draft Constitution of February 1948.

24.   T.T. Krishnamachari was a member of the Constituent Assembly from Madras. See, 'Constituent Assembly Membership', website of the Rajya Sabha. He later became the finance minister of India and had to resign after the LIC Mundhra scandal. See, Abhinav Chandrachud, *Republic of Rhetoric: Free Speech and the Constitution of India* (Gurgaon: Penguin, 2017).

25.   In support of this, Krishnamachari merely said: 'The words "final order" in the original article are sought to be removed and revised by the insertion of the words "determination, sentence or order".' CAD, vol. 10, p. 376.

26.   The entire debate on that day was focused on whether the Supreme Court should entertain appeals from court martials.

27.   See, e.g., *Maharani Inder Kumari v. Maharani Jaipal Kumari*, (1886) 14 IA 1.

28.   CAD, vol. 8, p. 596.

29.   Ibid., p. 614.

30.   Ibid., p. 607. Munshi was a prominent Bombay lawyer who served as home minister of Bombay state, member of the Constituent Assembly, India's political agent in Hyderabad, India's food minister, and Governor of Uttar Pradesh. He was also a prolific Gujarati writer and founded the Bharatiya Vidya Bhavan. See, K.M. Munshi, *India's Constitutional Documents: Pilgrimage to Freedom, 1902-1950* (Mumbai: Bharatiya Vidya Bhavan, 2012), vol. 1.

31.   CAD, vol. 8, p. 851.

32. They were referring to Article 112 of the draft Constitution.
33. Bhargava was a member of the Constituent Assembly from East Punjab. 'Constituent Assembly Membership', website of the Rajya Sabha. He was a lawyer, and had served as a member of the Central Legislative Assembly. See, profile of Pandit Thakur Das Bhargava, website of the Lok Sabha, available at: http://164.100.47.194/loksabha/writereaddata/biodata_1_12/619.htm (last visited 17 March 2018).
34. CAD, vol. 8, p. 638.
35. Ibid. pp. 638–39.
36. Motilal C. Setalvad, *My Life, Law and Other Things* (Gurgaon: LexisNexis, 2017 reprint), p. 213.
37. Mehr Chand Mahajan, *Looking Back* (London: Asia Publishing House, 1963), p. 196.
38. Ibid., p. 214.
39. Nehru to Pant, letter dated 8 November 1959. S. Gopal (ed.), *Selected Works of Jawaharlal Nehru*, 2nd Series (New Delhi: Jawaharlal Nehru Memorial Fund, 1989), vol. 54, p. 356.
40. Nehru's speech at the State Law Ministers' Conference, 18 September 1957. Gopal, ibid., vol. 39, pp. 275–76.
41. Nehru's message to the Incorporated Law Society of Calcutta on 16 December 1958. Gopal, ibid., vol. 45, p. 403.
42. Data is available in the 'Annual Reports' published by the Supreme Court. Available at: http://supremecourtofindia.nic.in/publication (last visited 18 February 2018). The Supreme Court classifies cases as 'admission' and 'regular' cases. I have assumed that 'admission' cases are cases which have not yet been admitted, while 'regular' cases are cases which have.
43. See, Supreme Court (Number of Judges) Act, 1956, and Supreme Court (Number of Judges) Amendment Acts of 1960 (6 May 1960), 1977 (31 December 1977), 1986 (9 May 1986) and 2008 (5 February 2009).
44. Nick Robinson, 'Structure Matters: The Impact of Court Structure on the Indian and U.S. Supreme Court', *The American Journal of Comparative Law*, 2013, vol. 61, pp. 173–208.
45. See, Alok Prasanna Kumar et al., 'The Supreme Court of India's Burgeoning Backlog Problem and Regional Disparities in Access to the Supreme Court', *Vidhi Centre for Legal Policy*, Consultation Paper, October 2015, available at: https://static1.squarespace.com/static/551ea026e4b0adba21a8f9df/t/560cf7d4e4b092010fff89b1/1443690452706/29092015_

Consultation+Paper+on+the+Supreme+Court%27s+
Burgeoning+Backlog+Problem.pdf (last visited 16 May 2017).

46. This is what Prasanna et al. conclude as well. Ibid.

47. Law Commission, 14th Report, 1958, vol. 1, p. 54.

48. Mitra Sharafi, 'South Asian Legal History Resources', https://hosted.
law.wisc.edu/wordpress/sharafi/research-guide-to-colonial-south-
asian-case-law/ (last visited 16 May 2017).

49. See, Rohit De, '"A Peripatetic World Court": Cosmopolitan Courts,
Nationalist Judges and the Indian Appeal to the Privy Council',
Law and History Review, November 2014, pp. 821–51, pp. 835–36.
In 1930, for instance, there were 229 appeals from India before the
Privy Council, but only twenty-seven from Canada.

50. This is what a high court chief justice informed the Law Commission,
as recorded in its 14th Report, 1958, vol. 1, pp. 49–50.

51. See, Abhinav Chandrachud, *An Independent, Colonial Judiciary:
A History of the Bombay High Court During the British Raj, 1862-
1947* (New Delhi: Oxford University Press, 2015).

52. *Pritam Singh v. State*, AIR 1950 SC 169.

53. Law Commission of India, 14th Report, 1958, vol. 1, p. 58.

54. Ibid., pp. 47–48.

55. Ibid., p. 49.

56. Ibid., p. 50.

57. Nick Robinson, 'A Quantitative Analysis of the Indian Supreme
Court's Workload', *Journal of Empirical Legal Studies*, vol.
10, Issue 3, September 2013, pp. 570–601. See further, Nick
Robinson, 'A Court Adrift', *Frontline*, 3 May 2013, available at:
http://www.frontline.in/cover-story/a-court-adrift/article4613892.
ece (last visited 17 May 2017).

58. FAQs, website of the US Supreme Court, available at: https://www.
supremecourt.gov/faq.aspx#faqgi9 (last visited 16 May 2017). This
has a 'signalling effect' on litigants. Simi Rose George, 'Releasing
India's Supreme Court from the Shadow of Delay: A Proposal for
Policy Reform', Master's Thesis at the Harvard Kennedy School
of Government, 2014, available at: https://www.hks.harvard.edu/
index.php/content/download/66823/1240102/version/1/file/
SYPA_SimiGeorge_2014.pdf (last visited 16 May 2017).

59. See, De, 'A Peripatetic World Court', p. 831.

60. See, Chandrachud, *The Informal Constitution*.

61. See, Law Commission of India, 14th Report, 1958, vol. 1, at pp. 49–50.

62. Robinson, 'A Quantitative Analysis of the Indian Supreme Court's
Workload'.

63. M. Hidayatullah, *My Own Boswell: Memoirs* (Bombay: N.M. Tripathi Pvt. Ltd, 1992), p. 203. P.B. Gajendragadkar, *To the Best of My Memory* (Bombay: Bharatiya Vidya Bhavan, 1983), p. 138.

64. Hidayatullah, *My Own Boswell*, p. 203.

65. Gajendragadkar, *To the Best of My Memory*, pp. 138–39.

66. Hidayatullah, *My Own Boswell*, p. 203.

67. Ibid.

68. Interview with Justice Y.V. Chandrachud (23 January 1980).

69. Interview with Justice P.N. Bhagwati (24 January 1980). Sinha claimed that when he was appointed to the Supreme Court in the 1950s, he had convinced the chief justice of India to stagger the hearing of SLPs to other weekdays apart from Monday. B.P. Sinha, *Reminiscences and Reflections of a Chief Justice* (Delhi: B.R. Publishing Corporation, 1985), p. 171.

70. Interview with A.N. Ray (29 June 1983).

71. Interview with Justice P.S. Kailasam (24 June 1983).

72. Interview with Justice A.P. Sen (11 May 1983). See further, Interview with Justice M.P. Thakkar (29 April 1983).

73. Interview with Justice M.P. Thakkar (29 April 1983).

74. However, Justice Pathak said that all the lawyers really wanted in SLPs was a stay order, not a final decision on the merits. Interview with Chief Justice R.S. Pathak (1 October 1988).

75. Interview with P. Jaganmohan Reddy (20 June 1983).

76. Interview with Justice N.L. Untwalia (3 December 1988).

77. Interview with Justice D.P. Madon (28 April 1983).

78. Interview with Justice Sabyasachi Mukharji (26 April 1983).

79. Interview with Justice M.H. Kania (23 April 1988).

80. Interview with Justice Sabyasachi Mukharji (26 April 1983).

81. Interview with Justice Chinnappa Reddy (10 May 1983); Interview with Justice Balakrishna Eradi (7 May 1988); Interview with Justice A. Varadarajan (13 May 1983). In his interview with Chief Justice R.S. Pathak (1 October 1988), Gadbois likened Mondays to a 'fish market', and Pathak agreed with the analogy. Justice Chinnappa Reddy also agreed with the analogy. Interview with Justice Chinnappa Reddy (9 November 1988).

82. Interview with Justice Varadarajan (13 May 1983); Interview with Justice A.C. Gupta (13 May 1983).

83. Interview with Justice A.C. Gupta (13 May 1983).

84. See, Coomi Kapoor, 'Supreme Court: The Conflicts Within', *India Today*, 15 November 1984, available at: http://indiatoday.intoday.in/story/has-chief-justice-y.v.-chandrachud-succeeded-in-his-

mission-to-win-prestige-back-for-sc/1/361161.html (last visited 17 May 2017).

85. Interview with Justice A.P. Sen (11 May 1983).

86. Of course, it is possible that judges like Justice Sen might have been perfectionists who might have never been happy with their judgments. However, the sense one gets is that judges did not really have much time to carry out substantial revisions of their judgments.

87. Interview with Justice A.P. Sen (11 May 1983).

88. Interview with Justice D.P. Madon (28 April 1983).

89. Interview with Justice Balakrishna Eradi (7 May 1983); Interview with Justice A.N. Sen (21 April 1983).

90. Interview with Justice P.N. Bhagwati (20 April 1983); Interview with Chief Justice R.S. Pathak (1 October 1988).

91. Interview with Justice Ranga Nath Misra (20 April 1983).

92. Interview with K.S. Hegde (13 January 1980); Interview with Justice Y.V. Chandrachud (23 January 1980).

93. Interview with Justice A. Varadarajan (13 May 1983). See further, P. Jaganmohan Reddy, *The Judiciary I Served* (Hyderabad: Orient Longman Ltd, 1999), p. 164.

94. Interview with Justice M.H. Kania (23 April 1988).

95. Recorded by Gadbois in his notes on the interview with Justice M.H. Kania (23 April 1988).

96. See, Abhinav Chandrachud, 'From Hyderabad to Harvard: How U.S. Law Schools Make It Worthwhile to Clerk on India's Supreme Court', *International Journal of the Legal Profession*, 7 October 2014, pp. 73–101.

97. Interview with Justice A.N. Grover (23 January 1980).

98. Interview with Justice P.N. Bhagwati (20 April 1983).

99. Interview with Chief Justice R.S. Pathak (1 October 1988).

100. Article 127, Constitution of India.

101. Mahajan, *Looking Back*, pp. 201–02. The other judges on that bench were the chief justice of the high court, R.S. Naik, and the most senior judge, Khalil-uz-Zama Siddiqui. Reddy, *The Judiciary I Served*, p. 40.

102. Article 128, Constitution of India.

103. George H. Gadbois, Jr., *Judges of the Supreme Court of India, 1950-1989* (New Delhi: Oxford University Press, 2011), pp. 162–63. However, it appears that the judges in the *Basic Structure* case heard other cases during that time as well. P. Jaganmohan Reddy, one of the judges in the *Basic Structure* case, wrote in his autobiography that '[w]hile the hearing of the Keshavananda case was going on

Justice Alagiriswami was sitting with us whenever we were not sitting in the Keshavananda case.' Reddy, *The Judiciary I Served*, p. 255.

104. Interview with Justice S.M. Sikri (6 May 1983).
105. Interview with Chief Justice Y.V. Chandrachud (3 May 1983).
106. Interview with Justice C.A. Vaidialingam (25 May 1983).
107. Interview with Justice A.N. Sen (24 October 1988).
108. Letter from Natarajan to Gadbois dated 19 August 2009. This letter enclosed a letter from Chief Justice E.S. Venkataramiah to the law minister dated 18 August 1989.
109. Letter from Chief Justice Venkataramiah to the law minister dated 18 August 1989. Something similar happened with P. Jaganmohan Reddy's attempts to get an ad hoc judge appointed to the Hyderabad High Court while he was the chief justice there, though he succeeded in getting other ad hoc judges appointed. Reddy, *The Judiciary I Served*, pp. 133–35, 139.
110. Justice Hardayal Hardy, the retired chief justice of the Delhi High Court, was quite critical of judges who dismissed SLPs quickly. Hardayal Hardy, *Struggles and Sorrows: The Personal Testimony of a Chief Justice* (New Delhi: Vikas Publishing House Pvt. Ltd, 1984), p. 141.
111. See, Chandrachud, 'From Hyderabad to Harvard'.
112. Robinson, 'Structure Matters', p. 192.
113. Interview with P. Jaganmohan Reddy (20 June 1983).
114. Reddy, *The Judiciary I Served*, p. 41.
115. Interview with Justice Sarkaria (15 July 1983).
116. Interview with Justice A.C. Gupta (13 May 1983).
117. Interview with Justice P.S. Kailasam (24 June 1983).
118. Interview with Justice Chinnappa Reddy (9 November 1988).
119. Upendra Baxi, *Courage, Craft and Contention: The Indian Supreme Court in the Eighties* (Bombay: N.M. Tripathi Pvt. Ltd, 1985), p. 30; Upendra Baxi, '"The Fair Name of Justice": The Memorable Voyage of Chief Justice Chandrachud', in V.S. Deshpande (ed.), *A Chandrachud Reader: Collection of Judgments with Annotations* (New Delhi: Documentation Center, 1985), pp. 71–99, 74.
120. Y.V. Chandrachud, 'We Are Not Spineless', *India Today*, 31 July 1985.
121. Baxi, *Courage, Craft and Contention*, p. 30.
122. Ibid.
123. Interview with Justice A.P. Sen (11 May 1983).
124. Interview with Justice M.P. Thakkar (29 April 1983).

125. Ibid.
126. Marc Galanter and Nick Robinson, 'India's Grand Advocates: A Legal Elite Flourishing in the Era of Globalization', *International Journal of the Legal Profession*, vol. 20, no. 3, 2013, available at: https://papers.ssrn.com/sol3/papers.cfm?abstract_id=2348699 (last visited 2 June 2017).
127. Interview with Justice P.N. Bhagwati (20 April 1983).
128. Interview with Justice M.H. Kania (23 April 1988).
129. This was not a new idea. Justice B.P. Sinha had raised the question of limits on oral arguments during the retirement of Chief Justice S.R. Das in September 1959. (1959) SCR vii, pp. ix–x. Das himself recalled stories of how judges in the 1950s ingeniously used different techniques to ask lawyers to stop arguing. Ibid., pp. xiv–xv.
130. Interview with Justice P.N. Bhagwati (20 April 1983).
131. (1980) 2 SCC 684.
132. Of course, since there were many judges on the bench, it is possible that some of them might have taken longer than others to grasp all the finer points of the case. However, the sense one gets is that this case dragged on for much longer than was actually necessary for all the judges to understand it.
133. Interview with Justice R.S. Sarkaria (15 July 1983).
134. Interview with Justice A.C. Gupta (13 May 1983).
135. Interview with Justice P.N. Bhagwati (3 October 1988); Interview with Justice P.N. Bhagwati (24 January 1980). Chief Justice Bhagwati had also suggested the bifurcation of the Supreme Court in this manner in *Bihar Legal Support Society v. Chief Justice of India*, (1986) 4 SCC 767. This was proposed by the Law Commission of India in its 95th Report, submitted under the chairmanship of Justice K.K. Mathew in March 1984, available at: http://lawcommissionofindia.nic.in/51-100/Report95.pdf (last visited 16 May 2017). A similar suggestion was made by the Law Commission more recently, in its 229th report submitted in August 2009, available at: http://lawcommissionofindia.nic.in/reports/report229.pdf (last visited 16 May 2017).
136. Supreme Court (Number of Judges) Amendment Act, 1986.

4. Decliners

1. A conversation (probably sometime between 1990 and 1991) between the chief justice of India, Ranga Nath Misra, and the chief justice of the Delhi High Court, Leila Seth, recorded in the latter's

autobiography, reveals how the chief justice of India probably thought of high court chief justices as his subordinates. See, Leila Seth, *On Balance: An Autobiography* (Kindle: Penguin, 2007), p. 4223.

2. Law Commission of India, 14th Report, vol. 1, pp. 49–50.

3. Interestingly, in Australia, the highest provincial courts are called 'Supreme Courts', whereas the Supreme Court is called the 'High Court'. Before the high courts were established in India in 1862, Calcutta, Bombay and Madras had 'Supreme Courts' which exercised original jurisdiction. See, Abhinav Chandrachud, *An Independent, Colonial Judiciary: A History of the Bombay High Court During the British Raj, 1862-1947* (New Delhi: Oxford University Press, 2015).

4. Earlier, the states of Manipur, Tripura and Meghalaya also shared the Gauhati High Court in Assam. However, they now have their own high courts. See, 'History', website of the Gauhati High Court, available at: http://ghconline.gov.in/history_more.html (last visited 21 February 2018).

5. In the city of Mumbai, there is a city civil court which exercises original jurisdiction in cases up to Rs 1 crore in value. Section 3, Bombay City Civil Court Act, 1948. In other words, in civil cases, the city civil court in Mumbai is not a court of appeal, but one where cases are to be filed in the first instance. Appeals from the city civil court are then heard by the Bombay High Court. The Bombay High Court exercises original jurisdiction in cases over Rs 1 crore. However, not all high courts exercise original jurisdiction. In civil cases typically involving disputes between landlord and tenant, the small causes court in Mumbai exercises original jurisdiction. In criminal cases, on the other hand, Mumbai has a number of metropolitan magistrates' courts peppered throughout the city. The city civil court is also the sessions court for the city (which is why it is referred to as the city civil and sessions court).

6. In Maharashtra, for example, apart from the city of Mumbai, civil subordinate courts are governed by the Maharashtra Civil Courts Act, 1869.

7. For example, in Maharashtra, there are, broadly speaking, three categories of civil judges: civil judges, junior division (who exercise original jurisdiction in civil cases up to Rs 5 lakh) [Section 24, Maharashtra Civil Courts Act, 1869]; civil judges, senior division (who exercise original jurisdiction in civil cases above Rs 5 lakh)

[Section 24, Maharashtra Civil Courts Act, 1869]; and district judges (who hear first appeals from all decisions of civil judges—whether junior or senior—so long as the value of the case is no more than Rs 1 crore) [Sections 8 and 26, Maharashtra Civil Courts Act, 1869 (as amended in 2015)]. Where the value of the case is over Rs 1 crore, the first appeal is to be filed directly before the high court [Section 26, Maharashtra Civil Courts Act, 1869]. However, a district judge is also considered the principal civil court of original jurisdiction [Section 7, Maharashtra Civil Courts Act, 1869], and as such he exercises jurisdiction under statutes like the Arbitration and Conciliation Act, 1996, intellectual property laws, etc. In Mumbai, the high court is the principal civil court of original jurisdiction. In other words, the high court is, in some respects, the 'District Court' for Mumbai.

8. In Maharashtra, the following system is prevalent: A civil judge (junior division) is selected on the basis of a competitive examination. A civil judge (senior division) is selected on the basis of promotion from the ranks of civil judge (junior division) by the high court on the basis of merit-cum-seniority. However, district judges can be selected on the basis of promotion (75 per cent of the posts are to be filled by this category) [either through merit-cum-seniority (65 per cent) or through merit on the basis of a competitive examination written by civil judges, senior division (10 per cent)]; or can be recruited directly from the bar on the basis of a written and oral test conducted by the high court (25 per cent). Maharashtra Judicial Service Rules, 2008.

9. Abhinav Chandrachud, *The Informal Constitution: Unwritten Criteria in Selecting Judges for the Supreme Court of India* (New Delhi: Oxford University Press, 2014), p. 31.

10. Law Commission of India, 14th Report, vol. 1, p. 77.

11. They are Justices Rohinton Fali Nariman, Uday U. Lalit and L. Nageswara Rao.

12. Indu Malhotra. If appointed, she will be the first female advocate to have been directly appointed to the Supreme Court of India.

13. Chandrachud, *The Informal Constitution*, pp. 185–214.

14. See, A.G. Noorani, 'The Prime Minister and the Judiciary', in B.D. Dua et al. (eds.), *Nehru to the Nineties: The Changing Office of Prime Minister in India* (London: Hurst & Company, 1994).

15. *Special Reference No. 1 of 1998*, (1998) 7 SCC 739 (paragraph 16). If the next in line to be the chief justice of India is not one of the

four most senior judges, then he too must be made a part of the collegium (paragraph 17).

16. The President can return the name once, but if the collegium submits it again, the recommendation is binding on the President.

17. *Special Reference No. 1 of 1998*, (1998) 7 SCC 739 (paragraph 30).

18. See, Nehru to Pant, letter dated 13 March 1960. S. Gopal (ed.), *Selected Works of Jawaharlal Nehru*, 2nd Series (New Delhi: Jawaharlal Nehru Memorial Fund, 1989), vol. 58, p. 185.

19. Interview with Justice Y.V. Chandrachud (8 December 1988). See further, Interview with Justice D.P. Madon (7 November 1988). Chief Justice Sikri did not offer a judgeship to Palkhivala, and said that 'he was earning six lakhs', meaning he was perhaps earning too much money in order to consider a Supreme Court judgeship offer seriously. Interview with Justice S.M. Sikri (17 October 1988).

20. Interview with Justice Y.V. Chandrachud (8 December 1988). His tenure as the chief justice of India would have begun when J.C. Shah retired in January 1971.

21. See, P.B. Gajendragadkar, *To the Best of My Memory* (Bombay: Bharatiya Vidya Bhavan, 1983), p. 153.

22. *Golak Nath v. State of Punjab*, AIR 1967 SC 1643.

23. This was according to his own son, who later became a Supreme Court judge himself. Interview with Justice L.M. Sharma (24 April 1988). See further, Gajendragadkar, *To the Best of My Memory*, p. 153. At least one of those offers came from Chief Justice Sikri. Interview with Justice S.M. Sikri (17 October 1988).

24. Hardayal Hardy, *Struggles and Sorrows: The Personal Testimony of a Chief Justice* (New Delhi: Vikas Publishing House Pvt. Ltd, 1984), p. 99.

25. Ibid.

26. See, profile of K. Parasaran, available at: https://archive.india.gov.in/govt/rajyasabhampbiodata.php?mpcode=2233 (last visited 21 February 2018).

27. See, *Purshottani Dass Tandon v. State of U.P.*, (1986) SCC OnLine All 264.

28. Interview with Justice Y.V. Chandrachud (8 December 1988). See further, Interview with Chief Justice R.S. Pathak (1 October 1988); Interview with Justice A.P. Sen (11 May 1983); Interview with Justice K.N. Singh (3 September 1988).

29. Interview with Justice A.P. Sen (11 May 1983).

30. See further, B.P. Sinha, *Reminiscences and Reflections of a Chief Justice* (Delhi: B.R. Publishing Corporation, 1985), p. 86.

31. Fali S. Nariman, *Before Memory Fades* (New Delhi: Hay House Publishers [India] Pvt. Ltd, 2016 reprint), pp. 136–37.

32. See, notes of Gadbois in Interview with Justice Y.V. Chandrachud (8 December 1988).

33. Nariman, *Before Memory Fades*, p. 198.

34. Interview with Justice D.P. Madon (28 April 1983).

35. Interview with Justice S. Natarajan (24 April 1988).

36. Law Commission of India, 14th Report, vol. 1, pp. 36–37.

37. Chandrachud, *An Independent, Colonial Judiciary.*

38. Ibid.

39. Gadbois, 'The Federal Court of India', footnote 7. See further, Section 201, Government of India Act, 1935.

40. Gadbois, ibid. Abhinav Chandrachud, 'My Dear Chagla', *Frontline*, 7 February 2014, available at: http://www.frontline. in/the-nation/my-dear-chagla/article5589838.ece (last visited 15 May 2017).

41. Chandrachud, *An Independent, Colonial Judiciary.* However, high court chief justices might not have always been paid the same salary. The chief justice of the Calcutta High Court, for example, was paid more than other high court chief justices. See, Chandrachud, ibid. See further, Section 221, Government of India Act, 1935.

42. See, speech of the Marquess of Zetland, on the Government of India (Federal Court) Order, 1936, available at: http://hansard. millbanksystems.com/lords/1936/nov/26/government-of-india-federal-court-order (last visited 22 May 2017).

43. Chandrachud, *An Independent, Colonial Judiciary.* Shanti Bhushan, however, said that even then, the salary of judges was more than enough and a chief justice earned more money than he could spend. Shanti Bhushan, *Courting Destiny: A Memoir* (Kindle: Penguin Books, 2008), p. 1361.

44. Earlier, Home Minister Patel had written a letter to all the judges of the country asking them to voluntarily agree to a cut in salaries at 15 per cent. Many had replied and voluntarily reduced their own salaries, though not to the full extent of 15 per cent. Patel did not prevail upon B.P. Sinha (later, a Supreme Court judge), to reduce his salary. Sinha, *Reminiscences*, p. 40. Justice B. Malik of the Allahabad High Court wrote a letter to President Rajendra Prasad in June 1949 which, among other things, complained about the reduction

in judges' salaries. Valmiki Choudhary (ed.), *Dr. Rajendra Prasad: In the Constituent Assembly* (New Delhi: Allied Publishers Ltd, 1994), vol. 20, letter from Justice B. Malik (Allahabad High Court) to Prasad, dated 25 June 1949, p. 333.

45. The salaries of Federal Court judges (including the chief justice) who stood over as Supreme Court judges, however, were not changed to their detriment. Chief Justice Kania wrote to Home Minister Patel about this, and Patel agreed that the salary reduction should only affect 'future incumbents'. P.N. Chopra and Prabha Chopra (eds.), *The Collected Works of Sardar Vallabhbhai Patel* (New Delhi: Konark Publishers Pvt. Ltd, 2015), vol. 13, p. 118. However, Justice S.R. Das, who was appointed to the Federal Court a few days before the Constitution came into being, had some difficulty getting the higher salary, until the President issued a clarificatory order in his favour. See, speech of S.R. Das at his farewell, (1959) SCR vii, p. xiii. Similarly, when Patanjali Sastri became the chief justice of India, there was some doubt about whether he would be entitled to the higher salary or the new lower one, until the President issued another clarificatory order, ensuring that he got the higher one. Ibid, pp. xiii–xiv.

46. Articles 125 and 221, read with Part D, Second Schedule, Constitution of India.

47. Compare Section 6, Indian High Courts Act, 1861; Section 104, Government of India Act, 1915; Sections 201 and 221, Government of India Act, 1935, with, Articles 125 and 221, Constitution of India.

48. Under the proviso to Article 125(2) of the Constitution, only the 'privileges', 'allowances' and 'rights in respect of leave of absence or pension' of a Supreme Court judge cannot be 'varied to his disadvantage after his appointment'. Similarly, under the proviso to Article 221(2) of the Constitution, the 'allowances' and 'rights in respect of leave of absence or pension' of a high court judge (high court judges do not have 'privileges' as Supreme Court judges do) cannot be 'varied to his disadvantage after his appointment'.

49. See, Ramachandra Guha, *India After Gandhi* (London: Macmillan, 2007), pp. 184–85; Durga Das (ed.), *Sardar Patel's Correspondence, 1945-1950* (Ahmedabad: Navajivan Trust, 1973), vol. 6, p. 300. In July 1949, Patel wrote to President Rajendra Prasad about Master Tara Singh and said: 'He is a fanatic and seems to suffer from some

hallucinations about the coming of Sikh Raj and . . . he even goes to the extent of saying that those who cannot reconcile themselves to the demands of Sikhs in East Punjab, should clear out.' Das, ibid., vol. 8, p. 279, and vol. 9, p. 145. See further, 'Tara Singh', *Encyclopedia Britannica*, available at: https://www.britannica.com/biography/Tara-Singh (last visited 25 May 2017).

50. Nehru to Patel, letter dated November 1948. Gopal, *Selected Works of Jawaharlal Nehru*, 2nd Series, vol. 8, p. 196.

51. Nehru to Patel, letter dated 23 November 1948, Gopal, ibid., p. 201.

52. Apart from the two letters above, see further, Nehru to Patel, letter dated 5 December 1948, Gopal, ibid., p. 202; Patel's correspondence with Nehru and the Premiers of the Provinces, between June and November 1949. Das (ed.), *Sardar Patel's Correspondence*, vol. 8, pp. 132, 134, 136.

53. Interview with K.S. Hegde (13 January 1980).

54. See, the Statement of Objects and Reasons of the Constitution (Fifty-Fourth) Amendment Act, 1986.

55. These statistics are based on the consumer price index. The data has been obtained from the website of the World Bank, available at: http://data.worldbank.org/indicator/FP.CPI.TOTL.ZG?end=1986&locations=IN&start=1960 (last visited 22 May 2017).

56. Interview with Justice R.B. Misra (1 June 1983).

57. Law Commission, 14th Report, vol. 1, pp. 82–83.

58. Ibid., p. 81.

59. This is because the Constitution itself provided what the salaries of judges were going to be.

60. See, Sinha, *Reminiscences*, p. 176.

61. Constitution (Fifty-Fourth Amendment) Act, 1986.

62. This amendment provided that the salaries of judges would now be determined according to a law made by Parliament, and until such a law was enacted, would be as per the Constitution.

63. The High Court and Supreme Court Judges (Conditions of Service) Amendment Act, 1998, available at: http://lawmin.nic.in/legislative/textofcentralacts/1998.pdf (last visited 20 May 2017). All legislations in India from 1851 onwards may be conveniently found on the following website arranged chronologically: http://lawmin.nic.in/legislative/textofcentralacts/index.htm (last visited 20 May 2017).

64. The High Court and Supreme Court Judges (Salaries and Conditions of Service) Amendment Act, 2018.

65. In fact, Chief Justice Sinha thought that it would be a good idea to appoint young lawyers as judges because those lawyers would not have large earnings at the bar. Sinha, *Reminiscences*, pp. 174–75.

66. Nehru's note to all ministries dated 27 July 1949, Gopal, *Selected Works of Jawaharlal Nehru*, 2nd Series, vol. 12, p. 211.

67. Nehru to Katju, letter dated 13 June 1952, Gopal, ibid., vol. 18, at p. 207. The letter was written in the context of a government proposal not to hire persons who had more than one wife. It seems that Katju might have had a lawyer's opinion saying that this would not be legal.

68. Remarks made by Nehru at the Chief Ministers' Conference on 23 October 1955. Gopal, ibid., vol. 30, p. 302.

69. Ibid.

70. '2016 Law Firm Salary Surveys Bonanza', *Legally India*, 9 December 2016, available at: http://www.legallyindia.com/law-firms/law-firm-salaries-2016-00011130-8145 (last visited 22 May 2017).

71. Prachi Shrivastava, 'How Much Do Delhi's Top Advocates Charge?', *Livemint*, 16 September 2015, available at: http://www.livemint.com/Politics/BvOZE6z7Oyl6LiHZxWVlzL/How-much-do-Delhis-top-advocates-charge.html (last visited 22 May 2017). See further, 'Which 9 Top Lawyers Easily Charge Rs. 15+ Lakh Per Hearing? 42 Delhi Seniors' Fees Revealed', *Legally India*, 8 September 2015, available at: http://www.legallyindia.com/the-bench-and-the-bar/revealed-delhi-rsquo-s-top-advocates-won-rsquo-t-even-touch-your-case-for-less-than-rs-5-lakh-20150908-6555 (last visited 22 May 2017); Priya Sahgal and Kaveree Bamzai, 'Rich Lawyers: The New Nawabs', *India Today*, 4 December 2010, available at: http://indiatoday.intoday.in/story/rich-lawyers-the-new-nawabs/1/122053.html (last visited 22 May 2017); Kritika Banerjee, 'Harish Salve, Who Charged Re 1 in Kulbhushan Jadhav Case, Drives a Bentley, Loves Playing Piano', *India Today*, 16 May 2017, available at: http://indiatoday.intoday.in/story/harish-salve-re1-fee-kulbhushan-jadhav-drives-bentley-plays-piano/1/954969.html (last visited 22 May 2017).

72. 'Judicial Compensation', *United States Courts*, available at: http://www.uscourts.gov/judges-judgeships/judicial-compensation (last visited 22 May 2017).

73. 'Ministry of Justice Judicial Salaries from 1 April 2016', *Ministry of Justice*, available at: https://www.gov.uk/government/uploads/system/uploads/attachment_data/file/518055/moj-judicial-salaries-1-april-2016.pdf (last visited 22 May 2017).
74. See, Judges' Remuneration (Annual Pensionable Salary) Order, 1994, as revised up to 2017, available at: http://statutes.agc.gov.sg/aol/search/display/view.w3p;orderBy=date-rev,loadTime;page=0;query=Id%3Accb6963b-fe58-4161-a455-c202a556dcf7;rec=0 (last visited 22 May 2017).
75. See, Rule 2-A, High Court Judges Rules, 1956, available at: http://delhihighcourt.nic.in/writereaddata/upload/CourtRules/CourtRuleFile_30T75TIT.PDF (last visited 2 May 2017). Rule 4, Supreme Court Judges Rules, 1959, available at: http://www.delhihighcourt.nic.in/library/acts_bills_rules_regulations/The%20Supreme%20Court%20Judges%20rules1959.pdf (last visited 22 May 2017). Rules 2B and 4B of these respective rules prescribe the maximum amount which can be spent for furnishing a judge's residence (Rs 2.50 lakh for the chief justice of India, Rs 2 lakh for Supreme Court judges or high court chief justices, Rs 1.50 lakh for high court judges).
76. Second Schedule, Constitution of India; Section 22A, High Court Judges (Salaries and Conditions of Service) Act, 1954; Section 23(1), Supreme Court Judges (Salaries and Conditions of Service) Act, 1958. However, it seems that the Federal Court judges who stood over as Supreme Court judges did not get a free official house. Consequently, Justice B.K. Mukherjea had to pay Rs 350 per month as house rent. Interview with Justice A. Mukherjea, son of B.K. Mukherjea (29 June 1983).
77. Second Schedule, Constitution of India. Section 22, Supreme Court Judges (Salaries and Conditions of Service) Act, 1958. Section 22, High Court Judges (Salaries and Conditions of Service) Act, 1954. Rule 7-A, High Court Judges Travelling Allowance Rules, 1956. Rule 6-A, Supreme Court Judges (Travelling Allowance) Rules, 1959.
78. Section 22C, High Court Judges (Salaries and Conditions of Service) Act, 1954 (first introduced in 1976). Section 23B, Supreme Court Judges (Salaries and Conditions of Service) Act, 1958 (first introduced in 1976).
79. Rule 2, High Court Judges Rules, 1956; Rule 6, Supreme Court Judges Rules, 1959. See further, Letter dated 9 May 2017 issued by the Government of India, Ministry of Law and Justice (Department

of Justice), on dearness allowance to Supreme Court and high court judges, available at: http://doj.gov.in/news/payment-dearness-allowance-judges-supreme-court-and-high-courts-0 (last visited 22 May 2017), citing the above rules for payment of dearness allowance to Supreme Court and high court judges.

80.   Section 23, High Court Judges (Salaries and Conditions of Service) Act, 1954; Section 23(2), Supreme Court Judges (Salaries and Conditions of Service) Act, 1958.

81.   This is subject to limits, at least for high court judges. For instance, the limit for high court judges (according to the latest rules which are available online, though the rules may have been updated thereafter) was 3600 kilo litres of water and 10,000 units of power per annum. Rule 2E, High Court Judges Rules, 1956. There does not appear to be a limit for Supreme Court judges (at least one which is prescribed in the rules). See, Explanation to Rule 4, Supreme Court Judges Rules, 1959.

82.   See, First Schedule under the High Court Judges (Salaries and Conditions of Service) Act, 1954, and Supreme Court Judges (Salaries and Conditions of Service) Act, 1958.

83.   Section 23D, High Court Judges (Salaries and Conditions of Service) Act, 1954 (first introduced in 1976); Section 23C, Supreme Court Judges (Salaries and Conditions of Service) Act, 1958 (first introduced in 1976).

84.   It was for this reason that Chief Justice B.P. Sinha wanted to increase the retirement age of judges, so that they would get a higher pension at the end of their longer period of service. Sinha, *Reminiscences*, p. 176.

85.   The High Court and Supreme Court Judges (Salaries and Conditions of Service) Amendment Act, 2005. Section 13A was inserted into the Supreme Court Judges (Salaries and Conditions of Service) Act, 1958, by virtue of this amendment. In fact, it was only after this amendment that three lawyers were directly appointed to the Supreme Court for the first time in India's history: Justices R.F. Nariman, U.U. Lalit and L. Nageswara Rao. However, correlation is not causation, and one doubts whether the 2005 amendment to the pensions of direct bar appointments to the Supreme Court really had anything to do with these lawyers accepting direct appointments to the bench.

      The Law Commission in its 14th Report had recommended that lawyers be appointed at a younger age to the high court bench so that they will have sufficient years in service in order to earn a full pension. Law Commission, 14th Report, vol. 1, p. 83.

86. Thus, the maximum pension that a retired chief justice of India can draw today is Rs 16.80 lakh per annum, a retired Supreme Court judge or high court chief justice can draw no more than Rs 15 lakh per annum as pension, while a retired high court judge is limited to Rs 13.50 lakh per annum as pension. See, First Schedule, High Court Judges (Salaries and Conditions of Service) Act, 1954; Schedule, Supreme Court Judges (Salaries and Conditions of Service) Act, 1958. Earlier, the maximum pension drawn by an Indian judge was one third of his annual salary. The Law Commission in its 14th Report (vol. 1, pp. 43–44) observed that in the UK, pensions were equal to half the judges' salaries, whereas in the US, they were equal to the annual salaries if ten years of service had been put in by the judge in question.

87. Section 22B, inserted by the High Court Judges (Conditions of Service) Amendment Act, 1976. Section 23A, inserted by the Supreme Court Judges (Conditions of Service) Amendment Act, 1976.

88. The Supreme Court and High Court Judges (Conditions of Service) Amendment Act, 1996. However, if the judges use less than 200 litres, the statute does not specifically permit them to encash the unused petrol.

89. Section 22B, High Court Judges (Salaries and Conditions of Service) Act, 1954. Section 23A, Supreme Court Judges (Salaries and Conditions of Service) Act, 1958.

90. M. Hidayatullah, *My Own Boswell: Memoirs* (Bombay: N.M. Tripathi Pvt. Ltd, 1992), p. 213.

91. Interview with K.S. Hegde (13 January 1980).

92. Section 22D, High Court Judges (Salaries and Conditions of Service) Act, 1954. Section 23D, Supreme Court Judges (Salaries and Conditions of Service) Act, 1958. These were inserted by the High Court and Supreme Court Judges (Conditions of Service) Amendment Act, 1980 (with effect from 1975). These provisions were made even more liberal by the High Court and Supreme Court Judges (Conditions of Service) Amendment Act, 1988.

93. Interview with Justice P.N. Bhagwati (20 April 1983); Interview with Justice P.N. Bhagwati (on 31 March 1988).

94. Law Commission, 14th Report, vol. 1, p. 82. Justice Hardy said that the salary of high court judges after taxes was around Rs 2000,

which is why he initially declined a high court judgeship, but was persuaded by Chief Justice Subba Rao to accept. Hardy, *Struggles and Sorrows*, p. 96. The salary paid to Federal Court judges who stood over as Supreme Court judges was, after taxes, reduced from Rs 5500 per month to Rs 2600 per month. Interview with Justice A. Mukherjea, son of B.K. Mukherjea (29 June 1983).

95. Very Important Person.
96. Interview with Justice P.N. Bhagwati (31 March 1988).
97. Travancore-Cochin was a 'Part B' state in the First Schedule to the Constitution, as originally enacted.
98. Gopal, *Selected Works of Jawaharlal Nehru*, 2nd Series, vol. 30, p. 302.
99. Interview with Justice A.N. Sen (24 October 1988).
100. Interview with Justice D.P. Madon (28 April 1983). See further, Interview with Justice R.B. Misra (1 June 1983); letter from H.M. Seervai to Chief Justice A.M. Ahmadi dated 12 December 1995, in Feroza H. Seervai (ed.), *Evoking H.M. Seervai: Jurist and Authority on the Indian Constitution* (Delhi: Universal Law Publishing Co. Pvt. Ltd, 2005), p. 329.
101. Interview with Justice A.N. Sen (24 October 1988). See further, Interview with Justice R.B. Misra (1 June 1983).
102. Interview with Justice Balakrishna Eradi (28 October 1988).
103. Interview with Justice A.P. Sen (11 May 1983).
104. Interview with Justice R.B. Misra (1 June 1983).
105. The Supreme Court offer probably came from Chief Justice Sikri. See, Interview with Justice S.M. Sikri (17 October 1988). However, this is not certain because Gadbois wrote that Sikri 'possibly' tried to recruit Seervai, in his interview notes.
106. Feroza H. Seervai, 'H.M. Seervai', in Feroza H. Seervai (ed.), *Evoking H.M. Seervai*, p. 4. The fact that Seervai declined an offer of judgeship was confirmed by Gajendragadkar in *To the Best of My Memory*, p. 153.
107. Interview with Justice A.P. Sen (11 May 1983).
108. Ibid.
109. See further, Interview with Justice Raghubar Dayal (2 June 1983).
110. Interview with Justice A.M. Ahmadi (1 January 89).
111. Seth, *On Balance*, p. 3369.
112. Ibid., p. 3391.
113. Interview with Justice G.K. Mitter (28 June 1983). However, Mitter advised his son to decline a high court judgeship because the pay

was too low and one had to have independent wealth and a house in order to become a judge.

114. Interview with Justice M.M. Dutt (24 April 1988).
115. His health had been poor since the age of thirteen. He had spondylosis, a spinal disease. He also had high blood pressure, failing kidneys and heart trouble. Interview with Mrs Archana Subimal Roy (29 June 1983). See further, Interview with Justice D.G. Palekar (4 November 1988).
116. He had also become bored of practising at the Calcutta High Court and thought that the Supreme Court would be a nice change. Interview with Mrs Archana Subimal Roy (29 June 1983).
117. Interview with Justice M.H. Kania (23 April 1988).
118. Section 220(2), Government of India Act, 1935. This was also the retirement age of high court judges prior to the Government of India Act, 1935. See, Chandrachud, *An Independent, Colonial Judiciary.*
119. Section 200(2), Government of India Act, 1935.
120. Law Commission, 14th Report, vol. 1, p. 85. See further, Chandrachud, *The Informal Constitution.*
121. Chandrachud, 'My Dear Chagla'.
122. See, Articles 124(2) and 217(1), Constitution of India.
123. Constitution (Fifteenth Amendment) Act, 1963.
124. See further, Abhinav Chandrachud, 'The Need to Have a Uniform Retirement Age for Judges', *Economic and Political Weekly*, vol. 47, Issue 46 (November 2012).
125. Sinha, *Reminiscences*, p. 176.
126. Chandrachud, 'My Dear Chagla'.
127. M.C. Chagla, *Roses in December: An Autobiography* (Mumbai: Bharatiya Vidya Bhavan, 2016 reprint), p. 171.
128. Ibid.
129. Ibid.
130. Interview with M. Hidayatullah (17 June 1983).
131. Interview with Chief Justice Y.V. Chandrachud (3 May 1983).
132. Interview with Justice Ranganathan (24 October 1988).
133. Interview with Justice Kailasam (24 June 1983); Interview with Mrs Subba Rao (23 June 1983).
134. Interview with Justice Y.V. Chandrachud (8 December 1988). See further, Interview with Chief Justice Pathak (1 October 1988).
135. Interview with Justice Y.V. Chandrachud (8 December 1988).
136. Interview with Justice R.B. Misra (1 June 1983).

137. Interview with Justice R.B. Misra (27 October 1988). See further, 'Judge of Emergency Fame Passes Away', *The Hindu*, 25 March 2015, available at: http://www.thehindu.com/news/national/tamil-nadu/judge-of-emergency-fame-passes-away/article7029812.ece (last visited 25 February 2018).

138. *Union of India v. Gopal Chandra Misra*, (1978) 2 SCC 301.

139. Interview with Justice R.B. Misra (27 October 1988).

140. Interview with Justice K.N. Singh (3 September 1988); Interview with Justice M.H. Kania (23 April 1988*)*. See further, Bhushan, *Courting Destiny*.

141. See, 'Chief Justices of the High Court of Judicature at Allahabad (1967–1983)', available at: http://www.allahabadhighcourt.in/photogallary/Chief-justice/newcj_3.htm (last visited 21 May 2017).

142. See: 'Former Chief Justices', Calcutta High Court website, available at: http://calcuttahighcourt.nic.in/former_cj.htm (last visited 21 May 2017).

143. For more on Ismail, see, Hardy, *Struggles and Sorrows*, p. 97.

144. Interview with Justice Y.V. Chandrachud (8 December 1988); Interview with Chief Justice R.S. Pathak (1 October 1988). Sikri said that Ismail did not like the Delhi climate. Interview with Justice S.M. Sikri (17 October 1988). Similarly, B.P. Sinha declined the chief justiceship of the Gauhati High Court because he was 'a life-long sufferer from asthma' and thought that 'the damp climate of Gauhati on the bank of the River Brahmaputra' would 'not be congenial to [his] health'. Sinha, *Reminiscences*, p. 41.

145. Interview with Justice H.R. Khanna (3 October 1988).

146. P.S. Vaidyanathan, 'The Decision Was Mine', *India Today*, uploaded on 14 November 2013, available at: http://indiatoday.intoday.in/story/there-was-absolutely-no-question-of-anyone-asking-me-to-resign-chief-justice-m.m.-ismail/1/402083.html (last visited 21 May 2017). See further, 'The Honourable Chief Justices', website of the Madras High Court, available at: http://www.hcmadras.tn.nic.in/cjlist.html (last visited 21 May 2017); 'M.M. Ismail Dead', *The Hindu*, 18 January 2005, available at: http://www.thehindu.com/2005/01/18/stories/2005011814310500.htm (last visited 21 May 2017).

147. Interview with Justice Y.V. Chandrachud (8 December 1988).

148. Interview with Chief Justice Y.V. Chandrachud (3 May 1983).

149. Ibid.

150. Interview with Justice Y.V. Chandrachud (8 December 1988).

151. Ibid.; Interview with N.L. Untwalia (3 December 1988); Interview with Justice V. Khalid (21 November 1988); Interview with Justice L.M. Sharma (24 April 1988).

152. Interview with Justice V. Khalid (21 November 1988); Interview with Justice L.M. Sharma (24 April 1988).

153. 'Justice Seema Ali Passes Away', *Times of India*, 5 September 2013, available at: http://timesofindia.indiatimes.com/city/patna/Justice-Seema-Ali-passes-away/articleshow/22306888.cms (last visited 21 May 2017). B.P. Sinha initially did not accept the chief justiceship of the Nagpur High Court because, apart from the fact that he did not think the post held much prestige, he did not want to run two establishments, one in Patna (where his young children were growing up) and the other in Nagpur. He later agreed to go there when the chief minister told him that he had to go to Nagpur in the national interest. Sinha, *Reminiscences*, pp. 40–42.

154. Interview with Justice Y.V. Chandrachud (8 December 1988).

155. Ibid.

156. Law Commission, 14th Report, vol. 1, p. 85.

157. Ibid.

158. Interview with Justice Y.V. Chandrachud (8 December 1988). See further, Interview with Mr Izari, Registrar of Karnataka High Court (26 June 1983).

159. See, 'Former Chief Justices', Calcutta High Court website, available at: http://calcuttahighcourt.nic.in/former_cj.htm (last visited 21 May 2017).

160. Interview with A.C. Gupta (22 October 1988); Interview with Justice Sabyasachi Mukharji (1 October 1988); Interview with Justice B.C. Ray (22 April 1988); Interview with Justice M.M. Dutt (24 April 1988).

161. See, 'Former Chief Justices', Calcutta High Court website.

162. 'Rajya Sabha Members, Biographical Sketches, 1952–2003', available at: http://rajyasabha.nic.in/rsnew/pre_member/1952_2003.asp (last visited 23 May 2017).

163. Ibid.

164. Interview with S.M. Sikri (17 October 1988); Interview with Justice K.S. Hegde (14–15 November 1988); Interview with Justice Y.V. Chandrachud (8 December 1988); Interview with A.C. Gupta (22 October 1988); Interview with Justice M.M. Dutt (24 April 1988). According to Justice A.C. Gupta, Mitra attached conditions to his Supreme Court appointment; he said that he

wanted to be the Calcutta High Court chief justice for two years before going to the Supreme Court, and wanted nobody junior to be appointed to the Supreme Court before him. Mitra was born on 26 December 1917. See, 'Rajya Sabha Members, Biographical Sketches, 1952–2003'.

165. Interview with S.M. Sikri (17 October 1988).
166. Interview with Justice Y.V. Chandrachud (8 December 1988). Mitra's profile says that he was an independent candidate. See, 'Rajya Sabha Members, Biographical Sketches, 1952–2003'. However, Chandrachud believed that he was a Congress (I) candidate.
167. Interview with Justice D.A. Desai (29 September 1988); Interview with Chief Justice R.S. Pathak (1 October 1988); Interview with Justice E.S. Venkataramiah (2 October 1988); Interview with Justice Balakrishna Eradi (28 October 1988); Interview with Justice Sabyasachi Mukharji (1 October 1988); Interview with Justice V. Khalid (21 November 88).
168. Interview with Justice M.M. Dutt (24 April 1988); Interview with Justice S. Natarajan (24 April 1988); Interview with Justice M.H. Kania (23 April 1988); Interview with Justice K.J. Shetty (25 April 1988); Interview with Justice L.M. Sharma (24 April 1988); Interview with Justice Ranganathan (24 October 1988).
169. Interview with Justice G.L. Oza (22 April 1988).
170. Interview with Justice M.P. Thakkar (29 April 1983).
171. Interview with Justice K.N. Saikia (11 December 1988).
172. Interview with Justice M.N. R. Venkatachaliah (1 September 1988).
173. His son was Justice L.M. Sharma.
174. Interview with Justice G.K. Mitter (28 June 1983); Interview with A.C. Gupta (22 October 1988).
175. See, 'Former Chief Justices', Calcutta High Court website, available at: http://calcuttahighcourt.nic.in/former_cj.htm (last visited 22 May 2017).
176. Interview with M. Hidayatullah (4 November 1988). Justice Vaidialingam confirmed that Hidayatullah recommended Kotval's name, but did not confirm that Hidayatullah had recommended Menon. Interview with Justice C.A. Vaidialingam (24 October 1988).
177. Interview with J.C. Shah (3 November 1988). Shah said he only later learnt that Hidayatullah had recommended Kotval's name. However, Shah's memory during the interview, noted Gadbois, did not appear to be excellent.

178. Interview with Justice Y.V. Chandrachud (8 December 1988);
     Interview with Justice D.P. Madon (28 April 1983). Justice M.H.
     Kania, however, did not believe that Kotval was offered a Supreme
     Court seat by Hidayatullah. Interview with Justice M.H. Kania (23
     April 1988).
179. However, this is implausible because Sikri could not recollect
     anything about Hidayatullah's recommendations of Kotval and
     Menon. Interview with Justice S.M. Sikri (17 October 1988).
180. Hidayatullah thought that either of these was a possibility. Interview
     with Justice M. Hidayatullah (3 June 1983).
181. Interview with Justice M.M. Dutt (24 April 1988); Interview with
     Justice M.H. Kania (23 April 1988).
182. Interview with Justice M.M. Dutt (24 April 1988); Interview with
     Justice S. Natarajan (24 April 1988).
183. Interview with Justice A. Varadarajan (13 May 1983).
184. Interview with Justice G.L. Oza (22 April 1988).
185. Interview with M. Hidayatullah (17 June 1983).
186. Interview with Justice Sabyasachi Mukharji (26 April 1983).
187. Interview with Justice M.H. Kania (23 April 1988).

5. The Fictional Concurrence of the Chief Justice

1.   *Supreme Court Advocates-on-Record Association v. Union of India*,
     (1993) 4 SCC 441, decided on 6 October 1993.
2.   Sections 200(2) and 220(2), Government of India Act, 1935.
3.   Undated note of President Rajendra Prasad, probably prepared
     sometime in the late 1950s, titled: 'Procedure to Be Adopted in
     Connection with the Appointment of High Court Judges', Valmiki
     Choudhary (ed.), *Dr. Rajendra Prasad: Correspondence and Select
     Documents: Presidency Period* (New Delhi: Allied Publishers Ltd,
     1989), vol. 12, p. 292. After the Indian Independence Act, 1947, the
     role of the secretary of state was eliminated in this process.
4.   Abhinav Chandrachud, *An Independent, Colonial Judiciary: A
     History of the Bombay High Court During the British Raj, 1862-
     1947* (New Delhi: Oxford University Press, 2015).
5.   See further, letter from Kania to Nehru, dated 18 December
     1947, Durga Das (ed.), *Sardar Patel's Correspondence, 1945-1950*
     (Ahmedabad: Navajivan Trust, 1973), vol. 6, p. 274.
6.   Shukla to Patel, letter dated 3 May 1947. Ibid., vol. 5, p. 157.
7.   Patel to Shukla, letter dated 7 May 1947. Ibid., p. 158.

8.   Shukla to Patel, letter dated 20 May 1947. Ibid., p. 158.
9.   Patel to Shukla, letter dated 26 May 1947. Ibid, p. 159.
10. S. Varadachariar (a former Federal Court judge), Alladi Krishnaswami
     Ayyar (a prominent Madras advocate), B.L. Mitter (former advocate
     general at the Federal Court), K.M. Munshi (Bombay advocate
     and politician), B.N. Rau (constitutional adviser to the Constituent
     Assembly).
11. B.N. Rau thought of the Council of State as a kind of Privy
     Council. He said: 'It is a non-party body of elder statesmen and
     judges including the Chief Justice and every ex-Chief Justice of the
     Supreme Court.' 30 May 1947 memorandum on the principles of
     a model Provincial Constitution by B.N. Rau. B. Shiva Rao (ed.),
     The Framing of India's Constitution: Select Documents (New Delhi:
     Universal Law Publishing Co. Pvt. Ltd, 2012 reprint) ('BSR'),
     vol. 2, pp. 632, 640
12. Ibid., p. 590.
13. Ibid., pp. 609–10.
14. Ibid., pp. 558–59.
15. Articles 87(2) and 164(2), October 1947 draft Constitution. Ibid.,
     vol. 3, p. 4.
16. Mountbatten to Patel, letter dated 11 August 1947. Das (ed.),
     Sardar Patel's Correspondence, vol. 5, p. 154.
17. Patel to Mountbatten, letter dated 14 August 1947. Ibid., pp. 154–
     55.
18. Patel to Nehru, letter dated 14 August 1947. Ibid., p. 155.
19. Undated note of President Rajendra Prasad, Choudhary (ed.), *Dr.
     Rajendra Prasad*, vol. 12, pp. 292–93.
20. Ibid.
21. Kania to Nehru, letter dated 18 December 1947, enclosed in the
     letter from Kania to Patel dated 24 January 1948. Das (ed.), *Sardar
     Patel's Correspondence*, vol. 6, p. 274.
22. Chagla to Kher, letter dated 10 February 1948. Ibid., p. 182.
23. Patel to Kher, letter dated 17 February 1948. Ibid., p. 184.
24. Patel to Kania, letter dated 10 December 1948. Ibid., pp. 201–02.
25. Kania to Patel, letter dated 11 December 1948. Ibid., p. 202.
26. Patel to Kania, letter dated 11 December 1948. Ibid., p. 203.
27. Kania to Patel, letter dated 14 December 1948. Ibid., p. 164.
28. Kania to Patel, letter dated 16 March 1948. Ibid., p. 276.
29. Memorandum of Federal Court judges and high court chief justices
     (March 1948), BSR, vol. 4, p. 193.

30. Kania to Patel, letter dated 4 April 1948. Das (ed.), *Sardar Patel's Correspondence*, vol. 6, p. 277.
31. Patel to Kania, letter dated 8 April 1948. Ibid., p. 277.
32. See, Profile of Professor Ranga on the Lok Sabha website, available at: http://164.100.47.194/loksabha/writereaddata/biodata_1_12/1326.htm (last visited 4 June 2017).
33. Ranga to Patel, letter dated 10 September 1948. Das (ed.), *Sardar Patel's Correspondence*, vol. 6, pp. 412–13.
34. Patel to Ranga, letter dated 14 September 1948. Ibid., p. 414.
35. B. Pocker Sahib moved an amendment in the Constituent Assembly, seeking to make judicial appointments in the Supreme Court subject to the concurrence of the chief justice of India. He cited the memorandum prepared at the conference of Federal Court judges and high court chief justices in support of his amendment. The amendment was rejected. Constituent Assembly Debates of India (New Delhi: Lok Sabha Secretariat) (CAD), vol. 8, p. 232 (24 May 1949). A similar amendment was moved by Mahboob Ali Baig Sahib. CAD, vol. 8, p. 238 (24 May 1949).
36. Ibid., p. 258.
37. Article 124(2).
38. Proviso, Article 124(2).
39. Article 217(1), Constitution.
40. Prof. Shibban Lal Saksena's amendment sought to make the chief justice of India the only judge consulted by the President while appointing Supreme Court judges. This amendment was negatived by the Constituent Assembly. CAD, vol. 8, p. 231 (24 May 1949).
41. Undated note of Rajendra Prasad, Choudhary (ed.), *Dr. Rajendra Prasad*, vol. 12, p. 295. The memorandum of procedure was revised over the years. For example, in 1955, it was revised to include a format for a medical certificate to be provided for a proposed judge. Ibid, p. 303.
42. The same procedure was to be followed while appointing high court chief justices, but the initiative in such cases was to come from the chief minister.
43. Granville Austin, *Working a Democratic Constitution: A History of the Indian Experience* (New Delhi: Oxford University Press, 2003 reprint), pp. 124–35. A.G. Noorani discusses some of the incidents mentioned in Austin's book in greater detail. A.G. Noorani, 'The Prime Minister and the Judiciary', in James Manor (ed.), *Nehru*

to the Nineties: The Changing Office of Prime Minister of India (London: C. Hurst & Co., 1994), available on Google Books.

44. Nehru to Patel, letter dated 23 January 1950. Das (ed.), *Sardar Patel's Correspondence*, vol. 10, p. 377.
45. Nehru to Patel, ibid., p. 378.
46. Patel to Rajagopalachari, letter dated 23 January 1950. Ibid., p. 377.
47. Patel to Nehru, letter dated 23 January 1950. Ibid., p. 378.
48. See, Noorani, 'The Prime Minister and the Judiciary'. One can find several reported judgments thereafter to the credit of Justice Basheer Ahmed Sayeed.
49. Patel to Nehru, letter dated 3 December 1950. Das (ed.), *Sardar Patel's Correspondence*, vol. 9, p. 305.
50. Patel to Nehru, ibid.
51. Patel to Nehru, ibid.
52. Patel to Raja, letter dated 20 November 1950, P.N. Chopra (ed.), *The Collected Works of Sardar Vallabhbhai Patel* (New Delhi: Konark Publishers Pvt. Ltd, 2015 reprint), vol. 15, pp. 281–82.
53. Patel to Nehru, letter dated 3 December 1950. Das (ed.), *Sardar Patel's Correspondence*, vol. 9, p. 306.
54. See, AIR 1954 Madras. Umamaheshwaran moved to the Andhra Pradesh High Court and retired in 1963. See, 'Hon'ble Sri Justice K. Umamaheswaram', Andhra Pradesh High Court website, available at: http://hc.tap.nic.in/aphc/kuj.html (last visited 27 May 2017). The Andhra Pradesh High Court website lists him as 'Umamaheswaram', but AIR 1954 Madras calls him 'Umamaheswaran'.
55. See, Nehru to Patel, letter dated 21 November 1950, enclosing a note dated 21 November 1950 prepared by Nehru. Das (ed.), *Sardar Patel's Correspondence*, vol. 9, p. 502. Patel to Nehru, letter dated 1 December 1950. Ibid, p. 505. See further, Noorani, 'The Prime Minister and the Judiciary'.
56. Under the First Schedule to the Constitution, 'Part A' states were, broadly speaking, provinces in British India prior to independence, and had stronger institutions. 'Part B' states had been princely states prior to independence.
57. Austin, *Working a Democratic Constitution*, p. 126. Austin spells his name as 'Nawalkishore'. The note dated 21 November 1950 prepared by Nehru spelled his name as 'Nawal Kishore'. The website of the Rajasthan High Court, however, spells it as 'Naval Kishore': http://hcraj.nic.in/formerj.aspx (last visited 2 March 2018).

58. See, Nehru to Patel, letter dated 21 November 1950, enclosing a
     note dated 21 November 1950 of the prime minister's secretariat.
     Das (ed.), *Sardar Patel's Correspondence*, vol. 9, p. 502.
59. Ibid. See further, Choudhary (ed.), *Dr. Rajendra Prasad*, vol. 13, p.
     103.
60. Nehru to Patel, letter dated 21 November 1950, enclosing a note
     dated 21 November 1950 of the prime minister's secretariat. Das
     (ed.), *Sardar Patel's Correspondence*, vol. 9, p. 502.
61. Patel to Nehru, letter dated 1 December 1950. Ibid, p. 505;
     Choudhary (ed.), *Dr. Rajendra Prasad*, vol. 13, Patel to Nehru,
     letter dated 1 December 1950, p. 105.
62. See, 'Former Chief Justices', Rajasthan High Court website, available
     at: http://hcraj.nic.in/formercj.aspx (last visited 27 May 2017); George
     H. Gadbois, Jr., *Judges of the Supreme Court of India, 1950-1989* (New
     Delhi: Oxford University Press, 2011), p. 80.
63. See, 'List of Hon'ble Judges in Rajasthan High Court . . .', Rajasthan
     High Court website, available at: http://hcraj.nic.in/formerj.aspx
     (last visited 27 May 2017).
64. The order is available at: https://archive.org/stream/
     in.gazette.1949.15/O-2353-1949-0018-109290#page/n1/
     mode/2up/search/sinha (last visited 2 March 2018).
65. Nehru to Kania, letter dated 14 February 1950. Das (ed.), *Sardar
     Patel's Correspondence*, vol. 9, p. 331. See further, Kania to Nehru,
     letter dated 23 February 1950. Ibid, p. 333; Nehru to Kania, letter
     dated 26 February 1950. Ibid, p. 336.
66. Annexure to the letter from Home Minister Pant to Satyanarayana
     Rao dated 17 October 1957. Rajendra Prasad Papers, National
     Archives of India, File No. 47. Reuben's name does not find
     mention in the annexure. However, since the appointment came
     through in July 1953, when Reuben was the chief justice, I have
     assumed that the reference to the chief justice of the Patna High
     Court in the annexure was to Reuben.
67. See, 'Hon'ble Sri Justice K. Bhimasankaram', Andhra Pradesh High
     Court website, http://hc.tap.nic.in/aphc/kbj.html (last visited 28
     May 2017).
68. Annexure to the letter from Home Minister Pant to Satyanarayana
     Rao dated 17 October 1957. Rajendra Prasad Papers, National
     Archives of India, File No. 47. The annexure does not mention
     Mahajan's name. However, since Mahajan was the chief justice

of India when Bhimasankaram's appointment was made, I have assumed that he was the one who objected to the appointment.
69. After Satyanarayana Rao, who retired on 3 June 1954.
70. Prasad's note dated 2 July 1954. Choudhary (ed.), *Dr. Rajendra Prasad*, vol. 17, pp. 318–19.
71. The judge was either P. Basi Reddy or A. Ranganadham Chetty. The website of the Andhra Pradesh High Court suggests that these two were the only puisne judges appointed to that high court in 1957.
72. Prasad to Pant, letter dated 10 July 1957. Choudhary (ed.), *Dr. Rajendra Prasad*, vol. 18, pp. 168–69.
73. Undated note of President Rajendra Prasad. Ibid., vol. 12, p. 292, p. 300.
74. Appendix B to letter from Pant to Setalvad dated 22 August 1957. Rajendra Prasad Papers, National Archives of India, File No. 47.
75. See, Allahabad High Court website, available at: http://www. allahabadhighcourt.in/Judges/ex-judge1900-1990.htm (last visited 25 June 2017).
76. He served as the chief justice between 1967 and 1971. See, Allahabad High Court website, available at: http://www.allahabadhighcourt.in/ photogallary/Chief-justice/newcj_3.htm (last visited 25 June 2017).
77. Appendix B to letter from Pant to Setalvad dated 22 August 1957. Rajendra Prasad Papers, National Archives of India, File No. 47. He held this position between 1969 and 1970. See, Karnataka High Court website, available at: http://karnatakajudiciary.kar.nic.in/ judges_former_cjk.asp (last visited 25 June 2017).
78. He was appointed on 9 March 1955, and he retired on 1 February 1959. See, 'Miscellaneous', *The High Court at Calcutta*, available at: http://calcuttahighcourt.nic.in/sesqui/HC_150_4.pdf (last visited 25 June 2017).
79. Appendix B to letter from Pant to Setalvad dated 22 August 1957. Rajendra Prasad Papers, National Archives of India, File No. 47. The appendix did not name Chakravartti. However, since Chakravartti was, according to the website of the Calcutta High Court, the court's chief justice between 1952 and 1958, I have assumed that he was the chief justice who objected to Sarkar's appointment.
80. Interview with S.K. Das (14 May 1983). In his interview notes, Gadbois quoted Das as having said that Menon was 'empty in the upper chambers'. Interview with S.K. Das (18 October 1988).

81. B.P. Sinha, *Reminiscences and Reflections of a Chief Justice* (Delhi: B.R. Publishing Corporation, 1985), p. 77.

82. Interview with T.V. Balakrishnan, son of T.L.V. Ayyar (25 June 1983); Interview with Asoke Sen (27 December 1988).

83. 'V.K. Krishna Menon', *Encyclopedia Britannica*, available at: https://www.britannica.com/biography/V-K-Krishna-Menon (last visited 2 June 2017).

84. Interview with M. Sankaranarayan (21 June 1983).

85. Interview with Justice B.P. Sinha (17 July 1983). Interview with Justice S.K. Das (14 May 1983). Sinha said that Kapur was a partyman both in the social and political sense. He also said that after retiring from the Supreme Court during Sinha's term as the chief justice of India, Kapur refused to vacate his house, and succeeded in getting his house taken out of the pool of judges' houses through his political connections. Interview with Justice B.P. Sinha (17 July 1983).

86. Interview with Justice Dalip Kapur (5 July 1983).

87. Kapur wanted two of his friends to be appointed chief justice of the Delhi High Court, which was not possible as long as Khanna was there. So, in a sense, thought Gadbois, Khanna had been 'kicked upstairs' to the Supreme Court. Gadbois later wrote, in red ink, on the margin of the typewritten notes of his interview with Justice Kapur's son, alongside the narration of this story, 'I wonder', which indicates that perhaps Gadbois did not think that this story was entirely accurate.

88. Law Commission, 14th Report, vol. 1, p. 72.

89. BSR, vol. 2, p. 630.

90. Das retired on 1 October 1959.

91. K. Subba Rao, originally from the Madras High Court, was at the Supreme Court at this time. However, since he had moved as the chief justice to the Andhra Pradesh High Court prior to his elevation, Prasad was thinking of him as an Andhra judge. The following Madras judges were no longer at the court when Prasad's letter was written: Patanjali Sastri (retired in January 1954), N.C. Aiyar (retired in January 1953), T.L.V. Ayyar (retired in November 1958) and P. Govinda Menon (died in October 1957).

92. Prasad to Pant, letter dated 28 August 1959. Choudhary (ed.), *Dr. Rajendra Prasad*, vol. 19, p. 146.

93. After retiring in September 1951, he was brought back as an Article 128 judge. Gadbois, *Judges of the Supreme Court of India*, p. 22.

94. Chief Justice Sinha felt that Hasan had been appointed because he was a Muslim, not on considerations of merit. Interview with B.P. Sinha (17 July 1983).

95. Motilal C. Setalvad, *My Life: Law and Other Things* (Gurgaon: LexisNexis, 2017 reprint), p. 165. Interestingly, P. Jaganmohan Reddy had not held judicial office for ten years or practised as an advocate for ten years. Even so, he was appointed a high court judge after an opinion was obtained from prominent Madras advocate Alladi Krishnaswami Iyer, who also had helped draft the Constitution. P. Jaganmohan Reddy, *The Judiciary I Served* (Hyderabad: Orient Longman Ltd, 1999), p. 45. See further, Sinha, *Reminiscences*, p. 74.

96. This is essentially what the Law Commission said.

97. Austin, *Working a Democratic Constitution*, p. 130.

98. Mehr Chand Mahajan, *Looking Back* (London: Asia Publishing House, 1963), p. 213. See further, Austin, ibid, p. 130.

99. Austin thought this could be either B.K. Mukherjea or S.R. Das. Austin, *Working a Democratic Constitution*, p. 132. However, Setalvad's autobiography contains a footnote that it was S.R. Das. Setalvad, *My Life*, p. 249.

100. Law Commission, 14th Report, vol. 1, p. 72.

101. Sinha, *Reminiscences*, p. 95.

102. Austin, *Working a Democratic Constitution*, p. 131.

103. Motilal C. Setalvad, M.C. Chagla, K.N. Wanchoo and P. Satyanarayana Rao.

104. Setalvad to Pant, letter dated 8 August 1957. Rajendra Prasad Papers, National Archives of India, File No. 47.

105. Pant to Setalvad, letter dated 22 August 1957. Ibid.

106. Setalvad to Pant, letter dated 27 August 1957. Ibid.

107. Pant to Justice Satyanarayana Rao, letter dated 17 October 1957. Ibid.

108. Setalvad to Pant, letter dated 10 November 1957. Ibid.

109. Setalvad, *My Life*, p. 248.

110. Ibid., pp. 248–49.

111. Law Commission, 14th Report, vol. 1, pp. 71–72. Setalvad, ibid, p. 249.

112. Law Commission, ibid, p. 34.

113. Ibid., p. 69.

114. Ibid., p. 69.

115. Ibid., p. 70.

116. Ibid., p. 71.

117. Ibid.

118. Ibid.

119. Ibid.

120. Ibid., pp. 71–73.

121. Ibid., p. 74. At a meeting of Supreme Court judges in the 1960s, it was resolved that the government should not initiate names on its own. Gajendragadkar to Home Minister Nanda, letter dated 7 June 1966. Austin, *Working a Democratic Constitution*, p. 130 (note 21). Gajendragadkar in his autobiography said that the initiative for high court appointments always came from high court chief justices. P.B. Gajendragadkar, *To the Best of My Memory* (Bombay: Bharatiya Vidya Bhavan, 1983), pp. 164–65.

122. Law Commission, 14th Report, vol. 1, pp. 74–75.

123. Ibid., p. 75.

124. See, Law Commission of India, 80th Report, available at: http://lawcommissionofindia.nic.in/51-100/Report80.pdf (last visited 28 May 2017), p. 19.

125. Ibid.

126. Ibid. The Law Commission in its 80th Report expressed no opinion on whether the state governments should be able to suggest their own names, since it had already been decided that the chief minister would be entitled to suggest another name in case he disagreed with the one suggested by the chief justice. Law Commission, ibid, p. 24.

127. Nehru to Pant, letter dated 8 November 1959. S. Gopal (ed.), *Selected Works of Jawaharlal Nehru*, 2nd Series (New Delhi: Jawaharlal Nehru Memorial Fund, 1989), vol. 54, p. 356.

128. Nehru to Pant, letter dated 13 March 1960. Ibid., vol. 58, p. 185.

129. Ibid.

130. Profile of Chief Justice S.T. Desai on the website of the Gujarat High Court, available at: http://gujarathighcourt.nic.in/cjjfull?jid=400 (last visited 20 October 2017).

131. Nehru to Pant, letter dated 13 March 1960. Gopal, *Selected Works of Jawaharlal Nehru*, vol. 58, 2nd Series, p. 186.

132. Sinha, *Reminiscences*, p. 95.

133. Ibid., p. 98.

134. Ibid.

135. Ibid., p. 96.

136. Ibid., pp. 168–70. This could have been the incident he was referring to on pp. 93–94 of his autobiography.
137. Ibid., pp. 94–95.
138. Ibid., pp. 167–68.
139. Gajendragadkar, *To the Best of My Memory*, pp. 164–65. Gajendragadkar described the process of appointing high court judges as follows. He said that 'the initiative to recommend . . . names . . . was always taken by the Chief Justice of the High Court'. The Governor 'expressed his opinion' on the recommendation, 'in consultation with the chief minister'. The recommendations then went to the home ministry, which forwarded the matter to the chief justice of India for his recommendation. If the chief justice of India agreed, the candidate was appointed, but not otherwise. If the state government wanted to suggest a name apart from the ones put forward by the high court chief justice, then the opinion of the high court chief justice was first sought on that name. Then the recommendation of the government with the chief justice's opinion was sent to the home ministry, which sent it to the chief justice of India. 'No name was sent by the Chief Justice without the knowledge of the Governor, nor by the Governor without the knowledge of the Chief Justice.' Gajendragadkar, *To the Best of My Memory*, pp. 164–65.
140. Biographical details of Asoke Sen are available at: http://rajyasabha. nic.in/rsnew/pre_member/1952_2003/s.pdf (last visited 2 March 2018). However, it must be borne in mind that it was the home minister, not the law minister, who dealt with judicial appointments at that time.
141. Interview with Asoke Sen (27 December 1988).
142. Interview with Justice Vivian Bose (21 June 1983).
143. Interview with Justice S.K. Das (14 May 1983).
144. Ibid.
145. Interview with Justice A.K. Sarkar (28 June 1983).
146. Gadbois, *Judges of the Supreme Court of India*, pp. 77–78.
147. Interview with Justice K.N. Wanchoo (24 May 1983). Wanchoo, who succeeded Subba Rao as chief justice, said that he had nothing to do with Hegde's appointment.
148. AIR 1967 SC 1643.
149. Gadbois, *Judges of the Supreme Court of India*, pp. 77–78.
150. The others were P. Jaganmohan Reddy and I.D. Dua.
151. Interview with M. Hidayatullah (4 November 1988).

152. *Rustom Cavasjee Cooper v. Union of India*, (1970) 1 SCC 248.
153. *Madhav Rao Scindia v. Union of India*, (1971) 1 SCC 85.
154. Interview with M. Hidayatullah (4 November 1988).
155. Interview with Justice J.C. Shah (3 November 1988).
156. Gadbois, *Judges of the Supreme Court of India*, p. 153.
157. There was a rumour that Sikri might have been superseded as well. Interview with Justice G.K. Mitter (28 June 1983).
158. See, website of the International Court of Justice: http://www.icj-cij.org/en/all-members (last visited 3 March 2018).
159. Interview with Justice S.M. Sikri (6 May 1983). Sikri said that two names, Beg and Fazal Ali, were suggested to him. He implied that neither was very good, but he went with Beg. Interview with Justice S.M. Sikri (17 October 1988).
160. Reddy, *The Judiciary I Served*, pp. 229, 231. Reddy, who was a part of the bench, says that the rumours about Beg being given a draft judgment by the government to deliver were false. Reddy, ibid, p. 233. However, he believes that the government had anticipated the judgment. Reddy, ibid., pp. 242–43.
161. Ibid., p. 220.
162. Interview with Justice S.M. Sikri (17 October 1988).
163. Gadbois, *Judges of the Supreme Court of India*, p. 166.
164. Interview with Mrs Archana Subimal Roy (29 June 1983). Gadbois wondered whether the government had planned on superseding J.C. Shah with S.C. Roy. Apparently, there were rumours that Shah might have been superseded by an outsider.
165. Interview with Mrs Archana Subimal Roy (29 June 1983).
166. Reddy, *The Judiciary I Served*, p. 219. Reddy heard the story of Roy's elevation from Roy himself. Roy was Reddy's 'old friend from London'.
167. Interview with Mrs Archana Subimal Roy (29 June 1983).
168. Ibid. Sometime after he died, Roy's wife was told that the government had planned to supersede judges and make S.C. Roy the chief justice of India ahead of others. Mrs Roy did not think that her husband would have accepted the chief justiceship under such circumstances. However, A.N. Ray was senior to Roy, and Khanna was junior to Roy, so it is doubtful whether Roy would have superseded anyone. Had he lived, he would have served as the chief justice of India for a few months in early 1977. Gadbois wrote of Mrs Roy, 'Charming lady, obviously educated in England, very sophisticated.' However, Gadbois later told me

that he thought Mrs Roy was quite naive to tell him the story about the prime minister's papers being taken away from Roy's home, and suggested to her that this story should not be repeated to anyone else.

169. Interview with M. Hidayatullah (4 November 1988).
170. Interview with G.K. Mitter (28 June 1983).
171. Interview with B.P. Sinha (17 July 1983).
172. Interview with Justice Y.V. Chandrachud (8 December 1988).
173. Gadbois, *Judges of the Supreme Court of India*, pp. 278–79.
174. Ibid. Islam eventually felt vindicated by the judgment of the Supreme Court in the review petition holding in favour of Misra. He thought that Bhagwati's dissenting judgment in that case was just a political lecture. Interview with Justice Baharul Islam (4 October 1988). The cases are reported at *Sheonandan Paswan v. State of Bihar*, (1983) 1 SCC 438 and (1987) 1 SCC 288.
175. Chandrachud said that Justice Madon, however, was his choice (though he knew that Madon himself did not think so). Madon had been recommended by Hidayatullah, Palkhivala and Seervai.
176. See, Interview with Justice A.C. Gupta (22 October 1988); Interview with Fali S. Nariman (16 July 1983); Interview with Justice P.S. Kailasam (24 June 1983); Interview with Justice P.N. Bhagwati (31 March 1988).
177. Interview with Justice P.N. Bhagwati (3 October 1988).
178. Interview with Justice R.S. Pathak (22 December 1988).
179. Justice Vaidialingam identified 1971 as the year in which the method of appointing judges changed. Interview with Justice C.A. Vaidialingam (25 May 1983). Similarly, Justice Grover identified Chief Justice Sikri's tenure as the period from which the government started pushing its names on the chief justice of India. Interview with Justice A.N. Grover (23 January 1980).
180. See further, Abhinav Chandrachud, 'Supreme Court's Seniority Norm: Historical Origins', *Economic and Political Weekly*, vol. 47, no. 8, 25 February 2012, pp. 26–30.
181. BSR, vol. 4, p. 166.
182. Paragraph 861, Report of the States Reorganization Commission (1955).
183. It opined that the chief justiceship of high courts should not devolve solely according to seniority, and that high court judges must not constantly be transferred. Law Commission, 14th Report, vol. 1, pp. 76–77, 99.

184. Ibid., p. 100.
185. Ibid.
186. Austin, *Working a Democratic Constitution*, p. 136.
187. Reddy, *The Judiciary I Served*, p. 115.
188. Gajendragadkar, *To the Best of My Memory*, pp. 165–70. There is an interesting story about Gajendragadkar and Chandra Reddy. Reddy went to receive Gajendragadkar at the railway station with two garlands. At the station, Reddy was about to garland Gajendragadkar, but Gajendragadkar 'pushed the garlands away' with a wave of his hand. Reddy, *The Judiciary I Served*, p. 116.
189. Gajendragadkar, ibid, pp. 170–72.
190. Justice Koshal said that the transfer policy was being applied incorrectly in the 1980s. If a judge was corrupt, he ought to have been impeached, said Koshal, not transferred. Interview with Justice A.D. Koshal (27 November 1988).
191. Chandrachud, *An Independent, Colonial Judiciary*.
192. Nehru to Pant, letter dated 22 September 1959. Gopal, *Selected Works of Jawaharlal Nehru*, vol. 52, 2nd series, p. 134.
193. Gajendragadkar, *To the Best of My Memory*, pp. 168–69.
194. Gajendragadkar to Nanda, confidential letter dated 12 February 1964, Gajendragadkar Papers, Nehru Memorial Museum and Library.
195. Austin, *Working a Democratic Constitution*, p. 345.
196. Reddy, *The Judiciary I Served*, p. 118.
197. However, where consent for the transfer was not given, the risk was that a judge could be superseded. Interview with Justice M.M. Dutt (24 April 1988).
198. See, Austin, *Working a Democratic Constitution*, p. 344; H.M. Seervai, *Constitutional Law of India* (New Delhi: Universal Law Publishing Co. Pvt. Ltd, 2014 reprint), 4th edition, vol. 3, p. 2698. Austin catalogues several reasons why the remaining transfers may not have taken place. One interesting reason was that Justice P.M. Mukhi of the Bombay High Court suffered a heart attack when he heard the news of his transfer from Bombay to Calcutta, which spooked the Delhi establishment. Austin, ibid, pp. 346–47. However, Mukhi had suffered previous heart attacks as well. S.S. Ray, then the chief minister of West Bengal, apparently made special arrangements for Mukhi after learning of his heart ailment. Interview with Justice D.P. Madon (28 April 1983).

199. *A.D.M., Jabalpur v. Shivakant Shukla,* (1976) 2 SCC 521. Austin, *Working a Democratic Constitution,* p. 344.
200. *Union of India v. Sankal Chand Himatlal Sheth,* (1978) 1 SCR 423: (1977) 4 SCC 193. See, Chandrachud, *The Informal Constitution.*
201. Law Commission, 80th Report, 1979, pp. 25–26. The Law Commission was not persuaded by the argument that the policy of recruiting judges for another state high court would prevent lawyers from accepting judgeships. It said that after retiring as judges, lawyers would be able to return to their home states to practise law, which might encourage them to accept these judgeships.
202. Ibid., p. 28.
203. Ibid., pp. 24–25.
204. Interview with Justice Y.V. Chandrachud (8 December 1988).
205. Abhinav Chandrachud, *The Informal Constitution: Unwritten Criteria in Selecting Judges for the Supreme Court of India* (New Delhi: Oxford University Press, 2014).
206. *S.P. Gupta v. Union of India,* (1981) Supp SCC 87.
207. See, Chandrachud, *The Informal Constitution.*
208. Austin, *Working a Democratic Constitution,* p. 531. However, there have been exceptions to this rule. For example, Justice V. Khalid was transferred to the Jammu and Kashmir High Court as chief justice from the Kerala High Court where he was a puisne judge in August 1983, though he was scheduled to retire in July 1984. He said that the appointment was made because it had been pending for a long time. Interview with Justice V. Khalid (21 November 1988). Even in present times, there are instances where judges who have had less than one year to retire have been transferred as chief justices to other high courts. For instance, Justice K.R. Vyas was appointed chief justice of the Bombay High Court in February 2006 and he retired at the age of sixty-two in July 2006. See, profile of Chief Justice Vyas, available at: http://bombayhighcourt.nic.in/cjshow.php?auth=amdldGlkPTM0JnBhZ2Vubz00 (last visited 28 May 2017).
209. Austin, *Working a Democratic Constitution,* pp. 531–32.
210. However, the transfer of chief justices policy has sometimes not been followed. Justice Sujata Manohar, a puisne judge of the Bombay High Court, was appointed the court's first female chief justice in January 1994, when she still had several years left to retire. See, profile of Justice S.V. Manohar on the website of the Bombay High Court, available at: http://bombayhighcourt.nic.in/cjshow.

php?auth=amdldGlkPTI3JnBhZ2Vubz0z (last visited 3 March 2018).

211. See further, Interview with Justice J.C. Shah (3 November 1988).

212. Interview with Justice P.K. Goswami (4 June 1983). Gadbois wrote in the notes of his interview with Justice Goswami: 'Says whole transfer policy is because independent judges are not liked by the madam.'

213. Interview with Justice V.D. Tulzapurkar (14 July 1983).

214. Seervai to Ahmadi, letter dated 12 December 1995, in Feroza H. Seervai (ed.), *Evoking H.M. Seervai*, at p. 329.

215. See, Interview with Justice S. Fazl Ali (24 April 1983).

216. Interview with Justice K.J. Shetty (25 April 1988).

217. The first instance of this occurred in January–February 1976, with Justice U.R. Lalit of the Bombay High Court and Justice R.N. Aggarwal of the Delhi High Court. Austin, *Working a Democratic Constitution*, p. 344. In 1980, the government did not want to confirm the appointment of Justice R.C. Srivastava of the Allahabad High Court, who resigned thereafter. Austin, ibid, p. 518. In 1981, rather than confirming the appointments of three additional judges of the Delhi High Court, their terms as additional judges were extended for short periods of time. One of those judges had decided a case against Sanjay Gandhi. Chandrachud, *The Informal Constitution*. A similar fate met judges in other high courts as well. Austin, ibid, p. 523.

218. Chandrachud, *The Informal Constitution*.

219. Gajendragadkar to Desai, note dated 8 July 1977. Available at: Gajendragadkar Papers, Nehru Memorial Museum and Library. Gajendragadkar recommended the following procedure for appointing a high court judge: The chief justice of the high court, 'in agreement with his two senior colleagues', should send a name to the Governor. The Governor could consult the chief minister in order to determine the 'general reputation of the Judge outside the Court'. This opinion then had to be conveyed to the Union minister of law, justice and company affairs, who then had to consult the chief justice of India. The chief justice of India had to consult 'two of his senior colleagues and, if there happens to be on the Bench of the Supreme Court a Judge from the High Court from which the new appointment is proposed to be made', then that judge as well. It was to be 'their collective decision' which had to be communicated to the Union government. Gajendragadkar wrote that the opinion of the

chief justice of India 'thus communicated, coupled with the opinion of the Chief Justice of the High Court concerned, should be accepted by the Union Government and the person recommended should be appointed to the High Court'. He recommended a similar procedure for appointing Supreme Court judges at the central level. Gajendragadkar's note was probably written in anticipation of the Constitution (Forty-Fourth Amendment) Act, 1978.

220. *Supreme Court Advocates-on-Record Association v. Union of India*, (1993) 4 SCC 441, decided on 6 October 1993. *Special Reference No. 1 of 1998*, (1998) 7 SCC 739. See further, *Supreme Court Advocates-on-Record Association v. Union of India*, (2016) 5 SCC 1.

221. Interview with S.K. Das (14 May 1983).

222. Interview with Justice K.N. Wanchoo (24 May 1983).

223. Wanchoo said that even Chief Justice Gajendragadkar followed the practice of consulting his senior colleagues.

224. Interview with B.P. Sinha (17 July 1983).

225. Interview with A.K. Sarkar (28 June 1983). However, when Subba Rao urged him to appoint someone, he refused, stating that the candidate in question was too young.

226. Hidayatullah's letter to Reddy, asking if Reddy would be interested in joining the Supreme Court, has been reproduced in Reddy's autobiography, along with Reddy's response. Reddy, *The Judiciary I Served*, pp. 150–51. Reddy was upset about the fact that Ray, who was junior to him, was eventually given seniority over him. Reddy, ibid, p. 159; Interview with P. Jaganmohan Reddy (9 November 1988).

227. Interview with M. Hidayatullah (3 June 1983)/(17 June 1983).

228. Interview with J.C. Shah (3 November 1988). He did not know about Hidayatullah's recommendation in favour of S.P. Kotval and M.S. Menon.

229. Interview with Justice K.S. Hegde (14–15 November 1988).

230. Interview with S.M. Sikri (6 May 1983). Sikri confirmed that Chief Justice Wanchoo used to consult him. Justice C.A. Vaidialingam (25 May 1983) said that Sikri did not consult him on Supreme Court appointments (Vaidialingam was third in seniority), though he was consulted on high court appointments for high courts with which he was familiar. Justice K.S. Hegde (14–15 November 1988) confirmed that Sikri consulted Shelat and Hegde on nominations. Sikri also consulted P. Jaganmohan Reddy on the appointment of M. Hameedullah Beg. Reddy, *The Judiciary I Served*, p. 220.

231. Ray himself said that he consulted colleagues only while making appointments from Tamil Nadu. Interview with A.N. Ray (29 June 1983). Justice Palekar said that Ray consulted him only once, about Justice Untwalia. Interview with D.G. Palekar (4 November 1988). Ray also consulted P. Jaganmohan Reddy about Untwalia. Reddy, *The Judiciary I Served*, p. 256.

232. Interview with Y.V. Chandrachud (23 January 1980).

233. Interview with Y.V. Chandrachud (8 December 1988). Justice Fazal Ali (in 1983, the second most senior judge after Bhagwati) confirmed that Chandrachud did not consult his two most senior colleagues. Interview with S. Murtaza Fazal Ali (24 April 1983).

234. The names were probably D.P. Madon, Sabyasachi Mukharji, M.P. Thakkar and Ranga Nath Misra.

235. Interview with P.N. Bhagwati (20 April 1983).

236. Interview with R.S. Pathak (22 December 1988). Justice Venkataramiah confirmed that Pathak consulted him on judicial appointments. Interview with E.S. Venkataramiah (2 October 1988).

237. Interview with B.P. Sinha (17 July 1983).

238. Interview with S.K. Das (14 May 1983)/(18 October 1988).

239. Interview with M. Hidayatullah (17 June 1983). It was clear that Hidayatullah and Setalvad did not get along too well. Hidayatullah said that Setalvad was pompous and arrogant. He also felt that parts of Setalvad's autobiography had major inaccuracies.

240. Interview with S.M. Sikri (6 May 1983).

241. Law Commission, 80th Report, p. 22.

242. Ibid., p. 30.

243. Ibid., p. 24.

244. These were the words of Chief Justice S.R. Das in his deposition before the Law Commission. Law Commission, 14th Report, vol. 1, p. 72.

245. Article 124(2), Constitution.

246. Article 217(1), Constitution. Prior to the Constitution (Fifteenth Amendment) Act, 1963, it was sixty years. Thereafter, it became sixty-two years.

247. A majority of the total membership of the House as well as a two-thirds majority of those present and voting.

248. Articles 124(4) and 217(1)(b), Constitution.

249. Serious attempts were made, for instance, to impeach Supreme Court judge V. Ramaswami, which failed, and Justice Soumitra Sen

of the Calcutta High Court. Sen resigned before the impeachment could proceed very far. See, Chandrachud, *The Informal Constitution*.

250. Article 124(7), Constitution.
251. Constitution (Seventh Amendment) Act, 1956.
252. Article 220, Constitution.
253. Statement of Objects and Reasons to the Constitution (Seventh Amendment) Act, 1956.
254. See, http://cadindia.clpr.org.in/constituent_assembly_members/k_t__shah (last visited 24 March 2018).
255. CAD, vol. 8, pp. 239–40 (24 May 1949). K. Santhanam wanted to prevent judges from holding any 'office of profit' without the prior approval of the President. This included their 'taking office in private companies such as Chairman of the Board of Directors, etc'. CAD, vol. 8, p. 244 (24 May 1949). Jaspat Roy Kapoor proposed a similar amendment. CAD, vol. 8, pp. 240–41 (24 May 1949). Pandit Thakur Das Bhargava felt that judges ought to be allowed to become legislators after retirement. CAD, vol. 8, p. 245 (24 May 1949). See further, BSR, vol. 5, pp. 501–03.
256. CAD, vol. 8, pp. 259–60 (24 May 1949).
257. Article 128, Constitution.
258. Setalvad, *My Life*, pp. 190–91; Gadbois, *Judges of the Supreme Court of India*, p. 22.
259. Setalvad, ibid, pp. 190–91. Similarly, two members of the National Human Rights Commission, Fathima Beevi (who was also a former Supreme Court judge) and S.S. Kang, were appointed Governors of Tamil Nadu and Kerala respectively, which raised questions of constitutional propriety. See, Raju Ramachandran, *I've Been Around for Some Time: Analyses, Reflections and Reminiscences* (Gurgaon: LexisNexis, 2017), p. 45. Likewise, Chief Justice P. Sathasivam, after retirement, was appointed Governor of Kerala. J. Venkatesan, 'Former CJI Sathasivam to Be Kerala Governor', *The Hindu*, 30 August 2014, available at: http://www.thehindu.com/news/national/kerala/former-cji-sathasivam-to-be-kerala-governor/article6365390.ece (last visited 20 October 2017).
260. Law Commission, 14th Report, vol. 1, p. 45.
261. Ibid., p. 46.
262. Ibid., p. 45.
263. Ibid., p. 44.
264. Ibid., p. 46.

265. Ibid., p. 88.
266. Ibid., p. 87.
267. Setalvad, *My Life*, p. 261. Nehru invited Chagla to become India's ambassador to the US in his letter to Chagla dated 21 August 1958. Chagla accepted the offer in his letter to Nehru dated 25 August 1958. See, Gopal, *Selected Works of Jawaharlal Nehru*, vol. 43, 2nd Series, p. 576.
268. Gadbois, *Judges of the Supreme Court of India*, p. 70.
269. Setalvad, *My Life*, pp. 509–10.
270. Ibid., p. 510. Setalvad also felt that the Law Commission was akin to a department of the government under the ministry of law, and holding the chairmanship of the commission would be beneath the dignity of a Supreme Court judge.
271. Ibid., p. 593.
272. M. Hidayatullah, *My Own Boswell: Memoirs* (Bombay: N.M. Tripathi Pvt. Ltd, 1992), pp. 280–81. Hidayatullah felt it necessary to issue this clarification in his autobiography because there was a perception at the bar that he himself wanted a position at the World Court and because of the 'somewhat incomplete account' given by Setalvad in his autobiography about this incident. Setalvad, *My Life*, pp. 611–12. However, Hidayatullah later indicated to Gadbois that his role in the *Privy Purses* case might have cost him a seat at the International Court of Justice. Interview with M. Hidayatullah (17 June 1983).
273. Shanti Bhushan, *Courting Destiny: A Memoir* (Kindle: Penguin Books, 2008).
274. See further, Interview with Justice A.P. Sen (10 September 1988); Interview with Justice V. Khalid (21 November 88).
275. Interview with Justice Y.V. Chandrachud (8 December 1988).
276. Interview with Justice P.N. Bhagwati (on 31 March 1988).
277. Interview with Chief Justice R.S. Pathak (1 October 1988).
278. Gadbois, *Judges of the Supreme Court of India*, at pp. 278–79. See further, Kapoor, 'Supreme Court: Conflicts Within'.

6. Criteria for Selecting Judges

1. The Constitution formally provides that there are three categories of Indian citizens who can be appointed to the Supreme Court: high court judges with a minimum of five years of experience, high court lawyers with a minimum of ten years of experience, or 'distinguished

jurists'. Article 124(3), Constitution. On the selection criteria for judicial appointments, see further, Abhinav Chandrachud, *The Informal Constitution: Unwritten Criteria in Selecting Judges for the Supreme Court of India* (New Delhi: Oxford University Press, 2014).

2. See, Interview with Chief Justice Pathak (22 December 1988). The Law Commission in its 80th Report was ambivalent about such criteria. Law Commission, 80th Report, pp. 23, 30. It said that, ideally, candidates should be appointed on the basis of merit alone, but where such criteria are employed, an attempt must be made to appoint the best among available candidates.

3. See, Chandrachud, *The Informal Constitution*.

4. Interview with S.K. Das (18 October 1988).

5. Law Commission, 14th Report, vol. 1, pp. 34, 69, 72, 92.

6. Interview with Chief Justice Pathak (22 December 1988); George H. Gadbois, Jr., 'Indian Supreme Court Judges: A Portrait', *Law & Society Review*, vol. 3 (November 1968–February 1969), pp. 317–36, 328–29; Chandrachud, *The Informal Constitution*. Law Commission of India, 14th Report, 1958, vol. 1, p. 34, available at: http://lawcommissionofindia.nic.in/1-50/Report14Vol1.pdf (last visited 16 May 2017).

7. Interview with Justice A.M. Ahmadi (1 January 1989).

8. Interview with Justice K.N. Saikia (11 December 1988).

9. Interview with Vivian Bose (21 June 1983).

10. Motilal C. Setalvad, *My Life: Law and Other Things* (Gurgaon: LexisNexis, 2017 reprint), p. 205. Justice Bhagwati said that some Madras High Court judges in the 1930s or thereabouts used to remove their shoes before mounting the bench. The idea was that the bench was a 'temple of justice', and Hindus remove their footwear before entering a temple. Interview with Justice P.N. Bhagwati (24 January 1980).

11. Interview with Justice Chinnappa Reddy (9 November 1988).

12. Interview with Justice A.P. Sen (11 May 1983).

13. Ibid.

14. Interview with Justice D.P. Madon (28 April 1983).

15. Nick Robinson, 'A Quantitative Analysis of the Indian Supreme Court's Workload', *Journal of Empirical Legal Studies*, vol. 10, issue 3, September 2013, pp. 570–601.

16. Interview with Justice Ranga Nath Misra (20 April 1983).

17. Interview with Justice L.M. Sharma (24 April 1988). Sharma believed that President Rajendra Prasad and Chief Justice B.P.

Sinha had helped ensure adequate representation for Bihar at the
Supreme Court.

18. Gadbois, 'Indian Supreme Court Judges', p. 324; George H. Gadbois,
     Jr., *Judges of the Supreme Court of India, 1950-1989* (New Delhi:
     Oxford University Press, 2011), p. 350; Chandrachud, *The Informal
     Constitution.*

19. Chandrachud, Ibid.

20. Interview with C.R. Pattabhi Raman about N. Chandrasekhara
     Aiyar (24 June 1983).

21. Interview with B.P. Sinha (17 July 1983).

22. Interview with M. Hidayatullah (17 June 1983).

23. M. Hidayatullah, *My Own Boswell: Memoirs* (Bombay: N.M.
     Tripathi Pvt. Ltd, 1992), p. 181.

24. Ibid., p. 182.

25. Interview with B.P. Sinha (17 July 1983).

26. Interview with Justice G.K. Mitter (28 June 1983).

27. Interview with Justice M. Hameedullah Beg (2 May 1983). He told
     Gadbois that there was a Muslim puisne judge at the Calcutta High
     Court, with a little more seniority than him, but the government
     wanted Beg, not him. Hegde said that Beg was the most senior
     Muslim judge in the country at the time of Beg's appointment
     to the Supreme Court. Interview with Justice K.S. Hegde (14–15
     November 1988). Perhaps his appointment as chief justice of
     the Himachal Pradesh High Court made him more senior to the
     Calcutta puisne judge.

28. Interview with Justice A.N. Grover (23 January 1980).

29. Interview with Justice R.S. Pathak (17 April 1983).

30. Interview with Justice M. Hameedullah Beg (2 May 1983).

31. Interview with K.S. Hegde (13 January 1980). He was the son
     of Justice Fazl Ali, one of the first judges of the Supreme Court.
     According to Gadbois, '[h]e chose to spell his surname differently
     than his father's to avoid confusion.' Gadbois, *Judges of the Supreme
     Court of India*, p. 233.

32. Interview with Chief Justice R.S. Pathak (22 December 1988).

33. Gadbois's notes in Interview with Justice A.M. Ahmadi (1 January
     89). Gadbois noted that Justice Kuldip Singh told him that Ahmadi
     was a Bohra. As we will see below, Justice Leila Seth wrote in her
     autobiography that even Justice Fathima Beevi believed that Justice
     Ahmadi was not really a Muslim. Leila Seth, *On Balance: An
     Autobiography* (Kindle: Penguin, 2007), p. 4296 (Kindle).

34. Interview with Justice V. Khalid (21 November 1988).
35. Ibid.
36. Interview with Justice L.M. Sharma (24 April 1988).
37. Interview with Justice A.M. Ahmadi (1 January 89). Ahmad was appointed to the Patna High Court in May 1974 and served until May 1993 [see, website of the Patna High Court], whereas Ahmadi was appointed to the Gujarat High Court in September 1976.
38. Notes taken on D.P. Madon during his 28 May 1990 visit to Gadbois.
39. Ibid.
40. See: profile of G.S. Dhillon on the website of the Lok Sabha, available at: http://164.100.47.194/loksabha/writereaddata/biodata_1_12/1762.htm (last visited 8 March 2018).
41. Probably Justice Bhupinder Singh Dhillon, who was appointed to the High Court in February 1970. R.S. Sarkaria had been appointed to the high court in June 1967. See, website of the Punjab and Haryana High Court.
42. There was, at this time, a judge by the name of P.C. Pandit, who served in the high court between March 1960 and May 1974. It also appears that Pandit was, in fact, the most senior puisne judge at the court at that time. See, website of the Punjab and Haryana High Court.
43. Interview with Justice R.S. Sarkaria (15 July 1983).
44. Gadbois omitted to ask Kuldip Singh this question directly. Interview with Justice Kuldip Singh (1 January 1989).
45. Interview with Chief Justice R.S. Pathak (22 December 1988).
46. Interview with Justice S. Murtaza Fazal Ali (24 April 1983).
47. Interview with Justice P.K. Goswami (4 June 1983).
48. Interview with Justice Baharul Islam (4 October 1988).
49. Interview with Justice Balakrishna Eradi (28 October 1988).
50. Interview with Justice Rajagopala Ayyangar (25 June 1983).
51. Interview with T.V. Balakrishnan (son of T.L.V. Ayyar) (25 June 1983), described by Gadbois as a 'leading advocate'.
52. Interview with M. Sankaranarayan (son of Govinda Menon) (21 June 1983). Chief Justice Sinha said that Menons were half Brahmins. Interview with B.P. Sinha (17 July 1983).
53. Interview with M. Sankaranarayan (son of Govinda Menon) (21 June 1983).
54. Interview with Justice E.S. Venkataramiah (2 October 1988).
55. B.P. Sinha, *Reminiscences and Reflections of a Chief Justice* (Delhi: B.R. Publishing Corporation, 1985), pp. 172–73.

56. Interview with Justice A.P. Sen (10 September 1988).

57. Interview with P. Jaganmohan Reddy (9 November 1988). Gadbois wrote that he must '[t]est this' hypothesis empirically.

58. Interview with Justice Krishna Iyer (22 January 1980).

59. Notes taken by Gadbois on D.P. Madon's visit to Gadbois on 28 May 1990.

60. This rule had one exception, viz., if the judge sought to be appointed as chief justice had less than one year in office. In such cases, the judge could be appointed the chief justice of his own court.

61. Interview with Justice A. Varadarajan (20 November 1988). On V.S. Deshpande, see, 'Late Mr. Justice V.S. Deshpande', (1992) 3 SCC (Jour) 3.

62. (1985) Supp SCC 714. Decided by Y.V. Chandrachud, D.A. Desai, O. Chinnappa Reddy, A.P. Sen and E.S. Venkataramiah.

63. Interview with Justice D.A. Desai (29 September 1988).

64. (1989) 1 SCC 204. The judges were R.S. Pathak, E.S. Venkataramiah, Ranga Nath Misra, M.N.R. Venkatachaliah and N.D. Ojha.

65. Interview with Chief Justice R.S. Pathak (22 December 1988).

66. Gadbois's notes in Interview with Justice E.S. Venkataramiah (2 October 1988). Of course, not all judges knew about the castes of their colleagues. For instance, Justice Raghubar Dayal wrote Gadbois a letter on 1 March 1984, and said: 'I do not know the castes of the Judges of the Supreme Court and am unable to help you in the matter.' Gadbois had asked Dayal and others for help in identifying the castes of Supreme Court judges. Likewise, Justice V. Ramaswami did not think that caste had any role to play in appointments to the Supreme Court, though it might have had a role in high court appointments. Ramaswami to Gadbois, letter dated 10 March 1984.

67. Interview with Justice V. Khalid (21 November 1988).

68. Interview with M. Hidayatullah (4 November 1988) / (17 June 1983).

69. Interview with Justice A.N. Sen (24 October 1988).

70. Interview with Justice B.C. Ray (22 April 1988).

71. Interview with Chief Justice R.S. Pathak (22 December 1988).

72. Interview with Justice Sabyasachi Mukharji (1 October 1988). Chandrachud too said that '[T]he only place where there is no casteism is the Calcutta High Court.' Y.V. Chandrachud, 'We Are Not Spineless', *India Today*, 31 July 1985.

73. Interview with Justice M.H. Kania (23 April 1988).

74. Justice Chinnappa Reddy's letter referred only to 'my friend Mr. Justice Mukhtadar'. The website of the Andhra Pradesh High Court suggests that there was a judge by the name of Justice K.A. Muktadar who served at the court from 1971–82. Justice Chinnappa Reddy was also a judge of the Andhra Pradesh High Court for some part of that time. I have therefore assumed that this was the judge Justice Chinnappa Reddy was writing about in his letter to Gadbois.

75. Interview with Justice Y.V. Chandrachud (8 December 1988).

76. Ibid.

77. Interview with Justice Chinnappa Reddy (9 November 1988).

78. Interview with Chief Justice R.S. Pathak (22 December 1988). T.K. Thommen himself did not believe that his being a Christian was a factor in his appointment to the Supreme Court. Interview with Justice T.K. Thommen (17 November 1988).

79. Interview with N.L. Untwalia (3 December 1988).

80. Interview with Justice Balakrishna Eradi (7 May 1983).

81. Interview with B.P. Sinha (17 July 1983).

82. Interview with Justice Y.V. Chandrachud (8 December 1988); Interview with Justice R.S. Pathak (17 April 1983). See further, Interview with Justice R.B. Misra (27 October 1988); Interview with Justice M.H. Kania (23 April 1988).

83. Interview with Justice Y.V. Chandrachud (8 December 1988). Shanti Bhushan's profile is available here: http://rajyasabha.nic.in/rsnew/pre_member/1952_2003/s.pdf (last visited 9 March 2018).

84. Interview with Justice R.S. Pathak (17 April 1983).

85. Granville Austin, *Working a Democratic Constitution: A History of the Indian Experience* (New Delhi: Oxford University Press, 2003 reprint), p. 519. Interview with Chief Justice R.S. Pathak (22 December 1988). Shiv Shankar had the ear of Prime Minister Rajiv Gandhi. Shankar's profile is available at: http://rajyasabha.nic.in/rsnew/pre_member/1952_2003/s.pdf (last visited 9 March 2018). He was himself a judge of the high court of Andhra Pradesh between 1974 and 1975, before joining Parliament. Apart from Scheduled Castes, he also wanted to appoint Marxists to the bench.

86. His profile is available here: http://164.100.47.194/loksabha/writereaddata/biodata_1_12/1956.htm (last visited 9 March 2018).

87. On Shankaranand's preference for Scheduled Caste judges, see further, Interview with Justice E.S. Venkataramiah (2 October 1988); Interview with Justice R.B. Misra (27 October 1988).

88. Interview with Chief Justice R.S. Pathak (1 October 1988); Interview with Chief Justice Pathak (22 December 1988). Dubey's profile is available here: http://rajyasabha.nic.in/rsnew/pre_member/1952_2003/d.pdf (last visited 9 March 2018).

89. Interview with Chief Justice R.S. Pathak (22 December 1988).

90. Interview with Justice R.B. Misra (27 October 1988).

91. Interview with Justice Y.V. Chandrachud (8 December 1988); Interview with Chief Justice R.S. Pathak (22 December 1988). Pathak said that while he initiated Pandian's name, his caste background was a factor which went into his appointment.

92. Interview with Justice B.C. Ray (22 April 1988).

93. Interview with Justice Kuldip Singh (1 January 1989).

94. Interview with Justice P.N. Bhagwati (3 October 1988); Interview with Chief Justice R.S. Pathak (22 December 1988). Bhagwati said that Ray was selected because he was the most senior Scheduled Caste judge in the country, while Pathak said that Singh being a Sikh was a major consideration which went into his appointment.

95. Seth, *On Balance*, p. 3391.

96. 'Former Judges', website of the Kerala High Court, available at: http://highcourtofkerala.nic.in/frmrjudges.html (last visited 22 May 2017).

97. (1959) SCR vii, at p. xii.

98. If her appointment goes through, Indu Malhotra will be the first female advocate to have directly been appointed to the Supreme Court of India.

99. Seth, *On Balance*, at p. 4321.

100. Interview with Justice Y.V. Chandrachud (8 December 1988).

101. Interview with Chief Justice R.S. Pathak (22 December 1988).

102. Seth, *On Balance*, p. 4257.

103. Ibid., p. 4288.

104. Ibid., p. 4299.

105. Ibid., p. 4299.

106. Ibid., p. 3369.

107. Ibid., p. 3437.

108. Law Commission, 14th Report, vol. 1, pp. 69, 72.

109. Chief Justice K. Subba Rao wrote the majority judgment for himself and Justices J.C. Shah, S.M. Sikri, J.M. Shelat and C.A. Vaidialingam. Justice M. Hidayatullah wrote a concurring judgment. Justices K.N. Wanchoo (for himself, V. Bhargava and G.K. Mitter), R.S. Bachawat and V. Ramaswami wrote separate dissenting judgments.

Oddly, the SCC online version of this case does not indicate which judge voted with whom. [The cause title of the SCC online version also deceptively suggests that Justice Ramaswami did not write a separate judgment, which is incorrect.] Consequently, I have deciphered the voting pattern of the judges of this case by reading the law report and relying on Seervai [H.M. Seervai, *Constitutional Law of India: A Critical Commentary* (New Delhi: Universal Law Publishing Co. Pvt. Ltd, 2014 reprint), 4th edition, vol. 3, p. 2431] and Austin [Austin, *Working a Democratic Constitution*, p. 197].

110. AIR 1967 SC 1643.

111. See, Paragraph 53 of the judgment of Chief Justice K. Subba Rao (taken from the SCC Online version of the above judgment).

112. See, Austin, *Working a Democratic Constitution*, p. 209. The *Bank Nationalization* case, *R.C. Cooper v. Union of India*, (1970) 1 SCC 248, involved an attempt by the government to nationalize fourteen private banks. Though the Supreme Court struck the law down, the government re-enacted a law to nationalize the same banks, without the offending provisions. Austin, ibid., pp. 219–20. The *Privy Purses* case, *Madhav Rao Jivaji Rao Scindia v. Union of India*, (1971) 1 SCC 85, involved the government's attempt to abolish amounts paid to the rulers of the erstwhile 'Indian States' who had agreed to join the Union of India.

113. Austin, *Working a Democratic Constitution*, p. 269. The two other cabinet ministers who were rumoured to have been packing the court, apart from S. Mohan Kumaramangalam, were H.R. Gokhale, law minister (the first law minister who was responsible for judicial appointments—the role had earlier belonged to the home minister), and S.S. Ray, cabinet minister of education, youth services and culture. Gadbois, *Judges of the Supreme Court of India*, p. 153. Gokhale had also appeared in Golak Nath on the losing side.

114. S. Mohan Kumaramangalam, *Judicial Appointments: An Analysis of the Recent Controversy over the Appointment of the Chief Justice of India* (New Delhi: Oxford & IBH Pub. Co., 1973). See further, N.A. Palkhivala (ed.), *A Judiciary Made to Measure* (Bombay: M.R. Pai, 1973).

115. *Kesavananda Bharati v. State of Kerala*, AIR 1973 SC 1461.

116. 'Aerial Crashes: Many Leaders Died, Others Survived', *India Today*, 9 May 2012, available at: http://indiatoday.intoday.in/story/aerial-crashes-many-leaders-died-others-survived/1/187981.html (last visited 23 May 2017); 'Family Relives Air Nightmare', *Telegraph*,

9 March 2014, available at: https://www.telegraphindia.com/1140309/
jsp/frontpage/story_18061670.jsp (last visited 23 May 2017).
Tragically, Kumaramangalam's grandson was in the Malaysian
Airlines flight which went missing in 2014.

117. Interview with Justice R.S. Pathak (17 April 1983).
118. Interview with Asoke Sen (27 December 1988).
119. Interview with Justice Y.V. Chandrachud (8 December 1988).
120. See further, Interview with Justice D.A. Desai (29 September 1988).
Justice M.H. Kania confirmed that M.N. Chandurkar's name was
not accepted, but he did not say why. Interview with Justice M.H.
Kania (23 April 1988).
121. See, the profile of Justice M.N. Chandurkar, website of the
Bombay High Court, available at: http://bombayhighcourt.nic.in/
jshowpuisne.php?auth=amdldGlkPTE2NyZwYWdlbm89MTc=
(last visited 21 May 2017).
122. Justice D.A. Desai informed Gadbois that his name had been sent
up in 1982 as well. Interview dated 29 September 1988.
123. Interview with Justice Y.V. Chandrachud (8 December 1988).
Chandrachud said that after this, he avoided discussing
appointments with Bhagwati.
124. Ibid.
125. Ibid., and Interview with Justice A.P. Sen (10 September 1988). See
further, Justice Markandey Katju, 'Why Justice G.P. Singh Was
Not Elevated to the Supreme Court', *Satyam Bruyat*, 30 July 2014,
available at: http://justicekatju.blogspot.in/2014/07/why-justice-gp-
singh-was-not-elevated.html (last visited 21 May 2017).
126. Interview with Justice Chandrachud (8 December 1988). This was,
in substance, also what Chandrachud said in an interview with the
newspaper *Sunday*, upon retiring from office, published on 21 July
1985. See, A.G. Noorani, 'The Prime Minister and the Judiciary',
in James Manor (ed.), *Nehru to the Nineties: The Changing Office
of Prime Minister of India* (London: C. Hurst & Co., 1994), p. 111.
127. Interview with Justice A.P. Sen (10 September 1988). See further,
Noorani, 'The Prime Minister and the Judiciary', p. 112; Justice
Katju, 'Why Justice G.P. Singh Was Not Elevated to the Supreme
Court'.
128. Interview with Justice A.P. Sen (11 May 1983).
129. 'Who Was V.C. Shukla', *India Today*, 11 June 2013, available at:
http://indiatoday.intoday.in/story/who-was-vc-shukla/1/279571.
html (last visited 21 May 2017).

130. *P.L. Kaushik v. V.C. Shukla*, (1980) SCC OnLine MP 104.
131. *V.C. Shukla v. P.L. Kaushik*, (1981) 2 SCC 84.
132. Interview with Chief Justice R.S. Pathak (22 December 1988).
133. Ibid.
134. It is not clear from the interviews why the following candidates were rejected. Justice M. Hameedullah Beg had recommended the appointment of Chief Justice Shiv Dayal Shrivastava of the Madhya Pradesh High Court to the Supreme Court. However, his name was not accepted by the government. Interview with Chief Justice R.S. Pathak (1 October 1988) (Justice Pathak thought that there may have been other rejected Beg nominees too).
135. Interview with Justice Y.V. Chandrachud (8 December 1988). See further, Interview with Justice R.B. Misra (1 June 1983); Interview with Justice K.N. Singh (3 September 1988).
136. Interview with Justice P.N. Bhagwati (3 October 1988).
137. Interview with Chief Justice R.S. Pathak (1 October 1988). See further, Interview with Justice K.N. Singh (3 September 1988).
138. Interview with Justice Y.V. Chandrachud (8 December 1988).
139. Interview with Justice P.N. Bhagwati (3 October 1988).
140. However, Justice Y.V. Chandrachud said that the Crime Branch was involved in background checks for judicial nominees at the high courts, not the Supreme Court. He said that it was the Department of Justice of the government which did background checks on Supreme Court nominees.
141. Interview with Justice Chinnappa Reddy (9 November 1988).
142. Interview with Justice P.K. Goswami (4 June 1983).
143. Interview with Justice P.N. Bhagwati (24 January 1980); Interview with Justice Bhagwati (20 April 1983). See further, Interview with Justice S. Natarajan (24 April 1988).
144. See, the biographical note on Chief Justice Chittatosh Mookerjee, website of the Bombay High Court, available at: http://bombayhighcourt.nic.in/cjshow.php?auth=amdldGlkPTI0JnBhZ2Vubz0z (last visited 21 May 2017).
145. Interview with Chief Justice R.S. Pathak (22 December 1988); Debashis Konari, 'Grandson of Sir Ashutosh Mukherjee Upset at Mamata's Silence on Letter', *Times of India*, 25 March 2013, available at: https://timesofindia.indiatimes.com/city/kolkata/Grandson-of-Sir-Ashutosh-Mukherjee-upset-at-Mamatas-silence-on-letter/articleshow/19181275.cms (last visited 10 March 2018). For a biographical sketch of Sir Asutosh Mookerjee, *see*,

D.P. Sen Gupta, 'Sir Asutosh Mookerjee—Educationist, Leader and Institution Builder', available at: http://www.iisc.ernet.in/currsci/jun252000/HISTORICAL%20NOTES.pdf (last visited 21 May 2017).

146. Interview with Justice P.N. Bhagwati (3 October 1988).

147. Interview with Chief Justice R.S. Pathak (1 October 1988).

148. See, profile of Charan Singh on the website of the Lok Sabha, available at: http://164.100.47.194/loksabha/writereaddata/biodata_1_12/2336.htm (last visited 10 March 2018).

149. Interview with Justice P.N. Bhagwati (3 October 1988); Interview with Chief Justice R.S. Pathak (1 October 1988); Interview with Justice Y.V. Chandrachud (8 December 1988). Bhagwati said that Chandrachud tried to appoint Chief Justice B.N. Deshmukh of the Bombay High Court as well. However, Chandrachud said that he did not recommend Deshmukh's name.

150. Narain retired as chief justice of the Delhi High Court in August 1985. See, profile of Justice Prakash Narain on the website of the Delhi High Court.

151. Interview with Justice P.N. Bhagwati (on 31 March 1988); Interview with Justice Bhagwati (3 October 1988). Previously, Chief Justice Chandrachud had also objected to Narain's appointment to the Supreme Court (again, it is not clear why), though he had supported Narain's appointment as chief justice of the Delhi High Court. Interview with Justice Y.V. Chandrachud (8 December 1988).

152. Interview with Justice P.N. Bhagwati (3 October 1988).

153. H.R. Khanna in his interview wrongly said that Chief Justice Chandrachud ought to have insisted on appointing B.J. Diwan before D.A. Desai. In reality, Desai was appointed in September 1977, when M. Hameedullah Beg was the Chief Justice of India. Interview with Justice H.R. Khanna (3 October 1988).

154. Interview with Justice D.A. Desai (30 April 1983).

155. Interview with Justice H.R. Khanna (3 October 1988).

156. Interview with Justice D.A. Desai (30 April 1983).

157. Interview with Justice V.D. Tulzapurkar (14 July 1983).

158. Upendra Baxi, *Courage, Craft and Contention: The Indian Supreme Court in the Eighties* (Bombay: N.M. Tripathi Pvt. Ltd, 1985), p. 28.

159. Interview with Justice G.L. Oza (22 April 1988). However, many said that Oza was selected because he did what Chief Justice G.P. Singh of the Madhya Pradesh High Court refused to do. See, infra.

160. Interview with Justice P.N. Bhagwati (31 March 1988).

161. Interview with Justice P.N. Bhagwati (3 October 1988).

162. *Sheonandan Paswan v. State of Bihar*, (1987) 1 SCC 288.

163. *Sheonandan Paswan v. State of Bihar*, (1983) 1 SCC 438. Justices Baharul Islam and R.B. Misra were in the majority, with Justice V.D. Tulzapurkar dissenting. See further, Chaitanya Kalbag, 'Jagannath Mishra: Cleared by the Court', *India Today*, uploaded on 26 July 2013, available at: http://indiatoday.intoday.in/story/bihar-cm-jagannath-mishra-gets-reprieve-in-urban-bank-case-sc-judgement-draws-criticism/1/371277.html (last visited 25 May 2017).

164. The review petition was supposed to be heard by the same bench, but Baharul Islam had resigned. Islam was replaced by A.N. Sen on that bench. This time around, the review petition was admitted, with Sen writing the judgment. *Sheonandan Paswan v. State of Bihar*, (1983) 4 SCC 104.

165. Justice P.N. Bhagwati wrote a dissent (with which Justice G.L. Oza agreed). Justice V. Khalid wrote the majority judgment, with which Justice S. Natarajan agreed. Justice E.S. Venkataramiah wrote a concurring judgment, agreeing with Khalid.

166. Law Commission, 14th Report, vol. 1, pp. 70, 92.

167. Interview with Chief Justice R.S. Pathak (22 December 1988).

168. Interview with Justice S.M. Sikri (6 May 1983); Interview with Justice Sikri (17 October 1988). Sikri said that he read the last three years' judgments of potential judicial candidates.

169. Interview with Justice Y.V. Chandrachud (8 December 1988). Chandrachud said that he read twenty-five judgments of a candidate before deciding to recommend his appointment.

170. R.S. Bachawat was appointed to the Supreme Court in September 1964, during P.B. Gajendragadkar's chief justiceship.

171. P.B. Gajendragadkar, *To the Best of My Memory* (Bombay: Bharatiya Vidya Bhavan, 1983), p. 181. See further, Interview with Justice R.S. Bachawat (30 June 1983).

172. Interview with Chief Justice R.S. Pathak (22 December 1988). T.K. Thommen was appointed to the Supreme Court in December 1988, during Pathak's chief justiceship.

173. Interview with Chief Justice Y.V. Chandrachud (3 May 1983).

174. Gajendragadkar, *To the Best of My Memory*, p. 181.

175. Interview with Justice S.M. Sikri (6 May 1983). Sikri believed that Foreign Secretary T.N. Kaul wanted Singh appointed to the Supreme Court. Interview with Justice Sikri (17 October 1988). See further,

Interview with Justice C.A. Vaidialingam (25 May 1983). Justice
A.N. Grover said that Nagendra Singh wanted to be appointed
to the Supreme Court and had hoped that he (i.e. Grover) would
appoint Singh when he became chief justice (eventually, Grover
was superseded, so he never held the post of chief justice). Grover,
however, did not have a very high opinion of Singh. He said that
Singh had no particular legal acumen, and that he got on the World
Court through political connections. Interview with Justice Grover
(24 May 1983).

176. Interview with Justice S.M. Sikri (6 May 1983).
177. 'Nagendra Singh, Judge at the World Court, 74', *New York Times*, 13
December 1988, available at: http://www.nytimes.com/1988/12/13/
obituaries/nagendra-singh-judge-at-the-world-court-74.html (last
visited 22 May 2017).
178. Interview with Justice S.M. Sikri (6 May 1983).
179. Interview with Chief Justice R.S. Pathak (22 December 1988).
180. Ibid.
181. Interview with Justice R.S. Pathak (17 April 1983).
182. Interview with Justice Y.V. Chandrachud (8 December 1988).
183. Ibid.
184. Ibid. (Chandrachud said that this judge's file contained serious
allegations against him from the CBI and Intelligence Bureau
reports); Interview with Justice P.N. Bhagwati (3 October 1988)
(Bhagwati said that Law Minister Asoke Sen told him that the
intelligence reports said that the judge was a womanizer and that
there was possibly some corruption involved); Interview with Justice
D.A. Desai (29 September 1988) (Desai identified the judge and
said that his appointment was recommended but did not say why
the appointment did not go through); Interview with Chief Justice
R.S. Pathak (1 October 1988); Interview with Chief Justice Pathak
(22 December 1988) (Pathak said that there was some controversy
about this judge, that he was informed that this judge had some
skeletons in the closet); Interview with Justice A. Varadarajan (20
November 1988) (Varadarajan identified the judge and said that he
would not be appointed because there was some controversy about
him).
185. Interview with P. Jaganmohan Reddy (20 June 1983). See further,
Reddy, *The Judiciary I Served* (Hyderabad: Orient Longman Ltd,
1999), p. 137.
186. Seth, *On Balance*, p. 3369.

187. Interview with M. Hidayatullah (4 November 1988). Apparently, P. Satyanarayana Raju, appointed to the Supreme Court in October 1965, had been unwell prior to his appointment, and his ill health had been kept a secret in order to ensure that it did not get in the way of his elevation. Reddy, *The Judiciary I Served*, p. 125.

188. Interview with M. Hidayatullah (17 June 1983).

189. Interview with Justice I.D. Dua (6 July 1983). See further, Interview with Justice K.S. Hegde (14–15 November 1988).

190. Interview with Justice P.N. Bhagwati (3 October 1988).

191. Interview with Chief Justice R.S. Pathak (1 October 1988).

192. Seth, *On Balance*, p. 4278.

193. Interview with Justice D.G. Palekar (4 November 1988).

194. B.P. Sinha used the euphemism 'agriculturist' to describe his father's occupation. When Gadbois asked him whether that meant that his father had been a zamindar, Sinha agreed. This suggests that Sinha obviously wanted to mask his father's elite background. Interview with B.P. Sinha (17 July 1983).

195. Interview with S.K. Das (18 October 1988).

196. Interview with B.P. Sinha (17 July 1983). J.R. Mudholkar's father had served as president of the Bankipore session of the Indian National Congress in 1912. Gadbois, *Judges of the Supreme Court of India*, p. 101.

197. Interview with Chief Justice R.S. Pathak (22 December 1988).

198. Ibid.

199. Ibid.

200. Interview with Justice A. Varadarajan (20 November 1988).

201. Interview with Justice R.S. Sarkaria (15 July 1983).

202. Interview with B.P. Sinha (17 July 1983). Sinha was quick to point out that what bothered him about S. Mohan Kumaramangalam was not that he was a member of the communist party in particular, but that he identified himself with a political party, of whatever persuasion that might be. See further, Sinha, *Reminiscences*, pp. 167–68. However, some judges said that Kumaramangalam's appointment was blocked by Home Minister Pant, not Chief Justice Sinha. Chinnappa Reddy said that he was sure of this. See, Interview with Justice Chinnappa Reddy (10 May 1983). Gadbois recorded in his notes of this interview that even K.S. Hegde said so.

203. Shanti Bhushan, *Courting Destiny: A Memoir* (Kindle: Penguin Books, 2008), p. 1409.

204. See, Chandrachud, *The Informal Constitution*. The Law Commission, in its 80th Report, recommended that the age of appointment to the high courts ought to be between forty-five and fifty-four, and to the Supreme Court between fifty-four and sixty. Law Commission, 80th Report, 1979, pp. 22, 30.

205. Law Commission, 14th Report, vol. 1, pp. 36, 37, 83.

206. Bhushan, *Courting Destiny*, p. 1409.

207. Justice A.P. Sen believed that Gajendragadkar instituted this rule because he wanted a distant relative of his to be appointed to the Madhya Pradesh High Court, and that person was, in fact, appointed. Interview with Justice A.P. Sen (11 May 1983).

208. Justice A.P. Sen said that his papers were cleared during Chief Justice K. Subba Rao's time. Interview with Justice A.P. Sen (11 May 1983). However, Subba Rao resigned from the Supreme Court in April 1967, whereas Sen was appointed to the Madhya Pradesh High Court in November 1967, during Chief Justice Wanchoo's tenure.

209. Interview with Justice A.M. Ahmadi (1 January 89).

210. Interview with Justice S. Natarajan (24 April 1988). See further, Chandrachud, *The Informal Constitution*.

211. Interview with Justice J.C. Shah (3 November 1988).

212. *Supreme Court Advocates-on-Record Association v. Union of India*, (1993) 4 SCC 441; *Special Reference No. 1 of 1998*, (1998) 7 SCC 739.

213. Chandrachud, *Informal Constitution*.

214. Gadbois was unable to figure out the exact date on which Sastri was confirmed as the permanent chief justice of India. Gadbois, *Judges of the Supreme Court of India*, p. 38. See further, Abhinav Chandrachud, 'Supreme Court's Seniority Norm: Historical Origins', *Economic and Political Weekly*, vol. 47, no. 8, 25 February 2012; Chandrachud, *The Informal Constitution*. The Law Commission in its 80th Report suggested that where the seniority convention was proposed not to be followed at the High Court Chief Justice level, the supersession had to have proceeded after consulting with the Chief Justice of India and his four most senior colleagues. Where it was proposed not to be followed at the Supreme Court Chief Justice level, however, it had to have proceeded after consulting all the Supreme Court judges. Law Commission, 80th Report, pp. 27, 30.

215. Oddly, Chief Justice Mahajan mentioned nothing about this incident in his autobiography. Mehr Chand Mahajan, *Looking Back* (London: Asia Publishing House, 1963), p. 206.

216. Setalvad, *My Life, Law and Other Things*, p. 185.
217. Interview with Justice Sarkar (28 June 1983).
218. M.C. Chagla, *Roses in December: An Autobiography* (Mumbai: Bharatiya Vidya Bhavan, 2016 reprint), p. 171.
219. Interview with C.R. Pattabhi Raman, dated 24 June 1983.
220. Interview with Justice A.N. Grover, dated 24 May 1983. Justice Vivian Bose remembered nothing about the 1951 incident, except that he too was willing to resign. Interview with Justice Vivian Bose, dated 21 June 1983.
221. Interview with A. Mukherjea (son of B.K. Mukherjea), dated 29 June 1983. Nehru did not like Kania either, as we have seen in the previous chapter.
222. Justice Ranga Nath Misra, interview dated 20 April 1983.
223. Interview with Krishnamurthy Sastri (nephew of Patanjali Sastri), dated 25 June 1983.
224. Law Commission of India, 14th Report, 1958, vol. 1, pp. 39–40.
225. Chagla, *Roses in December*, p. 171.
226. Ibid.
227. Setalvad, *My Life, Law and Other Things*, p. 261.
228. Setalvad wrote harshly (and, in some cases, perhaps a little unfairly) about several judges, including Fazl Ali, B.P. Sinha, J.L. Kapur, P.B. Gajendragadkar and K. Subba Rao.
229. Interview with Justice A.N. Sen (21 April 1983); Kuldip Nayar, 'The 13th Chief Justice', in Kuldip Nayar (ed.), *Supersession of Judges* (New Delhi: Indian Book Company, 1973), p. 12; K.S. Hegde, 'A Dangerous Doctrine', in Kuldip Nayar (ed.), *Supersession of Judges*, p. 47. See further, paragraph 1.14, 121st Report of the Law Commission of India, July 1987, p. 4, available at: http://lawcommissionofindia.nic.in/101-169/Report121.pdf (last visited 13 May 2017). The report said: 'An impression gained ground that the Government of India was not in favour of him [Sastri] and it was of the opinion that another Judge from the Supreme Court should be promoted as Chief Justice of India.'
230. Interview with M. Hidayatullah (17 June 1983).
231. Gadbois's handwritten note alongside the typewritten notes of his interview with M. Hidayatullah (17 June 1983).
232. Justice Ranga Nath Misra, interview dated 20 April 1983.
233. Interview with A. Mukherjea (son of B.K. Mukherjea), dated 29 June 1983; Interview with Krishnamurthy Sastri (nephew of Patanjali Sastri), dated 25 June 1983.

234. See further, Sinha, *Reminiscences*, p. 71.

235. See, 'Sudhi Ranjan Das', *Journal of the Indian Law Institute*, January–June 1960, vol. 2, nos. 2–3, pp. 154–56 available at: http://14.139.60.114:8080/jspui/bitstream/123456789/14903/1/017_Sudhi%20Ranjan%20Das%20(154-156).pdf (last visited 23 May 2017).

236. Interview with B.P. Sinha, dated 17 July 1983.

237. Gadbois's notes on Interview with B.P. Sinha (17 July 1983).

238. *Kameshwar Singh v. Province of Bihar*, AIR 1951 Pat 246. Interestingly, Das was of the view that had he written this judgment in 1988 (when the interview with Gadbois was conducted), he would not have been appointed to the Supreme Court (i.e. because the government was now looking only for committed judges). Interview with S.K. Das (18 October 1988).

239. Interview with S.K. Das (14 May 1983).

240. Gajendragadkar, *To the Best of My Memory*, p. 153.

241. Law Commission of India, 14th Report, vol. 1, p. 73.

242. Gajendragadkar, *To the Best of My Memory*, p. 180.

243. Bose's term was extended under Article 128 of the Constitution between September 1957 and September 1958. Gadbois, *Judges of the Supreme Court of India*, p. 36.

244. Hidayatullah, *My Own Boswell*, p. 190.

245. Interview with Justice Bhagwati (3 October 1988). See further, Interview with Chief Justice Pathak (1 October 1988).

246. Interview with Justice A.C. Gupta (13 May 1983); Interview with Justice Balakrishna Eradi (28 October 1988); Interview with P. Jaganmohan Reddy (20 June 1983); Interview with M. Hidayatullah (17 June 1983).

247. See, Abhinav Chandrachud, 'From Hyderabad to Harvard: How U.S. Law Schools Make It Worthwhile to Clerk on India's Supreme Court', *International Journal of the Legal Profession*, 7 October 2014, pp. 73–101.

248. Rajagopalachari to Patel, letter dated 1 February 1949. Das (ed.), *Sardar Patel's Correspondence*, vol. 8, p. 107.

249. Patel to Rajagopalachari, letter dated 7 February 1949. Das (ed.), *Sardar Patel's Correspondence*, vol. 8, p. 108.

250. Mahajan, *Looking Back*, p. 217.

251. Setalvad, *My Life, Law and Other Things*, p. 567.

252. R.A. Jahagirdar was elevated to the Bombay High Court in October 1976, and he retired in 1990. He was accordingly a Bombay High

Court judge when Gajendragadkar's autobiography was published. He was married to Gajendragadkar's elder daughter, gynaecologist Dr Sharad Jahagirdar. See, speech of Chief Justice Mohit S. Shah at the reference for Justice R.A. Jahagirdar, 29 March 2011, available at: http://bombayhighcourt.nic.in/libweb/references/JahagirdaRA. PDF (last visited 30 May 2017).

253. Gajendragadkar, *To the Best of My Memory*, p. 137.
254. Interview with Justice D.G. Palekar (4 November 1988).
255. Seth, *On Balance*, p. 4557.
256. Gajendragadkar, *To the Best of My Memory*, pp. 182–83.
257. Hidayatullah, *My Own Boswell*, p. 191.
258. Ibid.
259. Interview with Justice A.N. Grover (23 January 1980).
260. Interview with Justice V. Khalid (21 November 88).
261. See, Abhinav Chandrachud, *Republic of Rhetoric: Free Speech and the Constitution of India* (Gurgaon: Penguin Random House, 2017).
262. Interview with Justice Chandrachud (8 December 1988).
263. Interview with Justice Balakrishna Eradi (28 October 1988).
264. Gadbois, *Judges of the Supreme Court of India*, p. 296.
265. The Bombay High Court website says that Lentin was appointed on 28 March 1973, while Sawant was appointed on 29 March 1973.
266. Author's telephonic interview with Justice P.B. Sawant on 27 July 2011 at 11.30 a.m.
267. Ibid.
268. Gadbois, *Judges of the Supreme Court of India*, at p. 296.
269. Interview with Justice K.J. Shetty (25 April 1988); Interview with Chief Justice R.S. Pathak (1 October 1988); Author's telephonic interview with Justice P.B. Sawant on 27 July 2011 at 11.30 a.m.
270. Author's telephonic interview with Justice P.B. Sawant, Ibid.
271. Interview with Justice Y.V. Chandrachud (8 December 1988).